Fair Game?

FAIR GAME?

INEQUALITY AND AFFIRMATIVE ACTION

John C. Livingston

CALIFORNIA STATE UNIVERSITY, SACRAMENTO

W. H. Freeman and Company
San Francisco

Sponsoring Editor: Richard J. Lamb

Project Editor: Pearl C. Vapnek

Copyeditor: John Hamburger

Designer: Sharon Helen Smith

Production Coordinator: Linda Jupiter

Compositor: Graphic Typesetting Service

Printer and Binder: The Maple-Vail Book Manufacturing Group

Library of Congress Cataloging in Publication Data

Livingston, John C
    Fair game?

    Includes index.
    1.   Race discrimination—Law and legislation
—United States.   2.   Affirmative action pro-
grams—Law and legislation—United States.
I.   Title
KF4755.L58   342'.73'085   79-13422
ISBN   0-7167-1131-1
ISBN   0-7167-1132-X pbk.

*For Alisha and Veronica,
that their generation might
inherit a fairer world*

Contents

Preface

I undertook the writing of this book in a mood of anxiety and with a sense of urgency. Affirmative-action programs, adopted in the face of adverse public opinion, seemed to operate in a conspiracy of silence on the part of public officials, whose behavior defied their responsibility to defend their actions publicly. The field of public discourse had been left largely to opponents of affirmative action, who, in their arguments, had preempted the appeal to the ideals of justice and equality. Moreover, when the argument against affirmative action was not met with silence, it was often countered by evasion. Were the weightiest arguments really on that side of the issue?

My strong inclination was to reject that conclusion. Affirmative action, my instincts informed me, was both desirable and necessary. But if so, why had the case for it so seldom been made? And why, when it was made, was it not more persuasive?

Equality before the law and equality of opportunity were the twin pillars on which opposition to affirmative action was built. These ideals are close to the center of the American creed.

Had I, then, been emotionally drawn to a policy that would undermine the very values for which affirmative action was instituted?

The sense of urgency with which I began reflected my conviction that the civil-rights revolution involves an imperative and unfinished agenda. Without affirmative action, the struggle for racial justice would be stalemated, at the price of both justice and social peace. But opinion polls confirmed that the American public, by large majorities, opposed those programs. Letters to the editor and casual conversation revealed that this opposition was vehement and expressed a sense of moral outrage. "The politicians who advocate quotas," one letter writer opined, "are the most dangerous racists this country ever had." This white backlash appears to have been ignored in the belief that direct confrontation of the issue would increase white resentment and hostility and trigger more backlash. Silence and evasion, however, were contributing to the very reaction that was feared.

Over the long term, no program will be effective in remedying the injustices suffered by minorities in a majoritarian democracy if it does not appeal to the majority's sense of justice. If a persuasive case for affirmative action could not be made, the rancor those programs were producing could only increase. And if that were the case, the programs had best be abandoned. If, on the other hand, a persuasive case could be made, this case was indeed urgent business.

The exploration to which I was led by those questions turned out to be longer, and over more complicated and difficult terrain, than I had anticipated. Equality before the law and equality of opportunity turn out to be elusive concepts— especially when we test their meanings against a problem like racial injustice. We are then led back, as I discovered, to the assumptions and values underlying majority rule, to the fundamental question of why men should obey laws, and to the sources of political obligation and legitimacy.

The ideas one brings to bear on such questions are bound to reflect intellectual debts that are larger than can be fairly acknowledged. Some of my own vast indebtedness is registered in the notes at the end of the book. But the ideas of many other writers, whose works are missing from or inadequately reflected in the notes, have provoked, stimulated, or heavily influenced my own. They include Hannah Arendt, Marshall Berman, Ronald Dworkin, John Rawls, John P. Scharr, David Spitz, Joseph Tussman, Michael Walzer, Garry Wills, Robert Paul Wolff, and Sheldon Wolin.

During the writing of the manuscript, Reverend Theodore A. Webb and the members of the Unitarian Universalist Society of Sacramento provided me with a warm and receptive critical audience on whom to try out some of my ideas. Edwin Klingelhofer, Emily Wright, and Jerry Tobey read and criticized parts of the manuscript. I profited from discussion of key issues with Joe Serna, Elizabeth Moulds, Richard D. Hughes, and Joel McBride. Those who read the entire manuscript, at one point or another in its development, included William R. Andersen, University of Washington Law School; Jacob Fuchs, California State University at Hayward; Arvo Van Alstyne, University of Utah Law School; J. Cleve Livingston, practicing attorney; and Paul N. Goldstene, Ernest J. Isaacs, Robert G. Thompson, Mansour Farhang, William Dorman, and Marc R. Tool, California State University at Sacramento. Their comments were often warmly supportive (and doubly welcome when they arrived during periods of gnawing self-doubt), as well as challenging and provocative. If they discover that some of their most incisive and telling criticisms did not find their way into the finished product, they should know that they did at least disturb my sleep.

I owe special gratitude to Marc Tool, whose friendship, encouragement, and criticism over a good many years were matched by his thorough and exceptionally helpful review of the manuscript. I cannot adequately thank Harold J. Spaeth of Michigan State University, who read the manuscript in its later stages, and whose encouragement and critical assistance have been invaluable. Richard J. Lamb, political science editor at W. H. Freeman and Company, has been uniformly supportive and helpful. John Hamburger, copyeditor, and Pearl C. Vapnek, project editor at W. H. Freeman and Company, performed skill-fully and helpfully. Leonard Larson and Esther L. Branthaver helped appreciably in tracking down sources.

All of the members of my family have been involved, and not merely in the usual sense of cheerful forbearance and forgiveness for parental neglect. Cleve, Michael, and George have each taught me much about the issues I discuss here. Rebecca and James Harris, from their own special perspective, have constantly tested and informed my sensitivity. Finally, my wife, Ethel, is as much responsible for this book as I. We have shared its ideas over the years; her unerring sense of the decent and the humane has been a continuing inspiration. In addition, she has typed and edited the manuscript and called me to account for pretentious, vague, or convoluted reasoning.

All of these persons, of course, are partially responsible for whatever virtues the book possesses. Fairness, if not academic protocol, dictates that they share the blame for its defects.

June 1979   JOHN C. LIVINGSTON

Justice

That Justice is a blind goddess
Is a thing to which we black are wise:
Her bandage hides two festering sores
That once perhaps were eyes.

Langston Hughes

Fair Game?

Prologue

Justice William O. Douglas, in the 1974 case of a white law school applicant who had been rejected in favor of allegedly less qualified minority applicants, argued that:

> There is no constitutional right for any race to be preferred. . . . There is no superior person by constitutional standards. A DeFunis who is white is entitled to no advantage by reason of that fact; nor is he subject to any disability, no matter his race or color. Whatever his race, he has a constitutional right to have his application considered on its individual merits in a racially neutral way.[1]

Four years later, in 1978, Justice Thurgood Marshall offered a diametrically opposing view in the *Bakke* case:

> For it must be remembered that, during most of the past 200 years, the Constitution as interpreted by this Court did not prohibit the most ingenious and pervasive forms of discrimination against the Negro. Now, when a state acts to remedy the effects of that legacy of discrimination, I cannot believe that this same Constitution stands as a barrier.[2]

1

How is it that two such concerned and conscientious Justices, each with a well-earned reputation for judicial vigilance in protecting civil rights, can hold such divergent views on the constitutional issues in affirmative action? Social scientists and citizens, similarly committed to civil rights, are polarized on the moral and social issues involved. Why? What are the sources of their disagreement? All parties to the dispute invoke the same symbols of equality, liberty, and justice. To which side of the issue does the most plausible meaning of those symbols call us?

Our analyses of such issues, of course, are influenced by our experiences. Two events stand out in memory as having had a significant impact in my own case. The first occurred many years ago when Paul Robeson came to my undergraduate campus to debate the question of race relations. The problem, one of the speakers—an anthropologist—argued, is deeply rooted in tradition and the human psyche; anthropologically and sociologically it must be understood that it would take several generations for race prejudice to be overcome. Robeson's response has remained clear in memory. It struck me then, and still does, as irrefutable: "I'm not going to live that long."

The second event was more recent and more complex. A few years ago, as a member of the education committee of the local chapter of the NAACP, I was involved in an investigation of the case of a black family that had recently moved into a previously all-white neighborhood. The father was an airman stationed at a nearby base. The family had been subjected to a series of terrors and indignities—garbage had been dumped in the front yard, "Nigger get out" spray-painted on the front door, and finally a shot fired through a window. The children, not surprisingly, were having trouble at school. Their behavior problems were treated with the normal color-blind rules of discipline. They were failing academically, without receiving remedial help.

The committee sought a meeting with school personnel, including the principal, the school psychologist, and several teachers. We hoped the school officials would agree that the children's problems were linked to neighborhood racism, and that the schools were obligated to take into account the racial dimensions of the children's problems in order to devise appropriate and effective disciplinary and remedial measures.

The meeting was instructive, but not constructive. The school people insisted, vehemently and defensively, that they were not racists, though no one on the committee had suggested they were. The principal's response, accompanied by vigorous nods of approval from his staff, was to this effect:

> Here at this school we are color-blind. We do not look at the color of a child's skin. Every child is an individual. We treat them all equally, as individuals. If you have come here seeking special treatment for one of our pupils, you have come to the wrong place. Whatever your views may be, our commitment here to equality and to our children as individuals makes such a request impossible to honor.

It was, he intimated vaguely, both racist and un-American even to suggest it.

The committee members tried to shift the discussion to the circumstances of the case. It was, we tried to suggest, precisely the staff's color-blindness that was at the heart of the problem. These were not simply individual children, but *black* children. Far from being irrelevant, their blackness was the most significant feature of their lives—in the neighborhood and at that school. How could they conceivably be treated justly as individuals, subject to the impartial enforcement of color-blind rules and policies? Would not a commitment to racial equality require that their color be taken centrally into account in developing a response to their academic and behavior problems? Does not a blindness to their color reinforce the racist sources of their problems, and effectively obstruct the possibilities of their development as individuals?

We tried to question further the adequacy of color-blindness by raising broader issues. "What are the consequences," we asked, "of your position on the obligations of teachers and staff to respond to displays of racism among the children?" (The school yard is among the remaining public places where racist epithets and crude racist jokes are still exchanged freely, and teachers and administrators are compelled by their color-blindness to adopt an attitude of studied aloofness to the situation.) Does color-blindness imply a willful blindness to the social realities of racism? Is an indisputable sincerity and purity of motive enough, or are we accountable for the consequences of our behavior?

The meeting was a hopeless failure; minds and ideas never met, not even in contentious disagreement. Perhaps for that reason it remains vivid in memory, a metaphor for what has happened since and is still happening. Here was a black child, victim of vicious racism; the color-blindness of her teachers and school administrators, who were trying hard not to be racists, led them unwittingly into being accomplices. Most frustrating of all, the very sincerity of the teachers' and administrators' commitment to equality and individuality blinded them to the ways in which they were accomplices to inequality and obstructions to genuine individuality.

Those two events invite reflection on the assumptions and values that were at issue. Robeson's reply to a description of the glacial process of altering human prejudices had seemed to me irrefutable. And yet, the anthropologist was right; prejudice *is* an obstinate reality. That, of course, was not his main point. He had appealed to that reality to warn against the bitter recriminations and increased hostility he thought likely to result from frustrated hope built on overly optimistic assumptions. His appeal for lowered expectations, grounded in a sociological truth, was confronted by Robeson's demand, based on moral principle, for freedom *now*. How much justice is possible, and how soon? Evolution or revolution?

The gradualist position sees social reform as the art of the possible, and the recalcitrance of human nature as marking the boundaries of the possible. The radical position argues that, in order to introduce new possibilities, it is necessary to make an unconditional demand for what is morally required but presently impossible. Where ingrained prejudice and habits of thought are involved, to preach evolution is to encourage inertia; to demand revolution is to make evolution possible. Moreover, where basic human rights are denied by prejudice, to argue for an evolutionary approach to realizing them is to deny

4

their status as basic rights. The result is to encourage those responsible for their denial to persist in their prejudices.

A similar choice confronts us in the situation involving the school. The stance of color-blindness appeared to me to be an obstruction to justice, proposed in the name of justice. But the position of the school people cannot be dismissed as bigoted or self-serving. As in the case of the argument between Robeson and the anthropologist—as in the divergent positions of Justices Douglas and Marshall—the conflict is not between bigotry and equality, but between views claiming the same high moral ground of equality.

How are these conflicting claims to the same ideal to be understood? Clearly, the answer must lie in an effort to clarify and evaluate the divergent meanings of equality underlying the conflicts. This effort will lead us back to the history of the idea of equality in America, and to the philosophical assumptions underlying rival historical and contemporary versions of the egalitarian creed. At the same time, these divergent theories of equality lead to differing attitudes toward the general distribution of wealth and power in American society.

The question of racial justice is connected in basic but complex ways to the broader question of economic and social justice. The plight of the poor in America is not the same as the plight of colored minorities (who are, of course, disproportionately poor), but their conditions are connected by ties of ideology as well as economics.

I hope to show that if we attend seriously to the undeferrable problem of racial injustice, we will be led to a larger meaning of equality that is applicable to poverty as well. And we will have embarked on a venture that will lead us back to a more humane and nobler vision of the egalitarian possibilities and promises of our own cultural past.

1

The Crisis
of Equal Opportunity

The liberal world has come apart at the seams. The struggle for racial justice, which seemed to be going tolerably well, is at an impasse. There's no reliable way of telling who stands where anymore. Old standards no longer apply; old labels no longer fit. Friends, who once confidently shared a way of seeing the world and reacting to its problems, find themselves at odds—sometimes at bitter odds—over the question of affirmative action. Old liberals become new conservatives, seeing recent efforts to put minorities into the American mainstream as assaults on standards, on excellence, and on the rule of merit. Blacks and Jews, fellow victims of racism and partners in the historic struggle to end it, engage in bitter rivalry over quotas.[1] Justice Douglas, beacon of the liberal spirit, took a position on the issue that attracted the applause of bigots.[2]

The problem of getting a focus on such perplexing phenomena is deepened by the rapidity with which the problems have developed. Only a very few years ago liberal hope and confidence abounded. The pace of change had quickened. It had taken over two hundred years to eliminate slavery, and about ninety years more before the Supreme Court forbade us to pursue further the South African "solution." And that was not even three decades ago. Then, in a few short years, legal and extralegal barriers to opportunity in various areas of life were dismantled: in public accommodations, education, housing, voting rights, and employment. Things were better then; we were on our way. And because you could recognize a liberal when you heard one, we knew where we stood. The Douglases and the bigots were on opposite sides of issues. The progressive forces in society shared a vision of the meaning of progress. Only racists believed in the use of race as a criterion for opening the doors of opportunity. Only egalitarians insisted on the need to be color-blind.

The New Crisis: Equality of Group Results

A small cloud on the liberal horizon appeared in 1965, with the publication of a Department of Labor monograph entitled *The Negro Family; The Case for National Action*.[3] The opening sentence was prophetic: "The United States is approaching a new crisis in race relations." In the "new period" we were entering, the success of the struggle for civil rights had led blacks to new expectations that go beyond civil rights. "Being Americans, they will now expect that in the near future equal opportunities for them as a group will produce roughly equal results, as compared with other groups." Unless the challenge is met of insuring that "the distribution of success and failure within one group [is at least roughly] comparable to that within other groups . . . there will be no social peace in the United States for generations."

The Moynihan Report, as it came to be called, notes that the currently accepted meaning of equality of opportunity in the United States requires and insures inequality of individual results ("winners imply losers"). But when the achievement levels of one group differ significantly from others, the logic of the report implies, there are only two possible explanations. Either the competitive game has been unfairly played because the

8

group with lower achievement levels has been denied equal opportunity through prejudice and discrimination, or the results reflect group differences in natural ability.[4] The report cites two reasons for believing that the game has been unfair, and that "a new and special effort" to achieve at least roughly proportional group results is now necessary. First, "the racist virus in the American bloodstream still afflicts us" and produces continuing prejudice. Second, three centuries of oppression have "taken their toll on the Negro people" in a way that makes them less able than other groups "to win out in the competitions of American life."

If disproportionate group results are an index of unjust treatment, the situation of colored minorities in the United States cried out for redress. The formal and legal equality of opportunity achieved by the reforms of the 1960s was not enough. As the president of the National Urban League put it, "What happened in the 60's was just a beginning. The 70's are much more difficult because they deal with making real those things defined and conferred on black people in the 60's. White people never understand that the 60's were about checking into the hotel while the 70's are about getting the wherewithal to check out of the hotel."[5] The League's report, "The State of Black America," notes that, in spite of the apparent advances in civil rights in the 1960s: (1) more than twice as many blacks are unemployed today as ten years ago; (2) there were as many black families below the poverty line in 1977 as there were in 1967, although the number of poor white families decreased during the decade; and (3) the gap between median incomes of white and black families narrowed by only one percentage point in that period, black income having risen from 58 to 59 percent of white income.

The extent to which inequalities of group results make a hollow mockery of "equal opportunity" is further revealed in the data cited by Justice Marshall in his separate opinion in the *Bakke* case:[6]

- The life expectancy of a black child is five years shorter than that of a white.

- The infant mortality rate among blacks is twice that of whites.
- Black women are three times more likely to die during childbirth.
- The proportion of blacks living below the poverty line is nearly four times that of whites.
- The unemployment rate for black adults is twice that of whites.
- Unemployment among black teenagers is nearly three times that of white teenagers.
- Black males with college degrees average only $110 per year more than white males with only a high school diploma.
- While blacks are 11.5 percent of the population, they constitute only 1.2 percent of the lawyers and judges, 2 percent of physicians, 2.3 percent of dentists, 1.1 percent of engineers, and 2.6 percent of college and university professors.

If equal opportunity requires at least roughly proportionate group results, the facts reveal how very unfair the game has been. What justice in the abstract seems to require, the plight of black Americans makes urgent.

Affirmative Action: The Soft Sell

The new and special effort called for by the Moynihan Report was affirmative action. It was designed to produce the group results required by the doctrine of equal opportunity, based on the assumption of racial equality. The battle lines in the struggle for racial justice in the future would be different and less clearly drawn.

From the beginning, the affirmative-action forces were a motley coalition: minority groups, who had liberated themselves from white oppression ("black is beautiful") by refusing to define themselves any longer in white racist terms, and whose sense of moral indignation had been fired by their rising

expectations; politicians, who were frightened by the racial violence of the 1960s, or who rose above principle to the new opportunities of the ethnic vote; and the affirmative-action liberals
(including some politicians), who knew what results had to be
achieved and were unwilling to live with the continuing effects
of white racism, convinced that 250 years was long enough to
wait and that time was running out. Together, these architects of
affirmative action set out to short-cut the road to racial equality.[7]
They aimed to produce the required results without waiting for
the intolerably slow process of healing past wounds and inform-
ing white consciences.

From the beginning they were hard-pressed to defend their
approach, and as a result their programs lacked visible means of
ideological support. Affirmative-action programs, after all,
seemed to fly directly in the face of the master myth of American
culture—the ideal of equality of opportunity and the closely
related principle of individual merit and achievement in gaining
rewards. That ideal had originally been the weapon for attacking
a status system based on inherited aristocratic rank. But its logic
proscribes all forms of ascribed status, including status based on
race, color, or sex. According to this thinking, only individual
achievement is entitled to count. Expressed as a formal rule for
just treatment, it would seem to follow that every discrimination on the basis of race is equally reprehensible. Affirmative action, with its programs of racial preference, seemed almost un-
American on its face. To portray it otherwise required hard
justification—which it very rarely received.

Instead, supporters of affirmative action tended to meet the
challenge to their democratic credentials by evading the issues
affirmative action raised. To those for whom advertising had
become a way of life, manipulation seemed a quicker and surer
route to acceptance than reasoned persuasion. The Madison Avenue mentality had apparently lost any sense of limits. Clever
slogans could gloss over real difficulties; affirmative action was
assumed to require no more than a good image. From the beginning, the programs relied more on the efforts of image-
makers and on the power of the government's fist than on efforts at reasoned persuasion.

If the economy had not slowed down at the same time, "image politics" might have worked. But recession, and the more general crisis of growth, deprived liberals of their pet solution for all problems. Growth in America had always been the magic formula by which a crowded ladder to success could be turned into an escalator, with room for all and running room for the more ambitious and able. Growth made it possible to bring up those at the bottom without taking anything away from those at the top. Growth could make the remedy for injustice painless, even to those who had been reaping its benefits. If the rate of economic growth had been high enough, it might have been possible to conceal the fact that where jobs, income, and status are at stake, minority advantage means white disadvantage. But with the economic downturn, jobs were unmistakably at stake, as was the question of whose sons and daughters would make it through the golden but narrowing door to the professions.

Ideals as well as interests were involved. Affirmative action meant preference on the basis of race, or it meant nothing. But, hadn't we, at long last, invoked the ideals of equality before the law and equality of opportunity to abolish racial preference? Can "reverse discrimination" be a means of ending discrimination? These questions demanded a response but, by and large, none was forthcoming.

The manipulative defense of affirmative action had sought to evade both the adverse effect on white interests and the ideological and moral issues involved. Even the label attached to the programs—affirmative action—reflects the approach of the image-makers. A transparent euphemism for preferential treatment, it seeks to conceal the fact of preference, as well as the hard and obvious truth that nonwhites can be treated preferentially only at the expense of whites. And when the opponents of affirmative action invented the phrase "reverse discrimination" to describe that truth, its supporters sought to conjure it away by inventing a distinction between quotas and goals.

The ostensible basis of all this phrase making appears to have been the belief that the moral case for racial preference, however sound it might be in principle, would not sell and that the white majority could never be persuaded to relinquish white advantage voluntarily. But every American "knows" that it is unjust to reward people on any other basis than their individual accomplishments. Every person knows when his job is threatened or when his children or his friends' children are turned back at the gates to the American Dream.

In their willingness to play this game, the supporters of affirmative action, unwittingly perhaps, have turned the Constitution and the nation's conscience over to their opponents. The friends of affirmative action have had the power of the government, the threat of social disorder, the pressure of ethnic politics, and the weapons of public relations on their side. Most of the argument—the appeals to constitutional principle and to historic national ideals—have come from the other side. Even the ground of racial equality itself has been preempted by opponents of affirmative action: *They* now speak the language of the civil-rights struggle of the past—"the law must be color-blind." *They* now are the enemies of racism—"discrimination against nonwhites is wrong for the same reasons that reverse discrimination against whites is wrong."

The Appearance of Justice

When this seething conflict over the meaning of racial justice finally reached the Supreme Court in the *Bakke* case, the result was a historic nondecision. Allan Bakke, a white male, had been denied admission to the medical school of the University of California at Davis. Other applicants, whose grades and aptitude-test scores were lower than his, had been admitted under a special admissions program that set aside sixteen places in a class of one hundred to be filled by members of certain minority groups.

In addition to ordering Bakke's admission, the Court ruled that (1) the Davis special admissions program was invalid, but that (2) the university could constitutionally take race into account as one factor in its future admissions decisions.[8] Justice Powell, whose opinion announced the findings of the Court, was apparently the only member of the Court who believed that these findings could be reconciled. Justice Powell's effort at reconciliation, moreover, is not persuasive. A quota for which white applicants are not eligible to compete, he argued, violates the equal protection clause of the Constitution because it results in individuals being admitted or rejected solely on the basis of race. "The guarantee of equal protection," Powell agreed with the lower court, "cannot mean one thing when applied to one individual and something else when applied to a person of another color. If both are not accorded the same protection, then it is not equal."[9] But even if, as Powell argued, all applicants must compete for all available places, where race is used as one factor in the decision, it will sometimes be the decisive factor. If some borderline candidate is deprived of a seat simply because he is not the right color, then Justice Powell's definition of equal protection will be violated. Whenever the number of places is limited, if racial identity is a plus for colored applicants, it is a minus for white applicants.

In his effort to resolve this contradiction, Justice Powell took up the decisive question of whether a program that considers "race only as one factor is simply a subtle and more sophisticated—but no less effective—means of according racial preference."[10] Justice Brennan, joined by three of his colleagues, had addressed that question in his opinion and concluded that, whenever special consideration is given to race, "a determination of the degree of preference to be given is unavoidable, and any given preference that results in the exclusion of a white candidate is no more or less constitutionally acceptable than a program such as that at Davis."[11] Justice Powell denied this plausible conclusion by arguing that, whereas a quota system evidences "a facial intent to discriminate," this element of facial invalidity is not present "where race or ethnic background is simply one element—to be weighed fairly against other elements—in the selection process."[12] Powell seemed to be arguing that what is constitutionally required is a "facially nondiscriminatory" policy of according preference on the basis of race. Thus, facial appearances, not substantive consequences, are to be the constitutional test.

14

Why this intellectual sleight of hand in the highest judicial places? A plausible explanation was subtly suggested in the opinion of Justice Brennan and three of his colleagues: "But there is no basis for preferring a particular preference program simply because . . . it proceeds in a manner that is not immediately apparent to the public."[13] Was Justice Powell, following the techniques of obfuscation and evasion already established in public discourse on the matter, engaged in plying the ad-man's art? There is a strong hint, if not a confession, to that effect in this footnote in his opinion:

> There also are strong policy reasons that correspond to the constitutional distinction between petitioner's preference program and one that assures a measure of competition among all applicants. Petitioner's program will be viewed as inherently unfair by the public generally as well as by applicants to state universities. Fairness in individual competition for opportunities, especially those provided by the state, is a widely cherished American ethic. . . . As Mr. Justice Frankfurter declared in another connection, "justice must satisfy the appearance of justice."[14]

Apparently, if justice requires ethnic preference, the appearance of justice requires "a subtle and more sophisticated" means of accomplishing it while denying that it is being done.[15] We have become familiar with the use of this technique by recent national administrations in other contexts; in the Nixon White House it was given the name of "plausible deniability." Whatever else may be said for it, it is hardly a way of advancing the public understanding of the meaning and the requirements of justice—the office, in its better moments, of the highest court in the land.

The Supreme Court's nondecision in the *Bakke* case was the logical culmination of the public nondebate of the issues underlying affirmative action. It is true, as opponents of affirmative action have pointed out, that the public generally and the demographic groups within it—whether defined by race, sex, region, income, or education—oppose the principle of preferential treatment in hiring or in college admissions. "No wonder," says Thomas Sowell, who shares that view, "proponents of affirmative action try to achieve their goals (and timetables) through non-elected officials in politically insulated institutions like administrative agencies and the federal courts. Put it to a vote and the whole game would be over."[16] Such a vote, of course, would be no measure of either constitutional or moral truth on the matter—not even from a majoritarian perspective. No majoritarian has ever argued that an "engineered" majority opinion, formulated in an arena of manipulation, has any claim to prevail.

Thus, the nation's highest tribunal, to whom its people look as keeper of its constitutional—and, to a considerable extent, its moral—conscience, did little to resolve the issues, and even less to clarify them. The resulting confusion led partisans on both sides to claim victory and lament defeat. Any hope that the Court would resolve the issues, or even clarify the terms on which reasoned public discussion might proceed, was dashed —at least temporarily—by the *Bakke* decision. The issues remain, in all their immediacy and complexity—immediacy because fateful questions of public policy are at stake, and complexity, which will give us trouble enough in confronting the issues even if we pursue the arts of reasoned persuasion rather than those of manipulation and evasion.

The stakes are large. They involve the future of our quest for racial justice, and therefore the seams in our social fabric. Beyond that, the stakes reach to the meaning we will give to our binding historic myths—the ideals of equality and liberty—and the direction and limits of our collective hopes and aspirations.

A Preview of the Book

The analysis that follows is an effort to put a pressing issue of public policy into philosophical and historical perspective. The discussion begins with an effort to clarify some of the confusions that stand in the way of a clear view of the issues at stake:

- The confusion resulting from efforts by proponents of affirmative action to distinguish between racial quotas and goals.

- The confusion introduced by the ways opponents of affirmative action, consciously or unconsciously, gloss over the seriousness and the consequences of racist white attitudes toward colored minorities.
- The confusion inherent in the phrase "reverse discrimination."
- The confusion reflected in the view that affirmative action is simply white paternalism and is demeaning to the minorities who are its ostensible beneficiaries.
- The confusion leading to the conclusion that the Constitution must be color-blind and that equal protection is always incompatible with preferential treatment.
- The confusion surrounding the argument that affirmative action promises to balkanize American politics and lead us in the direction of a new "ethnic-group feudalism."

The root source of these confusions lies in the ideal of equality of opportunity and its hold on the American imagination. The nature of this ideal—its assumptions, its history, and its relationship to the closely associated idea of meritocracy and to a more radical tradition of equality—is the focus of the last several chapters.

To suggest, as I have, that major arguments against affirmative action rest on confusion implies that if we set things straight by reducing the confusion, we will be led to a defense of affirmative-action programs. That is the goal of this work. What follows, then, is a defense of affirmative action in general, and of racial quotas in particular. At bottom, I believe, if there is not a defensible and persuasive case for quotas, there is no case for affirmative action and no effective way to deal with racial injustice.

My defense of quotas, however, is something like Winston Churchill's defense of democracy as the worst of our alternatives—except for all of our other alternatives. But if affirmative action gets only two cheers from me, they are nevertheless resounding cheers. I give it only two because I find much of its merit in the flaws in the argument against it. The case for affirmative action has weaknesses too, but they are not those alleged by its enemies. They are rooted, rather, in the inadequacy of the ideals to which affirmative action is forced to appeal. As currently defined, equal opportunity, because of its internal contradictions, ends up setting the rules for a white man's game. A successful affirmative-action program would involve nonwhites in the game on an equal footing. The trouble is that, to contest the unfairness of the game's rules, one must act as if it were a fair game. Minorities have no alternative; it is the only game in town. But the trouble remains: The more fair the rules are made to seem, the more legitimate and defensible the game appears.

The system in which equal opportunity now operates has been labeled a *meritocracy*. The term describes a technocratic and bureaucratic social order in which individuals occupy places in a hierarchy of income, status, and power that they have earned exclusively on the basis of their demonstrated individual abilities. (The meaning of meritocracy is further refined and its implications explored in later chapters.) Without effective affirmative-action programs, meritocracy functions as a color-blind defense of the advantages of white elites. But, purified of its hidden racial bias, meritocracy would function as a defense of the advantages of integrated elites against the integrated poor and powerless. Affirmative action is not a populist conspiracy against the rule of merit. It would integrate the "elite of merit," nothing more. If we are to have an elite of merit, there is no alternative to integrating it. To refuse to take the necessary steps to do so is to insure its collapse. That, finally, is why I am uneasy about such programs. There is no chance that we might be ruled by a racially exclusive meritocracy, but a good chance that an integrated meritocracy might prevail. And the very process of integrating the meritocracy may facilitate its triumph. We need a nobler, more humane goal than an integrated meritocracy, drawn from the ranks of an integrated, anxious, climbing middle class that is blind to the plight of an integrated underclass of hopeless losers. For that nobler goal I reserve my third cheer.

2

Quotas and Goals: A Distinction Without a Difference

In recent public debate, the major effort to avoid the real philosophical and practical issues of affirmative action has taken the form of efforts to distinguish between quotas and goals. Most of these efforts are so loosely argued that they are nearly unintelligible. Two themes, however, emerge: (1) quotas are said to be rigid, while goals are flexible; and (2) quotas are exclusionary in their effects, denying benefits to whites solely on the basis of their skin color, while goals are not. The first distinction is tenuous at best; the second is false. A quota need not be rigid: quota positions need not be filled unless there are a sufficient number of qualified applicants; a quota need not deny positions to minority members who qualify through regular procedures; the quota number can be changed. A goal, on the other hand, is so vague that it can mean almost anything: a flexible quota; a quota in disguise; an alternative to quotas in the form of "catch-up programs" designed to improve the competitive chances of minority individuals by bringing them into competition on an equal basis; "talent-hunt programs" designed to search out exceptional minority individuals who can qualify under regular admissions procedures; or even no more than a vague hope that someday all racial prejudice and discrimination will disappear.

Those who labor at the distinction are remarkably unclear about what is meant by *goals*. The reason for this apparent muddleheadedness is obvious: The distinction they are reaching for does not exist. They want to avoid the exclusionary quality of quotas in the belief that any program having the effect of decreasing the opportunities of whites would be rejected as both unconstitutional and unjust.

Quotas, it cannot be denied, are exclusionary: When some nonwhite applicants are admitted under a quota, some white applicants who would otherwise have been admitted under regular procedures are excluded. And the white applicants are excluded on account of their race. Since excluding people on the basis of race is thought to be both unconstitutional and unfair, quotas are seen to be indefensible.

But goals that are more than mere dreams or vague hopes are also exclusionary. President Carter's euphemistic phrase, "flexible affirmative action programs using goals," for example, clearly suggests a range of compensatory and preferential programs for nonwhites. If affirmative action does not mean at least that, it means nothing. And insofar as it means that, it will have exclusionary results for whites. Any form of racial preference, from preschool head-start programs to compensatory quotas, that improves the competitive opportunities of nonwhites also decreases the opportunities of whites.

In matters of relative status, prestige, and income, the total amount of opportunity is finite and relatively fixed, so long as meritocracy prevails. Winners imply losers. This is true even of that most flexible and innocuous commitment to goals that takes the form of a nationwide talent search for gifted nonwhites to be funneled into the elite of merit through the Ivy League and other prestigious colleges, professional schools, and management training programs. Whenever an "upward-bound program" provides compensatory treatment to the gifted nonwhite, or whenever a talent search seeks to encourage the applications of superior nonwhite students, special treatment on a racial basis is involved. Some white who otherwise would have made it will be excluded. Affirmative-action programs that exclude whites cannot be distinguished from those that do not, for the simple reason that there are none of the latter sort.

The Allure of a Painless Morality

Why have so many Americans been hell-bent on making a distinction between goals and quotas when no difference can be found? Part of the answer lies in the "great American myth," the most fundamental tenet of which is not—despite our recent teaching—that *anyone* can be rich, powerful, and famous, but that *everyone* can be. This is a noble and democratic sentiment; in our early history it defined the meaning of equality and of opportunity. More recently, however, this view has fallen on hard times, having vied unsuccessfully with the quite different ideal of equality of opportunity to become unequal. Equal opportunity in America has long since come to mean competitive inequality: success evaluated in terms of the failure of others; and wealth, power, and fame defined by the relative poverty, powerlessness, and invisibility of the losers.

We live in a world of competitive inequality in which success requires the failure of others. We don't quite know what to do with that older ideal of a world that is congenial to the fullest development of the infinite promise of each of us. We do not let it go completely; we dare not, for we sense that it provides our only assurance of civic decency. Neither do we dare to take it seriously, for to take it seriously would involve challenging the whole structure of competitive inequality and its most recent expression as meritocracy. What we have done instead is to commit the ultimate crime against an ideal. By being unaware (or pretending to be unaware) of the conflict between these two radically different meanings of equal opportunity, we have allowed the original ideal to be used to legitimize its opposite. And in the process we have made it almost impossible to think clearly about our real problems and alternatives. We want to

21

believe in two incompatible propositions: that all persons should have equal opportunities to develop their potentialities, and that opportunity should be proportioned to relative individual merit; that *everyone* can become president, and that *anyone* can. Worse yet, we want to believe the two are not incompatible. In the resulting confusion we try to imagine that in the competition for power and fortune, opportunities for whites do not imply the exclusion of nonwhites, while, at the same time, increasing the opportunities of nonwhites does not decrease the opportunities of whites.

Serious discussion of the costs of eliminating racial injustice and of who should bear those costs is avoided by an analysis that denounces quotas as immoral and unconstitutional because they have costs for whites, while goals are assumed to provide a costless alternative. These efforts at evasion can only be explained by our infatuation with the idea of a painless morality, and our love affair with growth as the means to implement it. We would never have imagined that peasants could acquire land without the aristocracy losing it, or that the masses in an authoritarian state could acquire political power without their rulers losing theirs. As a matter of fact, we have always known better. We realized that women and blacks could not attain the right to vote without diluting the power of the white man's vote. We understood that minorities and women could not achieve equal opportunity in employment without white males sacrificing some of their employment advantages. That's why those reforms were resisted so long and so strenuously. How can we believe now that past and continuing injustice can be remedied without its beneficiaries being deprived of their benefits? The reason may be that it is very tempting from the perspective of the beneficiaries, which includes all those who are white.

Whether or not most of us yield to the temptation, the nation's leadership—its politicians, editors, and opinion-makers—generally assume that we have yielded, and so offer us false and misleading assurances that our interests and our ideals are not in conflict. The results of this intellectual and moral confusion are predictable. Politically, the struggle for racial justice is in a bad way. Affirmative-action programs are required if the legal victories of the 1960s are to be translated into social and economic reality. But, white backlash against reverse discrimination threatens social peace, the jobs of politicians, and the programs themselves. This context—which is political, not logical or philosophical—makes the effort to distinguish between quotas and goals an appealing one. Perhaps a public that rejects quotas as reverse discrimination will not notice that other forms of affirmative action have the same consequences; perhaps, even, quotas can masquerade as goals.

Quotas Masquerading as Goals

Perhaps those who insist on a distinction between quotas and goals are suggesting that we can dig Nigger Jim out of prison by following the example of Tom Sawyer in *The Adventures of Huckleberry Finn*.[1] The problem for Tom and Huck, Mark Twain readers will recall, was how to rescue Jim from the crude jail in which he had been put as a runaway slave. Tom, who was an authority on all matters of the right and proper and traditional ways for prisoners to dig themselves out, explained to Huck that "case-knives" (table knives) were the only appropriate tools: "It's the *right* way—and it's the regular way. And there ain't no *other* way, that ever *I* heard of, and I've read all the books that gives any information about these things. They always dig out with a case-knife." Huck, not knowing any better and not caring "shucks for the morality of it, nohow" was all for getting on with the job with picks. But Tom would not "stand by and see the rules broke—because right is right, and wrong is wrong, and a body ain't got no business doing wrong when he ain't ignorant and knows better." After digging until midnight with case-knives, but with little visible result except blisters, even Tom began to see the advantages of getting on, and said to Huck, "Gimme a case-knife." Huck tells the rest of the story:

> He had his own by him, but I handed him mine. He flung it down, and says, "Gimme a *case-knife*."
> I didn't know just what to do—but then I thought. I scratched around amongst the old tools, and got a pickaxe and

give it to him, and he took it and went to work and never said a word.

He was always just that particular. Full of principle.

And so they dug Jim out with case-knives that were really pickaxes, but form, precedent, and rules were followed. Most supporters of affirmative action have played Tom Sawyer to the rest of us Huck Finns. What other explanation is there for President Carter, supported by the Justice Department in its *amicus* brief in *Bakke*, declaring that "programs using rigid racial quotas are exclusionary and therefore unconstitutional," but that effective "flexible affirmative action programs using goals" are both constitutional and necessary?[2]

If pretending that the pickaxe of quotas is really a case-knife of goals seems necessary to reconcile the purity of constitutional categories with the demands of justice, it is also required by the cardinal rule of political success in America: Make promises to the "have-nots" in a form that is nonthreatening to the "haves." We can pretend that flexible affirmative-action programs using goals have no exclusionary consequences for whites by distinguishing them from quotas, which obviously do have such effects. The result is to make quotas (masquerading as goals) more palatable to whites. So, what's the harm?

The harm is that it is dishonest. Dishonest in the sense of proclaiming as true what one knows, or ought to know, is false. This dishonesty tends to destroy the common meaning of the terms that make political choice and political action possible. It leads to a manipulative approach to social relations, which reflects the same attitude toward people that leads employers to deal with employee theft by periodic and random application of lie-detector tests. The assumption is that the world can be made more moral without altering our consciousness or activating our consciences.

Majorities and Highwaymen

The long-run consequences of the political posture this semantic evasiveness reflects will be disastrous. A case for affirmative-action programs that do have exclusionary consequences for whites—that is, all effective affirmative-action programs—can be made to any white male who is still capable of distinguishing "I want" from "I ought to have." If, as all the talk of goals and quotas appears to imply, we and our children are no longer able to distinguish our interests from our moral obligations, no semantic magic will save us. For in a democratic society, the rights of minorities of all sorts (ethnic, racial, economic, religious) depend on the ability of the members of the majority to distinguish personal interests from moral obligations. On this also depends the hope of the majority itself to live in a decent, just, and justifiable society. If our children have lost the ability to make that distinction, we have deprived them of their democratic birthright. If that is the case, the only political task worthy of our efforts is reviving the capacity to share compassionately in the injustice suffered by others, so that interests might be subordinated to the pursuit of justice.

There is no better arena for that effort than the struggle for racial justice. If we have robbed our children of the moral sensitivity that makes the struggle possible, we only compound the felony by appeasing or manipulating their interests. And to no effective purpose. If quotas are unjust because of their exclusionary effect, then the practical test of the morality and limits of any effort to achieve racial justice will be whether it leaves white interests intact. Where interests wear the mask of justice, they will be pursued with smug complacency.

In summary, the effort to distinguish quotas from goals serves intellectual, legal, and social purposes, none of which is defensible. Intellectually, this effort seeks to make preferential treatment consistent with the demands of meritocracy; legally, it seeks to circumvent what are seen to be constitutional proscriptions of preferential treatment; socially, it seeks to placate or manipulate a misguided white indignation over reverse discrimination and to conceal damage to white interests. But meritocracy demands too much and takes too great a toll of other, more important, values. The meaning of constitutional principles is itself a moral issue, and precisely the question that must be faced.

25

Most important, the appalling state of public opinion on the question cannot be accepted as a given without disastrous consequences. Public opinion, V. O. Key argued in *The Responsible Electorate*, is like an echo chamber; its reactions are shaped and limited by the sounds it is fed. In this respect it resembles a computer: "garbage in—garbage out." Indeed, if we are to judge from the polls, the letters to the editor, and casual conversation, there is no public opinion on the issue of affirmative action in America. There are only mass attitudes. For, as Tom Paine, foremost spokesman for the American common man, put it, "That only is opinion which is the result of reason and reflection." A range of social critics, including Paine, Ortega y Gasset, and C. Wright Mills, have told us that when people are treated as a mass whose desires and impulses are to be manipulated, rather than as the "liberal public" (which Mills defined as "a body of reasoning men to whom reasoned appeals can be made"), the result is neither "public" nor "opinion."

But the functioning of democracy requires the rule of public opinion. In its absence, when public opinion is replaced by mass attitudes, there is no answer to the question posed some sixty years ago by A. Lawrence Lowell: How are we to distinguish between majority rule and robbery? Lowell put it graphically:

> If two highwaymen meet a belated traveller on a dark road and propose to relieve him of his watch and wallet, it would clearly be an abuse of terms to say that in the assemblage on that lonely spot there was a public opinion in favor of a redistribution of property. . . . The absurdity in such a case of speaking about the duty of the minority to submit to the verdict of public opinion is self-evident. . . .[3]

Unless public policies reflect a public opinion rather than mass attitudes, there can be no obligation on the part of minorities to accept majority decisions. Majority rule then becomes the age-old rule of "force and fraud" (as Jeffersonians were fond of describing it) in new garb.

The effort to distinguish quotas from goals is an exercise in providing a protective cover for our failings. In the general moral, social, and political crisis of our time, nothing is more important than a rediscovery of the difference, in Ray Ginger's words, between asking: "What is right?" and "Am I covered?"[4] Liberal intellectuals and politicians, seeking to make a manipulative case for the cause of racial justice, are destined to lose both their case and their cause.

3

The Case
Against Affirmative Action

With a few noteworthy exceptions, when the case for affirmative action has been made at all, it has been argued ineffectively, and sometimes deceptively. The moral ground of philosophic and constitutional principle, meanwhile, has been staked out by its opponents. These circumstances suggest that inquiry into the merits of affirmative action might most usefully be pursued through description and analysis of the arguments of its opponents.

The case against affirmative action is attractive. It is pro-equality, grounded in the Constitution, against discrimination and prejudice, mindful of past injuries, protective of private freedom against governmental intervention, and rooted in a commitment to equal opportunity and the rule of merit. Those are no mean goods; they claim a place in the very core of democratic values.

Putting the Past Behind Us

The fundamental proposition in the argument against affirmative action is that discrimination on the basis of race is unjust, and that when such discrimination is reflected in law or public policy it is unconstitutional as well. The argument recognizes the historic crimes of racism in America, from slavery through Jim Crow, and it does not seek to deny that our racist heritage continues to do grievous harm to whites and nonwhites alike.

It is time now, the critics of affirmative action propose, that we leave the past behind. We must not corrupt the idea of equal opportunity for all, limited only by individual abilities and inclinations, by reintroducing race as a basis for preference. The long, hard struggle to restore the Fourteenth Amendment to its original meaning—to insure that no one is deprived of the "equal protection of the laws," and that all are equal before the law—must not now be undermined by public programs of racial preference. To return to the use of race as a factor in determining the opportunities of individuals is to return to the ways of our racist past and to sacrifice the substantial gains we have made in the last generation.

Constitutional concerns do not exhaust the argument. The issue is also a moral one. Discrimination is morally wrong. If past discrimination against nonwhites was unjust, so also is discrimination against whites. We cannot cure ourselves of racism by invoking it, even for a moral end. As our whole experience with modern totalitarianism ought to have taught us, ends do not justify means; the means we employ determine the ends we will reach. Affirmative-action programs that discriminate in favor of nonwhites will discriminate against whites. "Reverse discrimination" is no more defensible on moral grounds than past discrimination. And even if it were, the constitutional guarantee of equal protection of the laws would not countenance it. Affirmative-action programs that establish minority quotas for hiring, promotion, or school admission are especially reprehensible, since they flagrantly discriminate against whites by excluding them solely on account of their skin color. Quotas were used as a major weapon of anti-Semitism in denying Jews

29

access to higher education and the professions. The infamous history of the use of quotas is an accurate clue to their character and their consequences.

Not only does reverse discrimination continue the injustice of the past in a new form, it exacts an additional price in the inefficiency it produces. For if the more qualified are excluded in favor of the less qualified, society must pay the price in the reduced level of competence of those who deliver its services. Patients, clients, students, customers, employees, and citizens in general will be deprived of the services of the best doctors, lawyers, teachers, managers, scientists, and politicians that would otherwise have been available. Standards will deteriorate; the quest for excellence will be eroded. Efficiency, no less than justice, requires that rewards be allocated solely on the basis of individual merit.

Affirmative-action programs that discriminate in favor of nonwhites are held to be unfair and insulting to the nonwhites themselves. Blacks admitted through a racial quota acquire a tainted advantage that will undermine their dignity and sense of self-esteem. Quota admissions, in Meg Greenfield's phrase, are "handout 'rewards,'" which stigmatize their recipients and require them to view their achievements as favors conferred by a white Lady Bountiful. They are therefore, Greenfield adds, "antiblack in impact and patronizing as hell."[1]

Finally, if quotas (or other preferential programs) are allowed, it will be impossible to decide which groups and individuals are entitled to preference. As Justice Douglas put it in his dissent in the *DeFunis* case: If a proportion of an entering class is to be set aside for minority groups, "one must immediately determine which groups are to receive such favored treatment and which are to be excluded, the proportions of the class that are to be allocated to each, and even the criteria by which to determine whether an individual is a member of a favored group."[2] No satisfactory answer, Douglas argued, can be found for any of these boundary-line questions. If those questions cannot be answered, the results will be disastrous. American politics will be balkanized as every ethnic minority stakes out its claims on public policy. The result will be a new "ethnic feudalism," an intensification of racial and ethnic animosity and conflict, the creation of "Nuremberg-style" government agencies to certify the ethnic identities of individuals, and the absence of any clear standards that courts could use to protect the rights of individuals.

But Is It Too Soon?

The moral credentials of many who make this case—Justice Douglas, for example, and the members of the Anti-Defamation League—are unimpeachable. They were front-line fighters in the battle for racial justice well before the *Brown* decision that ended the infamous "separate but equal" doctrine. And they continued on through the civil-rights struggles of the 1960s. They fought valiantly, and in a period when personal costs were high, for voting rights, equal access to public accommodations, open housing, and equal employment opportunity.

This is a powerful argument, then, put forward by intelligent, morally serious, and sensitive supporters. But something must be inherently wrong with a proequality argument that reaches a conclusion endorsed by racists. There must be a flaw somewhere in a case that opposes special treatment on the basis of race, but ends up protecting the special advantages of being white in America. Something must be wrong with a high-minded defense of racial equality that can so easily be turned into the message to nonwhites that fills the letters to the editor columns these days: "Sorry about all those historical injustices, but after all . . . two wrongs do not make a right."[3] These letter writers reduce a subtle and sophisticated argument to a cliché, and the authors of those sophisticated arguments cannot be held to be responsible for their abuse. But is this an abuse? Or are the arguments themselves an elaborate gloss on a cliché? I will argue that the latter is the case.

For all the apparent plausibility of the argument against affirmative action, it reaches a false and dangerous conclusion. The conclusion is false because the argument is flawed at several points:

- It takes inadequate account of the lingering consequences of our historic racism and of the extent, the
  gravity, and the immediacy of the injuries still sustained by nonwhites in America.
- Its claim that whites suffer reverse discrimination
  under programs of minority preference is just plain
  wrong.
- The color-blind, racially neutral solution for which it
  strives is premature and therefore impossible.
- Its fear of a new "ethnic feudalism" is misconceived
  and misplaced.

The analysis in the following chapters seeks to defend these
propositions.

A Matter of Perspective

A striking characteristic of the arguments considered here is that
they are advanced from a white perspective. By focusing on the
principles of meritocracy, they largely ignore the issue of racial
justice which gave rise to affirmative-action programs in the first
place. The problem can be illuminated by asking a few simple
questions. Is meritocracy a principle whose moral claims are so
weighty that it ought to be accepted even by those who are
excluded on racial grounds from competing on equal terms?
How does the principle of meritocracy appear from a nonwhite
perspective? Martin Luther King, Jr., tried to explain to whites,
in passionate and moving terms, "why we can't wait." Have the
opponents of affirmative action offered a persuasive argument
to nonwhites that they can, and ought to, wait?

  If it is to be persuasive, such an argument must be more
than a defense of the general, abstract principle of meritocracy. It
must also demonstrate that the principle has a binding claim on
the loyalties of those racial minorities who are denied equal
access to its rewards. The principle must be justified not only in
its application to individual white losers, but also in its applica-

tion to those who suffer under the obviously unfair handicap of group prejudice.

The fundamental question, then, is whether racism poses a crisis of political legitimacy of the sort described by Lowell. Is the relation between white majority and nonwhite minorities in the United States like the relationship between highwaymen and traveler? The test of the moral genuineness and the persuasiveness of white arguments against affirmative action is simple: If I were not white, and were in full sympathetic understanding of what it means in this society to be colored, would I find the argument compelling? The case against affirmative action is ordinarily advanced from a white perspective, precisely in the sense that this test is *not* made. But unless it is made, successfully, all that is left is the rationalizations of white highwaymen as they divide up the loot (on the high-minded principle of merit, of course).

Compensatory Action: A White Perspective

Although opponents of affirmative action almost never face squarely the problem of remedying racial injustice, they do not ignore it altogether. While they are generally suspicious of distinctions between quotas and goals—on the correct ground that goals provide camouflage for the preferential treatment that quotas make obvious—they are inclined to make a different distinction between "preferential treatment" and "compensatory action." The former (whether practiced through quotas or goals) makes race a preferential consideration at the point of hiring, promotion, or school admissions. Compensatory action, on the other hand, consists of efforts to enhance the competitive skills of minority individuals so that they can meet the normal standards of merit for employment and admissions. Preferential treatment is vehemently opposed as reverse discrimination; compensatory action is supported as a means to overcome racially imposed handicaps without doing violence to the principle of selection by individual merit. Compensatory action, however, as I have argued above, does involve preferential treatment.

The willingness of the philosophers of meritocracy to make this exception can be interpreted as their concession to the problem of racial injustice. The question is whether it is enough; whether it comes close to recognizing what is needed to make the political order itself legitimate; and whether it can make a claim, in Lowell's words, on "the duty of the minority to submit to the verdict of public opinion." Those who believe the answer is yes, I submit, are simply unable to approach the question from the standpoint of the minority.

Yet this position—involving rejection of preferential treatment, but support for compensatory action—is the prevailing attitude of white Americans. Lipset and Schneider summarize the results of recent public opinion surveys: "But the conclusive rejection of preferential treatment does not carry over to a rejection of compensatory action. Americans support strict adherence to meritocratic standards, but will countenance programs that help bring 'disadvantaged' groups up to the level set by those standards."[4]

These attitudes reflect a striking degree of consensus among almost all groups in American society. They reveal the hold of the values of meritocracy on the American mind, and they demonstrate how those values set limits on what are viewed as legitimate ways of achieving racial equality. These attitudes display the extent to which the ideal of competitive inequality has come to dominate the more fundamental and socially necessary ideal of racial equality. And they explain the ease with which—between periodic episodes of racial violence —white Americans can consider the racial crisis as a sort of minor blemish on a healthy political order.

This rejection of affirmative-action quotas and goals in favor of exclusive reliance on compensatory action is possible only from a perspective that minimizes the gravity of the evils of racism and denies that racism challenges the legitimacy of the political and social order. It is, however unconsciously, a white perspective. And in a multiracial society a white perspective will not do. Both justice and social peace require a human perspective, in which racial inequality is viewed as a violation of the fundamental principles necessary to transform highwaymen and their victims into a political community.

4

Turning Crimes into Misdemeanors

The argument against affirmative action, I have suggested, takes inadequate account of the seriousness and depth of the problem of racial injustice in America. The meritocratic principle can only be given priority over the principle of racial equality if the gravity of racial injustice can be minimized. This is the case when racism is viewed as a flaw in an otherwise healthy meritocratic social system, rather than as a denial of unalienable human rights and a challenge to the validity of the political order itself. The opponents of affirmative action have sought to establish the priority of the meritocratic principle by treating the "disadvantaged" as individuals, not as members of groups. This individualistic bias has permitted them to ignore or minimize (1) the difference between the "disadvantages" of race and of poverty, and (2) the difference between the prejudice directed against colored minorities and that directed against white immigrant groups. These differences, however, are critical to an understanding of what affirmative action is about.

Being Poor and Being Black in America

The disadvantage that goes with being born to poor parents simply expresses the inherent contradiction in an ideal of equal opportunity to become unequal. As R. H. Tawney persuasively argued some four decades ago, any real equality of opportunity would require so much equality of condition (income, access to health care, education, housing, diet, etc.) that there would be few prizes left for the winners.[1] In a regime of competitive inequality, opportunities cannot be equalized because opportunity is precisely the object of competition and the reward for success. Rewards (a job, a promotion, admission to a prestigious university or professional school) *are* opportunities. Those who win them early in life have an advantage in the later competitions in life. Especially in the "post-technological society," where merit is identified with cognitive intellectual skills developed through education, those who lose in the early going are effectively barred from making a stretch run later. The analogy of an equal start in a fair race, under these conditions, is absurd. There is no way of determining the start of the race, and no way of stopping it to equalize competitive conditions. The old folk adage, "them that has, gets," sums up the outcome of the meritocratic race.

Thus, to be white and disadvantaged is to be one of the inevitable casualties of a system that promises, but cannot deliver, genuinely equal opportunities. *Disadvantage* is simply a way of describing the condition of those in the lower ranks of the meritocratic pecking order—or those who have the misfortune to be born to parents in the lower ranks. Disadvantage of this sort is an inherent by-product of a competitive social system that requires losers and, through the institution of the family, inevitably visits the losers' disadvantages on their offspring. This is what it means, ordinarily, to be white and disadvantaged in America.

But to be black and disadvantaged is quite another matter. We find a clue to its meaning by recalling the dramatic climax of the 1968 Olympic Games in Mexico City, when Tommy Smith and John Carlos stood on the victory stand after the 200 meter dash, gold and bronze medals around their necks, and as the

American flag rose and the national anthem began, they defiantly lowered their heads and each raised a black-gloved fist. Both were expelled from the Games. When asked why this protest against a nation that gave them the opportunity to compete on equal terms, Smith replied: "Sure, I came here and proved that I'm the world's fastest human, but when I go home, I'll be the world's fastest nigger." Fast nigger . . . rich nigger . . . smart nigger . . . To be black in a white racist society is not merely to be disadvantaged in the competition, but to be judged by standards that are irrelevant to the competition, so that even success itself has a different meaning.

To be black and a failure is to suffer from both failure and the social stigma of blackness. To be black and successful now is still to experience something like the trauma suffered in the past by blacks who successfully "passed" as whites. It is not simply that black persons are not judged solely on their individual merits. In a fundamental sense, in a racist society, they cannot judge themselves solely on that basis. Successful individual blacks have always had to "pass" for white in a cultural sense. They have confronted relentless social pressures to abandon any claims for a black cultural identity. At the same time, they have been under equally compelling moral pressures not to abandon their blackness and its obligations. Upwardly mobile whites have nothing to lose but a "poverty identity," which can be left behind without regret or substantial guilt. The successful were never expected to torment themselves with doubts about making it or guilt about those who hadn't. But a successful black can never simply leave other blacks behind. The reason for the different cirumstances of white and black achievers is, of course, the fact that color is a different sort of stigma than poverty.

Nowhere is the blindness to the meaning of racial prejudice more evident than in a question likely to have been heard by anyone who has participated in discussions of affirmative action: "Isn't it possible, under a preferential admissions program, that a black who has passed might now come forward to claim black ethnic status in order to gain admission?" The question is asked innocently and rhetorically, as if it clinched the argument, and as if it expressed an obvious and serious injustice. The question is utterly lacking in any decent sense of the trauma of passing or the implications of "repassing."[2] It is blind to the psychologically devastating consequences of a racism so deeply entrenched that a person could be led to reject what he is in order to appear to be what he must be to acquire fully human status. The question ignores the abiding fear of being "found out," and the guilt of rejecting one's heritage and abandoning one's fellow victims. And, passing or repassing, the hypothesized black is a victim. He faces a crisis of identity, which, in its soul-wrenching implications, gives ordinary white meanings of that term the analogous importance of the common cold. From a black perspective—from the perspective of racial justice—the question of whether a black might reclaim his ethnic identity to take advantage of preferential admissions can only trigger an almost inexpressible sense of outrage.

The point, of course, is not that those who raise this question are consciously racist. It is, rather, that what is ignored in the question makes it possible to overlook the social and moral significance of racial prejudice, and to conclude that the meritocratic standard has a higher claim on justice than racial equality.

A Nation of Minorities?

The distinction between color prejudice and ethnic prejudice is also glossed over when the principle of meritocracy is invoked as the criterion for judging disadvantage. The issue here involves the boundary-line problem discussed earlier. Justice Powell, in his *Bakke* opinion, offered what had become a common analysis of the problem: America's history of ethnic diversity is also a history of pervasive ethnic discrimination. Italians, Poles, Jews, Irish—each new wave of immigrants—had to struggle and, as Justice Powell noted, "to some extent struggles still" to overcome prejudice.[3] Moreover, most of these groups have still not achieved a proportionate share of prestigious and highly rewarded positions in society. If the claims for the groups favored by special admissions programs are to be accepted, Justice Powell asked, on what basis are we to deny the parallel claims of other groups? No such standard, Justice Powell argued, was available in the circumstances of the *Bakke* case, and none, he suggested, is possible.

Justice Marshall, in his separate opinion, proposed the standard of color. He grounded his opinion in the claim that "the experience of Negroes in America has been different in kind, not just in degree, from that of other ethnic groups."[4] Justice Powell's analysis rejected Marshall's contention. "The Court's initial view of the Fourteenth Amendment," Powell stated, quoting from the *Slaughterhouse Cases*, "was that its 'one pervading purpose' was 'the freedom of the slave race, the security and firm establishment of that freedom, and the protection of the newly-made freeman and citizen from the oppressions of those who had formerly exercised dominion over him.'" Powell noted that the equal protection clause was "virtually strangled in its infancy by post-Civil-War judicial reactionism."[5] Powell then argued that when equal protection was subsequently rescued from "decades of relative desuetude," it was given a broader interpretation. This new view was consistent with the universal applicability of its terms, "responsive to the racial, ethnic and cultural diversity of the Nation," and thus "assuring to all persons 'the protection of equal laws.'" Powell concluded, quoting the Court's opinion in *Hernandez* v. *Texas*, that "the Fourteenth Amendment is not directed solely against discrimination due to a 'two-class theory'—that is, based upon differences between 'white' and Negro."[6]

Having concluded that a "two-class theory" may not constitutionally be used to countenance legalized discrimination against other ethnic minorities (a conclusion shared, of course, by all of his colleagues), Powell assumed that he had also established the quite different conclusion that a two-class theory represented an artificial line for purposes of distinguishing groups entitled to preferential treatment. He noted, "There is no principled basis for deciding which groups would merit 'heightened judicial solicitude' and which would not."[7] Insofar as Justice Powell provides a bridge between these two conclusions, he does so not on constitutional but on demographic grounds.

"During the dormancy of the Equal Protection Clause," he argued, with appropriate citations to the works of social historians, "the Nation had filled up with the stock of many lands." By the time the amendment was revived, "the United States had become a nation of minorities. Each had to struggle—and to some extent struggles still—to overcome the prejudices not of a monolithic majority, but of a 'majority' composed of various minority groups of whom it was said—perhaps unfairly in many cases—that a shared characteristic was a willingness to disadvantage other groups."[8]

The thrust of this language is the amazing suggestion that there is no white majority. The logic is that if there is no white majority, there is no colored minority whose oppression could serve as a boundary line for granting preferred status.[9] It is too bad for blacks that the equal protection clause was virtually strangled by a reactionary court in the historical period in which they had a legitimate claim for the special protection of the laws. Powell argues that, in the interim, the white majority against whom the blacks' claims could be made has disappeared. It has become a "majority" composed of white ethnic minorities, many of which also suffered discrimination. And now, Powell concluded, "It is far too late to argue that the guarantee of equal protection to *all* persons permits the recognition of special wards entitled to a degree of protection greater than that accorded to others."[10]

The argument is not persuasive. The fact that the white majority consists of white ethnic minorities in no way establishes that white prejudice against blacks is any the less marked or serious.[11] America's demographic history in no way establishes that the "one pervading purpose" of the Fourteenth Amendment is now any less valid or compelling. Nor does the fact that white ethnic groups have suffered social prejudice or economic and legalized discrimination argue against using the color line as a boundary line.[12]

Mary Ten Thor has made the relevant point: "The white majority was a majority of subminorities, granted, but on one thing they came together as a united front that never cracked: their conviction that colored minorities were innately inferior and not fit to be treated as first-class citizens and Americans."[13] Whether that oppression is of a different and special kind, or whether it represents a difference in degree so large as to approach a difference in kind, sufficient to justify using color as a standard for special treatment is a question to be resolved in light of our social history. The objective indicators of prejudicial and discriminatory treatment, including inequalities of group economic results, furnish relevant and persuasive data. Moreover, it is the color line, and not the divisions among white ethnic groups, along which our country threatens to come apart. But perhaps the most compelling argument is found when each of us consults our own humane impulses and honestly tests our own experiences against them.

If the color line is the basis for a uniquely grievous social injustice, then the problem is not one of increasing the opportunities of individual blacks in order to serve the meritocratic ideal more effectively. The problem is how to establish—for the first time in our history—the terms on which colored minorities might be expected to accept the legitimacy of the social order itself, and therefore to grant it their allegiance and loyalty. The problem takes us back to the beginnings of democratic theory and practice to the nature of a social contract through which persons agree to live together as fellow citizens, subject to a common legal and political order. A social contract, as its philosophers have always understood, is a voluntary agreement among equals. It is therefore incompatible with invidious group inequalities of any sort. Who would voluntarily and freely agree to be bound by a covenant that assigned him the status of nigger in a white society? For these reasons, the issue of racism is politically and morally prior to the issue of meritocracy.

Anti-affirmative-action arguments, if they are to be persuasive, must insist on making meritocracy the focus of the debate and the arbiter of its boundaries. They thus avoid the more fundamental question of legitimacy, which can only be done by minimizing the significance of racism. Such arguments must treat racial injustice as a mere boil on the otherwise healthy body of meritocracy. This purpose is usually accomplished by treating blacks as if they were simply one ethnic minority among others in a nation of immigrants. Consciously or unconsciously, this purpose is often served by three different techniques: (1) analyzing the racial issue using a style, language, and spirit that eschews passion in favor of "objectivity"; (2) describing the problem of racism in general and neutral—rather than in concrete social and historical—terms; and (3) portraying racism as mainly a historical phenomenon.

Objectifying Racism

While most arguments against affirmative action explicitly recognize and condemn the crimes of our racist past, they rarely do so with moral fervor. It is not that their authors are uniformly wanting in passion; discussions of reverse discrimination often bristle with indignation. But their recognition of the injustice done to nonwhites is rarely infused with the spirit of outrage that is morally appropriate to outrageous assaults on human dignity. They suggest a wrong, but hardly one that is unrivaled in our history in its enormity, in its defiance of our most cherished ideals, or in its dehumanizing consequences for oppressed and oppressor alike. To concede dispassionately the crime of white racism suggests that all wrongs are equally indefensible, a posture that makes moral priorities impossible, and effectively places all wrongs beyond our control. The world is so full of wrongs, and righting them is so complicated, that if they are all equally wrong, we have no place to start. The complexity of injustices in the modern world offers enough incentive to defeatism and disengagement; we don't need the additional excuse of having no place to start.

I am not criticizing a mood or a style of argument here. Not everyone has a passionate nature, and in higher intellectual circles passion is often viewed as a sin against scholarly objectivity. But I am suggesting that if one is to conclude that there is not much more we can do to eliminate white racism, then a lack of moral fervor is necessary—or at least useful. Dispassionate description of white racism makes more plausible the contention that discrimination against blacks and reverse discrimination against whites stand on the same moral footing.

Neutralizing Racism

Even when the argument concedes the moral enormity of historical discrimination on the basis of race, it often leaves it at that—discrimination on the basis of race. But that nice, formal, neutral statement of the matter conceals the concrete realities of our experience and grossly distorts our moral perspective. We have not merely been inclined toward some generalized tendency to discriminate on the basis of race. We have practiced white supremacy; whites have been guilty of systematic discrimination against people of color. White racism, not racial discrimination in general, is the crime that must be righted. Here, again, the specific language of the analysis is needed for a particular conclusion. Stating the problem as "a tendency to discriminate on the basis of race" not only conceals white racism, but provides a basis for describing affirmative action as "reverse racism," and putting it on the same moral scale.

Historicizing Racism

White racism, moreover, is often described as a historical phenomenon: "The use of race to limit the opportunities of whites now is no less reprehensible than its use to exclude blacks in the past." "It *was*, of course, wrong . . ." But affirmative-action programs are not reparations, nor are they some sort of revenge for past wrongs. Their object is to remedy the continuing consequences of past wrongs and the future consequences of present wrongs. Fewer than three decades ago we abandoned Jim Crow. A very few years ago a homicide detective explained to me at a dinner party that he was able to be there only because a reported killing the night before had turned out not to be a homicide, but "only a niggercide—one of them killed another." He clearly viewed this as a matter not important enough to interrupt his day off. Can anyone doubt that fear and hatred so deep in our innermost selves must continue to find expression in more subtle ways? Can anyone really believe that to be black in America does not still involve an enormous problem of self-definition? Can we doubt that white racism results in reduced opportunities for its victims or that it acts in more subtle ways, difficult to rectify through law? If it were not so, nonwhites would have already acquired their proportionate share of the American Dream. If it were not so, affirmative action would be unnecessary.

The foes of affirmative action know all this; they would deny none of it. But they don't often say it. This makes it easier to rationalize that a white excluded by a quota is a victim of a historical reversal of discrimination, that a Bakke is a "nigger" in whiteface, and that the rule of merit can now measure individuals against objective standards with a fine impartiality.

Being Black and Being White in America

The confusion and moral blindness to which all of the above tendencies often lead is illustrated by an apparently trivial matter that turns out to have significant implications. Wishing to illustrate the "cockeyed vision" to which affirmative action leads, Eliot Marshall paraphrases circular A-46 put out by the Office of Management and Budget in May 1977:

> You belong to a "minority group" if you had at least one grandparent who was an American Indian, Alaskan native, Chinese, Indian, Japanese, Korean, Filipino, Mexican, Puerto Rican, Cuban, Central or South American, Samoan or was of other Asian or Pacific Island heritage, or "Spanish culture of origin" or of black African descent. You are in the majority if you had neither parent nor grandparent who was one of these. In this case, you are "white," being defined as "a person having origins in any of the original peoples of Europe, North Africa or the Middle East." [14]

Marshall concludes that "this may look like an arbitrary division of the world, but it's the way the federal government sees us." Of course it's an arbitrary division of the world. We have known for a long time that *race* is an arbitrary social classification, not a biological category. But it is the way we have seen ourselves for several hundred years. The federal government didn't make it up. If the list of minority categories is long, that is because there is a great variety of skin pigmentation in the world, and whites have been consistent in their aversion to color. If the "one-grandparent test" is absurd, that is not because federal bureaucrats are inclined to absurdities (though they may be). It is rather because the system of racial classification on which white supremacy has rested is absurd.

It is not really difficult in America to decide who is black. The question was decided for us, in a fateful way, when our white ancestors opted for white supremacy. In a white supremacist society, to be white is to have *no* discernible Negro ancestry; to be black is to have *any* discernible Negro ancestry. The definition is simply another way of implying white superiority and the taint of black blood. In a society characterized by black supremacy, we can be sure, the definitions would be precisely reversed.

Critics have argued that racial definitions within affirmative-action programs lead to unmanageable and inane consequences. They suggest that such definitions could even lead to a situation in which the Supreme Court would deal with a question like: "Can a person qualify as black if his only black relative was a grandmother listed in the official records as mulatto?" But the Supreme Court has confronted just that question in the past, and answered it without apparent difficulty. In 1896 Vernon Plessy, a Negro, came before the Court to plead his case for equal access to seats in a railroad passenger car. Vernon Plessy was one-eighth Negro, which means that seven of his eight great-grandparents had no Negro ancestry— and we can't be sure that the eighth, "Negro" great-grandparent had no white ancestry. Albion Tourgée, in his brief for his client, Plessy, spelled out clearly for the Court the meaning of race: "Why not count everyone as white in whom is visible any trace of white blood? There is but one reason to wit, the domination of the white race."[15] But the Court had no difficulty in avoiding Tourgée's question and his conclusion. The Court merely noted, in reply, that "the proportion of colored blood necessary to constitute a colored person" is "to be determined under the laws of each state" and is "not properly put in issue in this case."[16]

What seemed obvious to the Court would not have been obvious at all to a common sense uncorrupted by racism. If we merely intended to construct noninvidious racial classifications we would obviously classify individuals by the racial origins of a majority of their ancestors. The world has never known a society in which race was thus sensibly defined, for the simple reason that if we define the race of an individual sensibly, there is no reason to define it in the first place.

Our tendency to cling to racist definitions of *race* points up our unconscious racism. However, we have no real alternative to those definitions; we are saddled with them because they still describe the reality of what it means to be black or white in America. We cannot change to a more sensible, egalitarian way of making the distinction. We can only work in the most effective ways available to create a world in which the distinction itself is viewed as nonsensical and inherently vicious.

We are, therefore, caught in an uncomfortable trap. *White* and *black*, carrying all the freight of our racist past, continue to describe our social reality in important ways. Recognizing those terms as racist epithets does not cause them to disappear as social categories, or create a heaven of cultural pluralism. The effort to wish them away most likely leads in the opposite direction. To point to the inanity of racial definitions as a reason for not pursuing affirmative-action programs is to forget that millions of our fellow citizens still suffer under those inane definitions. If our inanity produced no victims, we could stop being inane. But we have no right to stop seeming to be foolish at the expense of the victims of our continuing foolishness.

5

Reverse Discrimination?

So far, my critique of the argument against affirmative action may appear to deal more with style than substance, or to make too much of nuances of language. But style and language may cloak, as well as reveal, our most basic assumptions. I have argued that style and language do more to cloak than to reveal the unconscious assumptions in the case against affirmative action. This becomes even more strikingly apparent in an examination of the charge that affirmative action means reverse discrimination.

Preference and Discrimination

The charge of reverse discrimination is rooted in the high moral ground claimed by opponents of affirmative action. They appeal to the principle of color-blindness—the principle that individuals should be judged exclusively on their individual merits without regard to race or color. The principle of color-blindness challenges all historical forms of legalized and institutionalized preference for whites and proposed forms of preference for others. It proposes that racism can only be overcome by ruling out all forms of racial preference. Viewed in this light, a racial quota—or any form of racial preference—appears to be reverse discrimination.

Too often the supporters of affirmative-action programs have accepted the phrase "reverse discrimination" as describing the effects of racial preference, and then have sought to justify, or evade, it. But to do so is to accept an unfair and unnecessary burden. What needs to be challenged is the proposition that racial quotas or other forms of racial preference for colored minorities involve reverse discrimination. They do not. And in the claim that they do lies a basic flaw in the case against affirmative action.

However implausible it may appear at first glance, the point can be made without hedging: *a quota system that gives preference to minorities does not discriminate against whites.* Even a compensatory quota of 100 percent, I will later argue, would not discriminate against whites as a group.

The charge of reverse discrimination rests on the implicit premise that whites are denied access to advantages to which they are entitled, and which they would have achieved had not preference been given to minorities. This assumption appears to make obvious sense—until one stops to think about it. Consider, for example, the Bakke situation. Let's assume, for the sake of argument, that Bakke was qualified by past performance and motivation and that he stood next in line for selection so that his place could be said to have been taken by someone admitted under the minorities quota whose qualifications were inferior to his. On those assumptions, was Bakke discriminated against on the basis of his race? Was he treated unfairly? Was he a victim of reverse discrimination, of the same sort of denial of equal protection under which minorities have suffered in the past?

My argument is that the answer to all these questions is no. Quotas are not reverse discrimination, for the simple reason that they do not imply or result in discrimination.[1] To discriminate, in the relevant meaning of the word, is not simply to treat differently, but to treat unjustly or unfairly on the basis of prejudice. Our common sense and our common experiences teach us this difference. As every parent knows, one of the most striking and frustrating characteristics of children is their inability to distinguish between different treatment and discriminatory treatment—a deficiency of judgment that leads younger siblings to perceive their lesser privileges as clear instances of parental discrimination. As every parent learns, an important part of the parental role is to enable children to become adults by equipping them to judge between different and unjust treatment. By just this sort of judgment, after all, the issue of justice is tested.

It should be clear, then, that the question of whether white males are victims of discrimination under affirmative-action programs is not answered by merely noting that they are treated differently from ethnic minorities. The question is whether they are deprived, on the basis of prejudice, of what they are fairly entitled to have.

As Justice Brennan, joined by three of his colleagues, noted in the *Bakke* case:

> Nor was Bakke in any sense stamped as inferior by the Medical School's rejection of him. . . . Moreover, there is absolutely no basis for concluding that Bakke's rejection as a result of Davis' use of racial preference will affect him throughout his life in the same way as the segregation of the Negro school children in *Brown I* would have affected them. Unlike discrimination against racial minorities, the use of racial preferences for remedial purposes does not inflict a pervasive injury upon individual whites in the sense that wherever they go and whatever they do there is a significant likelihood that they will be treated as second-class citizens because of their color.[2]

Is Winning Enough?

If white males excluded by a quota are not victims of prejudice, it still may be claimed that they are deprived of places to which they are fairly entitled. What then is the basis of this claim to entitlement? It is not enough to say that the qualifications of a rejected white are superior to those of a minority person who was admitted. The argument must be the more general one that the only way to be fair to individuals is to act, in allocating rewards, as if racial (and other) differences are irrelevant, so that individual achievement is the only criterion.

But, if to the winners go the laurels because they have run a faster race, the race itself must be fairly run. If winners are to be selected and rewarded on the basis of individual achievement, without regard to race, color, or sex, then fairness requires that those characteristics cannot have been determinants of the losers' chances. Justice involves giving people, not what their achievements warrant, but rewards commensurate with their achievements *in a fair race*. This is not my conclusion; I find the view of life as a racetrack to be a perversion of human possibilities. I believe that a thoroughly meritocratic society would be an unlivable society. What I am describing is the logically necessary corollary of the argument for merit and against quotas. At issue is the question of what Bakke, for example, was entitled to on the basis of his claims and the arguments of his supporters. It is his own test that he must be judged to have failed. For, on his terms, there was no position in the Davis Medical School to which he was entitled—which, that is, he would have won in a fair race. And unless we insist that individual merit be fairly achieved, we are left with a fascist glorification of success, however achieved.

Where would Bakke have stood at the finish if the conditions of justice (as Bakke's supporters defined them) had been met, if the race had been run fairly, if opportunities had been genuinely equal, and if racial prejudice had not been a factor in the chances of some of Bakke's competitors? The answer must be that he would not have ranked higher than the quota applicants. For, unless we are prepared to accept the racist premise of genetic inequality, we must conclude that the performances of minority competitors reflected the social and cultural consequences of racism. And we must conclude that, in the absence of the arbitrary handicaps imposed by racism, colored minorities would have performed as competently on the average as whites.

Fair competition would have produced equality of group results, and the quota positions would have been filled by minorities through the normal processes of meritocratic competition.

The crucial fact is that Bakke would not have earned the qualifications for admission in a fair race (unless, of course, it was unfair to deny him admission on account of his age, which is another matter, and one between him and his younger white competitors). He was, therefore, not entitled as a matter of justice to the position and he had not originally been denied it for being white.

In the specific situation of the *Bakke* case a quota of sixteen minority positions in an entering class of one hundred deprived neither whites as a group, nor individual whites, of any rights for which a plausible moral claim of entitlement could be made. In fact, since 25 percent of the California population is made up of minorities, nine white applicants received admissions to which they were *not* entitled.[3] The Davis quota went part way, and only part way, in preventing whites (as a group and as individuals) from continuing to receive advantages that accrue entirely from skin color and from continuing discrimination against minorities. In effect, and by the logic of Bakke's own assumptions, he was demanding the place a black or brown person would have won in a fair race.

Brennan, joined by Justices White, Marshall, and Blackmun, reached this same conclusion. "If," they argued, "it was reasonable to conclude—as we hold that it was—that the failure of minorities to qualify for admission at Davis under regular procedures was due principally to the effects of past discrimination, then there is a reasonable likelihood that, but for pervasive discrimination, respondent would have failed to qualify for admission even in the absence of Davis' special admissions program."[4] Justice Powell took vigorous exception to this proposition:

> The breadth of this hypothesis is unprecedented in our constitutional system. The first step is easily taken. . . . : [the regrettable fact of] societal discrimination against various racial and ethnic groups [is denied by no one]. The second step,

however, involves a speculative leap: but for this discrimination by society at large, Bakke "would have failed to qualify for admission" because Negro applicants would have made better scores. Not one word in the record supports this conclusion.[5]

Is there a gap between "societal discrimination" and the relatively disadvantaged position of blacks that can only be bridged by a "speculative leap"? Or is an elementary understanding of the dynamics of color prejudice enough? What sturdier bridges could be built than are already available in the experiences of John Howard Griffin, and in the works of Ralph Ellison, James Baldwin, Claude Brown, Malcolm X, Martin Luther King, Jr., Nat Hentoff, Robert Coles, Robert Blauner, William Grier, and Price Cobbs—the list goes on.[6] This is the literature that, by laying bare the consequences of color prejudice, both promoted and showed the need for the "second Reconstruction." Should its lessons have to be put on the judicial record? Should it not by now be part of our understanding of the "societal discrimination" that Justice Powell recognized as an undeniable fact?

True, the existence of inequality of group results does not, in itself, prove that they were caused by prejudice and discrimination. If there were no evidence of pervasive racism, a speculative leap might be necessary. But the undeniable existence of group prejudice and discrimination—which Justice Powell granted—furnishes compelling evidence. At most, only a very small and not very speculative hop (a "permissible inference," in the language of the law) is required to make the connection.

Explaining Away the Effects of Prejudice

There are, I suggested earlier, ways of arguing against this conclusion by offering alternative explanations for existing inequalities of group results. Three such explanations have been advanced. One is that the relative disadvantage of minority groups is a function of the date of their arrival on the American scene and simply records the time necessary to overcome the prejudice directed against each new wave of ethnic immigrants, and to assimilate them effectively into the melting pot of American culture. (This explanation assumes that each immigrant group has moved a rung up the status ladder by planting its feet on the necks of the next new group of immigrants.) The fact is, however, that, except for Jews, prejudice against white ethnics tended to be justified by cultural rather than genetic differences. Thus Madison Grant's racist ideology, developed in *The Passing of the Great Race* in 1917 and popularized in the *Saturday Evening Post* in the 1920s, focused on the colored races and the Jew as the source of genetic degeneration of the white race: "The cross between a white man and an Indian is an Indian; the cross between a white man and a negro is a negro; and the cross between any of the three races of Europe and a Jew is a Jew."[7]

Prejudice rooted in cultural differences can be overcome by assimilation; prejudice rooted in assumed genetic differences prevents assimilation. Thus, whatever validity the "date of arrival" explanation may have for white ethnics, it is inapplicable to the condition of blacks and other colored minorities.

A second effort to explain away inequality of group results proceeds from statistical analysis of differences in age distribution among ethnic groups. "The median age of the population as a whole was about twenty-eight at the last census. Puerto Ricans and Mexican Americans average almost a *decade* younger than that. Blacks average about twenty-three years old." At the same time, the jobs that are at stake in affirmative-action programs tend to be "high-level," requiring "long years of education and/or experience."[8] The conclusion this analysis reaches is that the underrepresentation of these groups in such jobs is attributable neither to genetic inferiority nor to discrimination, but to the fact that the groups consist disproportionately of younger people.

This explanation will not take us far in understanding the disproportionately high share of colored minorities in unskilled jobs—or their disproportionately low representation among firemen or policemen—to which affirmative-action programs have also been directed. Even in those jobs requiring long preparation, the disproportionate age distributions among ethnic groups fall far short of explaining how it is that "at last count

54

there was one white physician for every 750 persons in the general population, but only one black doctor for every 3500 black citizens," and that there "appear to be only 250 Mexican-American and 56 American Indian physicians in the entire United States."[9] To suggest that the age distributions described above explain such gross inequalities of results is to stretch the limits of credulity.

A third effort to deny the causal connection between prejudice and group inequality of results (without attributing the latter to genetic differences) suggests that there is no reason to believe, or to desire, that the cultural values of different ethnic groups would produce proportional economic and occupational results. Ethnic cultures, according to this view, give differing priorities to the development of different human aptitudes. We ought not to expect, then, this cultural diversity to produce uniform results; and we should not attempt to homogenize the healthy cultural diversity that produces these different results. The trouble with this analysis is that it simply smothers the historical and social reality of white racism in the warm glow of a pluralistic heaven. Blacks and the other colored minorities, to whom affirmative-action programs are addressed, are more accurately to be described as "nations within a nation" than as "free and equal" ethnic cultures coexisting amicably and in mutual respect with others.

The question of whether to embrace this vision of a pluralistic utopia, or the "melting pot" ideal that informs the first two efforts to explain away the effects of color prejudice, is irrelevant to the question at hand. None of these "explanations" offers a plausible alternative to the conclusion that the inequality of group results for colored minorities reflects color prejudice. How could we have imagined they would?

Getting Upset About Racial Preference

An implicit, but subtle, racism in some reactions against affirmative action is suggested by another consideration. When the question is raised about reverse discrimination on the basis of race, we are inclined to discuss the issue as if racial preference were the only departure from a strict regime of competitive, individual merit. [10] This assumption, of course, is far from the truth. In prestigious universities and colleges, in professional schools, and in business and industry, a wide range of arbitrary criteria is invoked to offer advantage on other grounds than merit. Preference often goes to the boss's son, the foreman's friend, the alumni's offspring, the children of influential politicians and potential donors, the bed partners, the politically conventional, the con-artists, and the positive thinkers—anyone with experience in the competition for place and power in American society could add to the list. None of these practices, of course, is justifiable on the premises of meritocracy. We grumble to our wives, husbands, and close friends about their unfairness. But we find them tolerable. They do not give rise to a backlash or the sort of resentment that threatens social stability. But quotas do. Why? Clearly, it cannot be because quotas are more important in their overall effect. Probably, the arbitrary preference accorded to persons on the basis of who their parents are exceeds in magnitude the consequences of a full-fledged quota system.

Is it, then, because these other arbitrary criteria are somehow less arbitrary, more morally defensible, than preference on the basis of race? To ask the question is to answer it. It is morally irresponsible even to put racial preference for oppressed groups on the same moral plain as customary forms of preference—as the key opinion of Justice Powell reveals in the *Bakke* decision. In his effort to justify the use of race as a factor in admissions decisions, Powell found that the justifying public purpose lies in the university's goal of a diversified student body. As Justice Blackmun noted, the effect of this reasoning gives preference that serves the cause of remedying racial injustice the same constitutional standing as preferences accorded "to those possessed of athletic skills, to the children of alumni, to the affluent who may bestow their largess on the institutions and to those having connections with celebrities, the famous, and the powerful." [11] Our moral sense protests against this result. And our common sense tells us that our unconscious racism provides an unpleasant but plausible explanation of why we are so much more disturbed about racial preference than about preference derived from parentage or other arbitrary considerations.

Whatever's Fair

Most affirmative-action programs aim to assign a proportion of available positions to minorities on the basis of their proportions of the relevant population. They may be described as "fairness quotas," since they indicate what the results would be if the competition were fair—if, more specifically, white racism had not crippled the chances of nonwhite competitors. The upper limit of a fairness quota for minorities in the *Bakke* situation, for example, would have been 25 percent.

A second type of quota may be described as "compensatory." By setting the figure higher than the proportion of minorities to the total relevant population, a compensatory quota aims at reaching a proportional result in the profession or occupation more rapidly.[12] A compensatory hiring or admissions quota—even one of 100 percent—would not lead to reverse discrimination against whites as a group. Its goal is to achieve a proportional share for minorities in the particular profession—the share required by justice in a system of equal opportunity. A compensatory quota, however, would discriminate against white *individuals*—or, more accurately, against the class of young whites just entering the job or career market. The misperception that this discrimination occurs under fairness quotas has led to much of the white backlash and increased racial tension in recent years.

Who's Sitting in Whose Place?

But even under compensatory quotas, the injustice done to young white males does not result from the preference given to minorities. It results rather from the accumulated historical preference enjoyed by older white males. The grievance of young white males under a compensatory quota is against their fathers, uncles, and cohorts—not their colored contemporaries. For, among those older white males, some occupy their positions unfairly and undeservedly. Some of these older white males would not be where they are if their potential ethnic competitors had been able to compete fairly. True, we cannot identify these individuals in any satisfactory or just way, but that is irrelevant to the question of racial justice. Group larceny does not make its victims less victimized or deprive them of the right of redress. To say this is not to imply, of course, that older white males have gotten their unearned advantages through personal acts of discrimination or displays of prejudice. They may well have belonged to the NAACP and the ACLU. In a sense, they couldn't avoid being favored for the color of their skins.

The trouble with compensatory quotas, then, is not that they are unjust in imposing injuries on whites—remedying racial injustice can never be costless to its beneficiaries—but that they impose the entire cost on the generation of white males just entering the career market. To put the matter bluntly, under a system of fairness quotas, older, successful white males are able to hang onto their undeserved advantages at the same time that it goes unnoticed that they are the beneficiaries of group larceny. Our sons do not blame us for frustrated careers; they blame our victims. They don't say, "I want to be a professor and you're sitting in my chair." They don't even say, "There aren't enough chairs—create some more." They say, instead, "Those blacks and Chicanos are getting places that rightfully belong to me." And they use the slogans we've taught them, albeit innocently, to put a moral gloss on their careerism: Individual merit is the only legitimate test. Sure, blacks and others have been victimized in the past, but two wrongs don't make a right.

The Sins of the Fathers

Among white males, the problem of justice is a matter of the equitable distribution of costs and burdens (which are justified) among generations and social classes. Our failure to confront the inequitable distribution of these costs has tended to make the costs themselves seem unjustifiable. In an earlier version of my analysis I argued that, from the perspective of the ideal of equal opportunity in a fair race, the Bakkes of the world are poor sports. Sore losers in the competition with those who had similar opportunities, they now demand the places assigned to those who ran the race in shackles. They demand continuation of the affirmative action for white males which is written, not in programs and regulations, but in the racist fabric of the social order.

That is a harsh judgment, but one I still believe is accurate if kept in context. The problem, as several critics helped me to understand, is that the context is too narrow. From a broader perspective than that provided by equal opportunity, it is also an unfair judgment. And it may appear self-serving when it comes, as Robert G. Thompson has reminded me, from a member of "a generation which has profited from and practiced so enthusiastically the folkways of merit and racism." It is also a generation that arranges remedies for the results of its own practices in such a way that the price is paid by its children, and by those of its peers who received none of the advantages of its practices. The older generations—the "separate-but-equal generations"—have arranged things so that the entire burden falls on the younger generation. They propose not to tax themselves; they give up nothing—"not one crumb," Harold Spaeth points out, "of their own piece of the American pie." They demand that their children pay their elders' debts. Not surprisingly, their children react with something less than filial obligation.

Every generation does, of course, pay the moral debts—and bank the moral credit—of its ancestors. In this sense the sins (as well as the virtues) of the fathers are always visited on their children. This constitutes the social inheritance. Guilt, of course, is not part of the package—except in the important sense that we are led by the weight of our inheritance to continue in the sins of our forebears. Harold Spaeth notes that the young might be expected to feel shame for America's past. They do not feel guilt: "And indeed, why should they? They were not guilty."

The crucial point, however, is that, as inheritors of a political and cultural tradition, the young share responsibility with all those living for amending that heritage to correct its faults and redress its injustices. But they are likely to be able to recognize and assume that responsibility only if it is shared. If among the young there are sore losers, that is because among the living generations of white males, they are the only losers. If they seek to avoid paying the price, "it is because," in Spaeth's words, "they cannot and will not continue to bear alone the burden of their inheritance."[13] Why should they?

Free Lunch at the Moral Counter

Considered purely from the perspective of what, in the name of justice, ought to be done, fairness quotas may not go far enough. Certainly such quotas are more a deliberate, than a speedy, way to achieve the results that justice requires. The main thing to be said for them, as opposed to compensatory quotas, is that they provide a gradual means to a just end without exacting a price from white beneficiaries of our racist past. If justice is our main concern, that is not saying much. In practical terms, however, it has a powerful appeal to a people who make much of the fact that in economic matters there is no such thing as a free lunch, but who imagine that in moral matters justice can, and must, be achieved painlessly.

But are we not obligated to ask more than that of those who are older, white, male, and successful? In a system in which inequalities of opportunity flourish, is not every successful person obligated to ask the question Nietzsche wanted even his Superman to ask: "The one who is ashamed when the die has fallen in his favor and asks, 'Have I, then, been cheating?'"[14] This question triggers the moral sense and introduces the claims of justice into our assessment of a situation. Perhaps our children have learned from us that the question need not be asked; or they failed to discover, because they found no example in us, that such a question is conceivable.

Nietzsche's question is the starting point for concern about the problem of distributive justice. By putting our own advantaged positions on the defensive, it directs our attention to the fairness of the system through which differential advantages are distributed. An older liberalism had obligated individuals to put Nietzsche's question to themselves. Modern liberalism has made the question unnecessary. Modern liberalism has fostered an acceptance of self-interest as the motivating force of politics, and a reliance on the system of group rivalry to produce an automatic equilibrium of group interests. Thus liberalism has legitimized the tendencies toward egoism created by our consumer society. We have not been able to deal effectively with the problems of poverty and powerlessness. We have seen the creation, under liberal auspices, of an underclass shut off from majority affluence and influence. These phenomena reflect the failure of relatively affluent liberals—who believe that some people are too poor—to ask themselves: "Do I, then, make too much?" Similarly, the question avoided by opponents of affirmative action is: "If minorities have too few advantages, do not whites have too many?"

Our vaunted pluralism in politics can respond to new demands from groups at the bottom only if there is an annual increment large enough to satisfy also the expectations of the powerful and entrenched groups at the top. We should not be surprised, in these circumstances, to discover that questions of distributive justice have all but completely disappeared from the political agenda. The appeal of minorities to racial justice is lost in this political and moral vacuum.

Moral Indignation as a Scarce Resource

Compensatory quotas, of course, are not the source of the recent and continuing fervor over affirmative action. After a brief trial in a very few places in the late 1960s, compensatory quotas were rapidly abandoned in the face of a white, largely intellectual, backlash. The debate now rages over fairness quotas. And on that level, no question of discrimination is involved.

Quotas are not reverse discrimination in either an individual or a group sense, and the insistence on describing them that way serves only to protect white interests while soothing white consciences. In letters to the editor and in casual conversation, one is struck by the vehemence, the moral outrage, and the righteous indignation that accompanies the charge of reverse discrimination. A nation with such reserves of easily triggered moral indignation and such a keen eye for discrimination might be expected to be a little further down the road to racial justice by now! This capacity to get in a moral lather over reverse discrimination against whites (which does not exist), while whites continue to enjoy the advantage of a racist heritage (which still exists) says something about the adequacy of our perceptions and the seriousness of our moral claims.

But if quotas do not produce reverse discrimination, another and more valid charge may be made against them and against all other forms of racial preference. They seek to produce the conditions that would exist if there were no discrimination against minorities, without eliminating discrimination against minorities. They would thus approximate the results of equal opportunity without achieving the conditions of equal opportunities. This is a valid charge, but not a morally weighty one; if we can't have both—at least in the immediate future—we're better off with one than we would be without either. We have been tragically unsuccessful in eliminating racism, especially in its subtler forms. Very likely its roots go so deep in our culture, our institutions, and our psychological makeup that it will take generations.

So our choices for the near future involve continuing to live with racism and its social and economic consequences, or altering the social and economic consequences of racism without waiting for its roots to wither.

Is there not a serious moral flaw in a concept of meritocratic justice, advanced by whites, that argues that whites are morally justified in continuing to play with a loaded deck? Why, in any event, should aggrieved minorities be expected to wait patiently on the processes of cleansing white souls for changes in the objective economic conditions of their lives?[15] Moreover, a powerful case can be made that changes in the social and economic status of minorities will be, in the long run, a powerful factor in speeding changes in white attitudes. In the American gospel of equal opportunity, it is a short step from being poor and black to being judged poor because black. Whites are generally willing to accept equality before the law as a close enough approximation of social justice built into the law, a fair chance as a substitute for real equality of opportunity, and the results of unequal opportunities as a satisfactory measure of the relative merit of the competitors. Under these conditions, inequality of group results will continue to feed white prejudice and, however unconsciously, delusions of white superiority.

Equality of group results, even though achieved through programs of racial preference, may in the long run benefit from the great American tendency to use the slogan of equal opportunity to legitimize whatever the winners have come by. In the old American adage, "nothing succeeds like success." It's worked that way in the past for successful whites. Why not for blacks in the future?

Even if it is granted that fairness quotas produce a sort of justice, it still may be objected that they do it too crudely. It may be objected that not all blacks are equally disadvantaged, that there are other sources of disadvantage that are not touched by racial quotas, the chief of which is being poor.[16] There is truth in the objection, but such moral fastidiousness is unbecoming in a people who have been able to stomach without apparent distress the rough textures of success in American life. In any event, doing justice is always, for fallible man, a rough business. The old principle that the good should not be allowed to become the enemy of the better is still a solid ground for moral conduct.

6

White Paternalism
and Black Self-Image

Writing in 1965, the same year as the Department of Labor report that envisioned what was later to be called affirmative action, Donald E. Smith predicted that such programs were not feasible in the United States for two reasons. First, it would be regarded as "'patently unfair' to favor race groups with state aid." Second, such programs "would meet with strong objections from the Negro community itself, which would resent the official label of social or economic backwardness."[1] His predictions have been half-accurate. Affirmative action has been regarded, by a large majority of whites, as patently unfair.

A Stigma of Backwardness?

The predicted reaction of the Negro community has not proved to be as accurate. The assumption underlying this prediction was that blacks would choose to judge their rights not on the unfairness of their condition, but on the color-blind principle of individual merit. On that principle, to receive preferential treatment on the basis of race would be to accept a label of social or economic backwardness. But what does this mean? "Social and economic backwardness" may simply be a way of describing the consequences of racism: the growing social and economic gap between blacks and whites, the higher rate of unemployment among blacks (a horrendous 40 percent among young black males), and ghetto poverty.

Few blacks would have a problem accepting their "backwardness," if such were its meaning. But that, of course, is not its meaning. The official label of "backwardness" is a stigma that follows from applying the logic of meritocracy in a color-blind way. If blacks are given preference on the basis of their group identity, the color-blind principle decrees that the recipients of preference be labeled "backward" and their achievements stigmatized as tainted. But if blacks are treated as individuals, the meritocratic principle mandates that the group basis of their disadvantage be disregarded, and thus labels their disadvantage as "backwardness." Catch-22.

Are the victims of this perspective likely to share it? Or, should we expect that nonwhites, from the experience of their daily lives, are more likely to understand what many intellectuals and most white Americans have failed to understand—that "backwardness" is the label meritocracy places on real inequalities of opportunity? What, from the perspective of human equality, appears as racial oppression, appears as individual failure from the perspective of meritocracy. To expect blacks to acquiesce to the meritocratic view is to expect them to be accomplices to their own oppression. They can be expected to resent the label of "backwardness" as thinly disguised racism concealed in the color-blind rhetoric of meritocracy.

The issue here is whether affirmative-action programs are patronizing, and whether they undermine the dignity and self-respect of those who are presumably patronized by them. The claim that affirmative-action programs are patronizing has been widely and persistently made from the beginning. "The anti-Bakke argument," Meg Greenfield asserts, tends, however inadvertently, to be "anti-black in impact and patronizing as hell."[2] She describes as "mindless and damaging" the argument made by "so-called friends of minorities" that "a ruling for Bakke would undo all the gains made since enactment of the great civil rights statutes of the 60's." She views this argument as "mindless and damaging," presumably, because it implies that "those gains were strictly the product of special help and various props which, if removed, would spell the end of black achievement." And she characterizes it as "patronizing and wrong-headed to attribute the big changes that occurred after the enactment of those laws to something other than the talent and will of a people only lately liberated."

Affirmative Action: Prop or Foundation?

This analysis raises both an empirical and a theoretical question. The empirical question is raised by the claim that black achievement in recent years is the result of the talent and drive of individual blacks, and not at all a result of racial preference. It would follow from this premise that continued black achievement would not be affected by elimination of racial-preference programs. The evidence appears to be solidly against this supposition. The brief for the university in the *Bakke* case made a powerfully documented argument that, without affirmative action, the flow of black students into medical and other professional schools would be reduced to a trickle. McGeorge Bundy, reviewing the historical evidence on the admission of blacks to medical schools, reached the same conclusion. In the last year before special admission programs "began to be significant" (1967–1968), there were 735 blacks in medical schools, 71 percent of whom were in two black medical schools. In the hundred other medical schools with "racially neutral" admission standards, the 211 blacks enrolled constituted 0.6 percent of the total (blacks are 12 percent of the total population). There are now 3,000 blacks (5 percent of the total) in those schools. Bundy concluded that "what most close observers believe is that if these same mainly white medical schools were driven back to 'racially neutral' admissions, the number of blacks would slide back close to where it was in 1968." Moreover, he added, "a parallel impact would be felt in other professional schools and selective colleges."[3]

This conclusion is hardly surprising. It merely reflects the obvious fact that white racism is still a significant factor in black competitive disadvantage. Greenfield, and those who share her views, are surely too sensitive and knowledgeable to believe otherwise. One suspects that she is driven to her conclusion not by the evidence, but in order to defend what she sees as the necessary condition for black dignity and in order to avoid a patronizing position. The trouble with this analysis is that, in order to avoid stigmatizing black achievement, we are compelled to believe that race is not still a handicap. If, against the evidence, we accept that conclusion, we give support to the perverse logic of meritocracy. If color is assumed not to be a handicap, then relative black failure is a badge of black inferiority. Where, then, black dignity?

If, on the contrary, as the evidence clearly suggests, color continues to mean reduced opportunity, then racially neutral standards will produce relative black failure. Color-blind meritocracy, again, stamps its label on the losers, and their failure reinforces the racism that has caused it.

Because it is both color-blind and meritocratic, the assessment of the conditions of black dignity underlying this analysis is inadequate and misleading. It assumes that the problem of self-esteem is the same for everyone, and that the problem is defined by the logic of the meritocratic ideal. In a society dominated by the success ethic, and characterized by lifelong competition for status, no one's self-esteem is secure. No one experiences what Edmund Burke nostalgically described as "the unbought grace of life" that characterized societies in which status was largely inherited or ascribed. In modern meritocratic social systems, individuals earn self-respect and dignity by achieving success in the world.

For those who view the world from this perspective, success that is not earned by competitive demonstration of individual merit is not a legitimate basis for self-esteem. Even the achievers suffer continuing anxiety and self-doubt, since the race has no finish line and other competitors have a lead. But the perpetual crisis of self-esteem confronted by those who enter the race on equal terms (insofar, of course, as this misty slogan has any operational meaning) is not to be equated with the wounds to dignity and self-worth inflicted on minorities by racism. Those wounds are rubbed raw in a meritocratic milieu in which whites, having eliminated legal barriers, are smugly and self-righteously satisfied to leave the rest to individual achievement.

A Sense of Dignity

Self-respect, as J. R. Pole notes, is always "crucial to the balance and integrity of the human personality."[4] It is ordinarily maintained through a sense of recognition and belonging that is offered by social groups. This is ordinarily possible only when the groups one depends on are not "specifically deprived of respect by the rest of society." A sense of belonging to a group that is denied esteem and recognition from the larger society cannot be a source of self-respect—except for outlaws, or revolutionaries.

Here, again, there is a hidden and unconscious racist undercurrent in our attitudes. We worry, conscientiously, about undermining the dignity of minorities by conferring on them unearned and unmerited benefits. But, what of the dignity and sense of self-worth of those who owe their positions in the professions to the preferential advantages whites have enjoyed in the past? Or, more generally, what of those who have inherited success by inheriting wealth?[5] Are their situations any different? Why does their "success" not carry the stigma of an arbitrarily conferred benefit? Why do we not expect their sense of dignity and self-worth to be compromised? How is it that those whose success is the unfair consequence of injustice are able to feel a secure sense of self-esteem, while the compensation of its victims is expected to lead to self-deprecation and self-doubt? How, indeed, can this be—unless we somehow unconsciously connect white skin with self-esteem? Otherwise, the "equal-opportunity liberals" would share the same concern for the threatened self-images of the children of the rich and of those who presently occupy the positions that would have been filled by minorities in a fair race.

Is it, then, patronizing for whites to support affirmative-action programs? My dictionary defines a *patron* as "anyone who supports, protects, or champions." The Latin root of the word, of course, is *pater*, and hence another meaning of patronize: "to treat in an offensively condescending manner." Affirmative-action programs will appear to minorities in that light only if they are seen as exceptions to meritocratic principle, rather than as remediation of racial injustice. Does it make sense to believe that a nonwhite who has become a qualified physician will feel a weakened sense of self-esteem because he took the place of a white who, without the advantage of race, would not have been better qualified for admission than he? It is a white presumption that a black, admitted under a quota, will accept the stigma attached by whites to his admission, or will feel that his admission is somehow a denial of the ability, enterprise, and determination that won him his quota place. To become qualified for a quota position, against the racist odds of American society, is a greater individual accomplishment—more meritorious, in a nonmeritocratic sense—than to have won a regular position as an upper-middle-class white. Why should we expect a black person to judge himself by a criterion of equal opportunity that he has never experienced?

Nor should we expect minorities to experience pangs of guilt over their complicity in an alleged affront to a meritocratic definition of social efficiency. A black, admitted to medical school under a quota, has every right to feel that he is, in fact, redressing the color-blind meritocratic inefficiency that has resulted in a grossly unequal distribution of doctors in white suburbs and black ghettos.

Black dignity is simply not achievable on white terms, and the terms of color-blind competition are white terms. It is true that blacks and other minorities have acquired a remarkable sense of dignity and self-esteem in recent years. But they are not peoples only lately liberated. They gave up the hope of being liberated by the white majority a decade ago, and proceeded to liberate themselves. "Black is beautiful" was not a white slogan, nor even one addressed to whites, but a declaration of independence from white judgments—a self-affirmation, a unilateral declaration of the meaning of color. This self-liberation—the decision to fulfill no longer the oppressor's role definition—is the historical prelude to social and economic liberation. The course of the struggle is inexorable, once that decision is firmly made—it ends in social and economic liberation, or in revolution. During the struggle, the terms of human dignity for the historically oppressed group are no longer under the control of the oppressors. It is, therefore, fruitless for whites to presume to specify for nonwhites the ground on which they are entitled to experience a sense of dignity and self-esteem. Is there not something patronizing about whites presuming to determine when a nonwhite is patronized?

Beyond Paternalism

Still, in some sense, white paternalism is unavoidable—so long, at least, as the actions of whites are informed by the moral imperative of racial justice. Whites have no alternative to acting like *pater*. They are *pater* in the sense that, being a majority and occupying the centers of power in society, they make and change the rules. If we are in earnest about racial equality and racial justice, we have no alternative to being do-gooders, and to running the risk of condescension that the role implies. Whites must be patrons, if they are not to be patroons. The difference between these roles, again, is measured by the extent to which white interests—those advantages accrued from a heritage of racism—are impaired. And, again, the test of our moral commitment is whether we entertain a deep and abiding suspicion of any interpretation of nonwhite interests that leaves white advantage intact. The same argument applies, of course, to the attitudes of the affluent toward the poor, of men toward women, and of the politically powerful toward the politically invisible.

The problem of paternalism is that the more successfully whites meet this test, the greater the risk they will act in a patronizing manner toward those who have been unfairly disadvantaged and to whom they now propose to give up their unfair advantages. But the only way to avoid the risk is to do nothing, to wait for the oppressed to claim their inheritance by force, or to yield to the threat of social disorder what is owed to justice. Who can believe we are not better off to run the risks of condescension? The hope is, of course, that the risk is temporary, since whites will be deprived of the vantage point from which their whiteness makes condescension possible.

The issue, then, is not whether blacks will feel stigmatized by the preference they enjoy under affirmative-action programs. The issue is whether the stigma, applied by whites, amounts to a white conspiracy to continue to rob blacks of dignity. The remedy is clear: let whites stop stigmatizing blacks in that way. But, if the remedy is clear, it is not simple. It requires no less than a fundamental reexamination of the values and attitudes that give rise to the stigmatizing in the first place. If we follow through on this reexamination, we will be led to a discovery of the internal contradictions, the false promises, and the alienating and dehumanizing consequences of some of our most cherished ideals. Such an inquiry reaches beyond the issue of race to the terms of human dignity generally. It questions the adequacy and the humanity of an ideal of equal opportunity that makes dignity a prize available only to the winners. It opens the possibility of returning to a more radical ideal of equality, which could serve a more egalitarian purpose than the defense of the advantages of whites, males, the rich, and the powerful. Only through such an ideal can the question of dignity be cast in human rather than meritocratic terms, and so become available to all.

7

But Some Are More Equal than Others

In 1928, in his speech accepting the Republican presidential nomination, Herbert Hoover offered his version of the American Dream:

> The founders of our Republic propounded the revolutionary doctrine that all men are created equal and all should have equality before the law. This was the emancipation of the individual. And since these beginnings, slowly, surely and almost imperceptibly, this nation has added a third ideal almost unique to America—the ideal of equal opportunity. This is the safeguard of the individual. The simple life of early days in our Republic found but few limitations upon equal opportunity. By the crowding of our people and the intensity and complexity of their activities it takes today a new importance.
>
> Equality of opportunity is the right of every American—rich or poor, foreign or native-born, irrespective of faith or color. It

is the right of every individual to attain that position in life to which his ability and character entitle him.[1]

The intervening four decades have not materially altered the authentic tone of these phrases. Here, in all its ringing ambiguity, is the American doctrine of equality, the very center of the great American consensus. It starts out by offering hope to the losers and ends up blessing and protecting the advantages of the winners. The words sound plausible and meaningful; yet they are shot through with contradiction and ambiguity. If we think they make sense, it is only because we confuse familiar sounds with intelligible meaning.

Our national faith has come to be summed up in equal opportunity, which is in turn seen to be adequately protected by "equality before the law." The shortcomings of these ideals, in their current interpretation, go far toward explaining a whole range of symptoms of political and social crisis:

- The fact that we have been unable to relate ourselves meaningfully to the revolutionary ferment in the rest of the world.

- The fact that increasing numbers of poor people, colored people, and young people are alienated from the political process.

- The fact that a middle class—including both the working poor on the verge of penury and the affluent on the verge of opulence—can make common cause in a "taxpayers' revolt."

- The sporadic and inadequate concern for the problem of poverty and the pervasive absence of resentment toward the very rich.

- Our dependence on growth.

- The disappearance of the question of redistribution from our political agenda.

Each of these symptoms reflects the fact that equality, as it is currently understood, no longer functions as an ideal. It no longer provides us a basis for judging any of the actual inequalities in the world. Not surprisingly, racial injustice is protected by the same myth that protects all existing inequalities.

Rich or Poor

Consider some of the questions raised by Herbert Hoover's authentic statement of the American creed. "Equality of opportunity is the right of every American . . . to attain that position in life to which his ability and character entitle him." It is his right whether he is rich or poor. But how can the poor child's opportunities be made equal to those of the rich child without making him (or his parents) rich? In the absence of equal conditions, equal opportunity means only that the poor child's poverty will not be an insurmountable barrier, and that poverty will not be legally used to establish caste barriers to mobility. Thus, it turns out that the poor man's "equality before the law" is all that is required by the principle of equal opportunity.[2]

Is this because Americans have not taken seriously enough the ideal of equal opportunity or, as seems more likely, is it because the promise of equal opportunity to become unequal is an absurdly contradictory proposition? Was Hoover's invitation to the poor to share in the American Dream genuine? Or was it, for most of them, "the impertinent courtesy of an invitation offered to unwelcome guests in the certainty that circumstances will prevent them from accepting it"?[3]

Hoover extended the invitation not only to the poor, but to those of every "faith or color." Nineteen twenty-eight was a time when Jews were barred by quotas from vocational opportunity and suffered from social and economic bigotry, when blacks were still being lynched by white mobs and Congress would not even consider a federal antilynching law, when segregation was the law of the land, and when overt and vicious racism was accepted social practice. The remarkable fact is that neither Hoover nor most of his countrymen regarded those conditions as barriers to equal opportunity or as violations that cried out for redress. It was enough that all Americans, "irrespective of faith or color," were equal before the law. And they were. The Supreme Court had said so.

Irrespective of Faith or Color

Hoover affirmed the right of the individual to rise "irrespective of faith or color." He proposed, in essence, that we can treat people equally without treating them as equals. Hoover's position, considering the condition of blacks in America in 1928, is logically absurd and morally obtuse.

But it differs in degree only—not in principle—from the attitudes of "equal-opportunity liberals" today. It is still absurd to believe—as the American consensus still appears to hold—that nonwhites have equal opportunity to attain those positions in life to which individual ability and character entitle them, even though color is an important determinant of opportunity. Although the Court has revised the meaning of "equality before the law," it is still absurd to believe that legal equality is a sufficient guarantee of equality of opportunity. And it is still moral effrontery to offer blacks the social ladder on the same formal terms as whites. In those circumstances, in the words of John Plamenatz, "the ladder, as they see it, is there less for them to climb than to advertise to all and sundry their lack of ability to climb it."[4]

The Right of Every Individual

Hoover's—and our own—conception of equal opportunity affirms the principle of individualism. But it ignores "the coordinate principle of interchangeability," which is required by the "equal" part of the doctrine. J. R. Pole defines the principle this way:

> The interchangeability principle in turn means simply that, if the requisite training and experience were given—which for

reasons of social history, oppression, and privilege has not usually been the case—a white and a black, a Protestant and a Roman Catholic, a Jew and a gentile, as well as a peasant and a nobleman, could take each other's places in work, in sport, in intellectual discourse, and in the respect their personal bearing could command from others.[5]

Unless the individualistic principle, that each person is entitled to be judged on individual merit, is linked to the egalitarian principle of interchangeability, individualism can serve only to conceal the social effects of birth, race, sex, or class. To assume that individualism automatically produces interchangeability is to put the opportunity cart before the egalitarian horse. Equal opportunity can function to measure the relative merits of individuals only in a society that regards individuals as having equal *worth*.

For these reasons, equal opportunity as it has developed in America is, strictly speaking, not an ideal at all. Short of the case of a caste system that denies opportunities altogether (including such variations as the legal enforcement of the "separate but equal" doctrine), the dominant version of equal opportunity provides no standards for identifying or criticizing actual inequalities of opportunity.[6]

It is easy to detect the way in which equal opportunity served both the president and his white countrymen to conceal and rationalize the racism of America in the age of apartheid. Why is it more difficult to discern the same effects of the identical rationale in the arguments against affirmative action?

Yet, public-opinion surveys reveal that Americans are still able to believe today what they were able to believe in 1928. Then and now, because of its inherent ambiguity and internal inconsistencies, equal opportunity has functioned in America more as a consoling myth than as an operative ideal. Its effect has been to justify existing inequalities and to make them tolerable to those at the bottom. It has concealed the reality of actual inequalities of opportunity so effectively that, until very recently, it has distorted reality even for blacks themselves.

"Negroes Are Treated Fairly"

In postbellum America, Booker T. Washington, born a slave and himself a model for black achievement, proposed to lead his people up from slavery through individual self-improvement. The essence of Washington's position was that the individualistic, competitive virtues of diligence, persistence, and hard work, exercised and developed by individual blacks, would result not only in the improvement of black conditions, but in the elimination of prejudice as well. "Say what we will," he wrote, "there is something in human nature which we cannot blot out, which makes one man, in the end, recognize and reward merit in another, regardless of colour or race."[7]

Sixty-five years later, in 1966 (just before the inauguration of affirmative-action programs), a Louis Harris opinion survey reported that only 33 percent of American blacks felt that they "don't have nearly as good a chance to get ahead as most other people." Two years later, in 1968, some of the power of the myth was gone: the figure had increased from 33 percent to 56 percent. While fewer blacks accepted the myth, the blind and contradictory faith of American whites was undisturbed. A National Opinion Research Center (NORC) survey in 1966 revealed that many whites believed *both* that blacks are discriminated against *and* that blacks are treated fairly! (Although 73 percent felt that "Negroes are treated fairly" in their communities, over half of those 73 percent also believed that there was "a large amount" or "some" discrimination against blacks in those communities.)[8] This glaring, and self-serving, contradiction is apparently conjured away, in the minds of the white majority, by the magic of equal opportunity and the romantic myth of individualism. The exploitation of opportunity, as long as *some* opportunity exists, is held to depend uniquely on individual effort. Real inequalities of opportunity, even those rooted in racial discrimination, can be disregarded. The race is fair, or fair enough, as long as every individual has a fair—not necessarily an equal—chance. And since sufficient individual effort can overcome obstacles, some chance is fair enough. (There is probably also, in these attitudes, more than a little of the belief, rooted in the American gospel of success, that overcoming obstacles is itself both character-building and character-certifying. Obstacles are, according to this thinking, good for you.)

These white attitudes have not changed, even though whites have come in the last decade to "sympathize with blacks over past mistreatment" and to be "increasingly aware of the continuing vestiges of discrimination." Earlier, I argued that it was almost self-evident that relative black failure could only be attributed either to innate black inferiority or to discrimination. While a majority of whites now reject the first explanation, they also reject the second! In a 1977 survey, the NORC found that only 25 percent of whites explained black economic disadvantage on the grounds of racial inferiority ("most blacks have less inborn ability to learn"). Only 39 percent attributed black disadvantage mainly to discrimination. The alternative, chosen by 65 percent of whites, was that black problems resulted from the moral failings of individual blacks ("because most blacks just don't have the motivation or will power to pull themselves up out of poverty").

This is not a logically admissible alternative; it is, in fact, complete nonsense. For, if those individuals who are black lack the "motivation or will power" of those who are white, there are still only two possible explanations. Either the relative absence of motivation is an innate characteristic of blacks, or it is a consequence of discrimination. Only a remarkable doctrine enables whites to believe otherwise; "equal opportunity" *is* a remarkable doctrine. Before the issue of race occupied our attention, it had functioned for decades to blame the poor—and to get the poor to blame themselves—for their condition. The cause of poverty is viewed as lying, not in the disadvantages of poverty, but in the moral failings of the individual poor. Using the same logic, racial discrimination does not mean that minorities are treated unfairly! The credit of the poor and the nonwhites in the equal opportunity bank is guaranteed—so long as they don't try to cash a check.

Sweeping Racism Under the Rug

The conditions of colored minorities have changed in the fifty years since Herbert Hoover summed up the American creed. But from the perspective of the most fundamental white attitudes—on which the prospects for further improvement and future social peace depend—things have not changed at all. Hoover's moral blindness is still ours. And our recognition of the racial crimes that were glossed over by his rhetoric has not helped us recognize that same duplicity in the ideas in our own day. Thus equal opportunity serves us in the same way—though not, admittedly, in the same degree—to sweep racism and its victims under the rug.

Hoover's version of the American creed—and our own generation's version, as well—speaks at most to the necessity of providing greater opportunities for disadvantaged individuals to rise. It says nothing about those forms of group discrimination that still separate a black lawyer from his white counterpart. It takes no account of the ways in which the stigma of racial inferiority may affect the motivation of blacks to become lawyers. It can be silent on those questions only because it assumes that "the ideal of equal opportunity" is an addition to, rather than a denial of, "the revolutionary doctrine that all men are created equal."

George Orwell's description of the hierarchy in *Animal Farm*—"all animals are equal, but some are more equal than others"—is not simply a comment on the failed promises of "classless societies," as so many of his readers have believed. The book accurately represents the outcome of the victory of the slogan of equal opportunity over the more radical claim of natural human equality. And that victory is at the very center of the American dilemma. Because the meaning of equality has been limited to opportunity for social ascent, there is no longer an appeal, beyond a specious equality of individual opportunity, to a principle of equal human dignity and human worth.

Thus, Hoover could believe, as we can, that equality demands no more than giving minorities a formally equal chance.

Equality is no longer a weapon against the grossest social assaults on human dignity, but provides only that prejudice must not take the form of legal barriers to opportunity. The revolutionary principle that human equality is dictated by man's nature has simply been conjured away by the magic of equal opportunity.

8

Color-Blindness and the Constitution

In *Plessy* v. *Ferguson* in 1896 a near-unanimous Court, with only ex-slave-owner Justice Harlan dissenting, put its constitutional blessing on state laws and local ordinances requiring segregation of the races. At immediate issue was a Louisiana statute requiring separate but equal accommodations for Negro and white passengers traveling on railroads within the state. The Court rested its case on the distinction between the "equality of the two races before the law" which was "the object of the [Fourteenth] Amendment to enforce," and social inequalities which "it could not have been intended to abolish."[1] In a memorable tribute to judicial ingenuity, the Court went on to add that "the enforced separation of the two races does not stamp the colored race with a badge of inferiority"; if inferiority is inferred, "it is not by reason of anything found in the Act, but solely because the colored race chooses to put that construction upon it."[2]

Justice Harlan, in dissent, challenged the premises of the majority opinion and the narrowness of its interpretation of equality before the law:

We boast of the freedom enjoyed by our people above all other peoples. But it is difficult to reconcile that boast with a state of the law which, practically, puts the brand of servitude and degradation upon a large class of our fellow-citizens, our equals before the law. The thin disguise of "equal" accommodations for passengers in railway coaches will not mislead anyone, nor atone for the wrong this day done.[3]

In a ringing and majestic phrase that was to become the rallying cry of civil-rights forces decades later, Harlan based his opinion on the proposition that "our Constitution is color-blind." This phrase became the touchstone for undoing the infamous doctrine of enforced racial segregation. In recent years it has been invoked as almost a sacred text by judges and civil-rights leaders, black as well as white, to root out legalized racial preference and discrimination in all areas of public life. And now, its antiracist credentials apparently firmly established, the color-blind doctrine is claimed to be the final ground of appeal on the issue of affirmative action, the bulwark against "reverse racism" and reverse discrimination, and the only solid foundation on which to insure genuine equality before the law. To resist or oppose it now puts those who earlier invoked it in the struggle for racial justice in a difficult position, opening them to the charge of changing the rules in the middle of the game and of abandoning a principle when it becomes an inconvenience. The mistake was in ever imagining that constitutional color-blindness could serve as a first principle. It was an honest and well-intentioned mistake, but a mistake nonetheless.

Honor Among Thieves and the Dishonor of Thievery

The argument that the Fourteenth Amendment requires that the Constitution be color-blind confuses a narrowly legal meaning of justice with its broader social and moral meaning. These two meanings, Paul Freund suggests, may be seen as manifestations of individual and social justice: "The individual . . . may be treated justly if the existing rules are applied to him impartially, but the rules themselves may be inequitable and therefore unjust. This is the familiar dichotomy between internal and external standards, between honor among thieves and the dishonor of thievery."[4] By the first standard, the judges who denied the right to vote to women "were dispensing justice as long as they denied the vote to ladies of Republican and Democratic persuasion alike." So also, in the same sense of justice, we may say that antimiscegenation laws were just as long as the penalties for interracial marriage were applied equally to blacks and whites. The Court applied this narrow legal meaning of justice in *Plessy*. Separate facilities were saved because, in the myopic eye of individual justice, they do not imply unequal status before the law. But, Freund points out, the suffragettes—and, of course, a few decades later the civil-rights activists—were seeking justice in a broader sense.

That broader justice is not always an extension of individual equality before the law, and may, in fact, be in conflict with it. Equality before the law, in its narrow sense, was the achievement of the courts in the period from *Plessy* in 1896 to *Brown* v. *Board of Education* in 1954. Even the narrowly individual meaning required that separate facilities be equal, a proposition to which the Court paid lip service in the years immediately following *Plessy*, but without inquiring into the actual equality of separate facilities. (They were, of course, almost never equal.) In a series of decisions leading up to *Brown*, the Court increasingly undertook, unlike earlier Courts, to determine whether even the minimal test of justice was met in particular cases by examining whether separate facilities were, in fact, equal.[5]

From Plessy *to* Brown

Finally, in *Brown* v. *Board of Education* in 1954, the Court ordered the desegregation of schools on the grounds that separate facilities are inherently unequal. In retrospect, the Court's conclusions in *Brown* seem to have been a logical and necessary extension of its earlier efforts to take the *Plessy* formula seriously. In those earlier decisions the Court had applied the *Plessy* test with increasing rigor, but without challenging its underlying assumption that individual justice defines the limits of judicial concern. But by insisting on the impartial application of segregation laws, the Court found it increasingly difficult to avoid taking notice of the social injustice embodied in the laws. By 1950, for example, the inequality of black and white law schools in Texas was held to be a matter not only of buildings and other tangible considerations, but of "position and influence of the alumni, standing in the community, traditions and prestige."[6] This and similar decisions gradually paved the way for the Warren Court's frontal assault on the separation of individual from social justice.

Because the effort to overturn the *Plessy* decision had to operate within the terms of that decision, it was virtually inevitable that it would rest on an appeal to the principle of a color-blind Constitution. Forced to make their case in the courts of law, rather than in the sovereign court of public opinion or its legislatures, the partisans of racial equality had to make their claims in the language of individual justice. Moreover, since all legal classifications based on race that came to the Court's attention (or existed in fact) were invidious expressions of white racism, it was tempting to believe that the solution lay in applying the color-blind principle of Harlan's dissent in *Plessy*. This was a solution only to the problem of justice in its narrow individual meaning, a limitation that appealed to those who believed that only individual justice is the business of the courts, and a limitation that was forced on those who had a broader vision, but lacked a broader forum to which a broader appeal might be made.

In *Brown*, the Warren Court was forced by the logic of its decision to go further. It argued, in effect, that social injustice, reflected in state laws, made individual equality under the law a practical impossibility. "Separate educational facilities," Chief Justice Warren said for a unanimous Court, "are inherently unequal . . . even though the physical facilities and other 'tangible' factors may be equal . . . ." The policy of separating persons "solely because of their race," Warren noted, must be understood to denote "the inferiority of the Negro group." Applied to school children, it "generates a feeling of inferiority as to their status in the community that may affect their hearts and minds in a way unlikely ever to be undone."[7] The Court thus challenged the conclusion in *Plessy* that the Constitution does not address the broader question of the social justice of the relationships embodied in the law.

Warren's analysis appears to parallel the argument of Harlan's dissent in *Plessy*. But where Harlan argued that equal protection of the laws is a pretense when the laws themselves reflect social inequality, Warren went further to imply that social injustice makes a mockery even of the formal justice that Harlan had championed. It is not enough, Warren's argument implies, that the law be color-blind. In a society that practices racism, color-blind laws will reinforce the social injustices of racism. The Warren Court was led by the logic of this understanding to a color-consciousness that could confront and redress the wrongs embodied in a segregated social order. Thus, the development of a legal remedy for the injuries inflicted by racism must take into account the racial mix of school populations. Equal protection demands, not color-blindness, but a conscious effort to eliminate the invidious consequences of racism.

Color-Blind Racism

Because the principle of a color-blind Constitution was the lever for demolishing the legal protection of white privilege, and because this principle seems to imply a commitment to racial equality, it is easy to lose sight of its historical meaning and its logical limitations. Often the radical and liberating principles of one generation become the bastions of reaction and exploitation of the next. So it is with the principle of color-blindness, as the context in which Harlan developed it makes clear.

Unlike many of those who now champion it, Harlan did not regard color-blindness as a synonym for racial equality. The paragraph in his dissent in which he uses the phrase begins with a recognition of the social dominance of the white race, and suggests its innate superiority. He goes on to profess his own faith in the future security of white supremacy. The "white race," he notes,

> deems itself to be the dominant race in this country. And so it is, in prestige, in achievements, in education, in wealth, and in power. So, I doubt not, it will continue to be for all time, if it remains true to its great heritage and holds fast to the principles of constitutional liberty. But in view of the Constitution, in the eye of the law, there is in this country no superior, dominant ruling class of citizens. There is no caste here. Our Constitution is color-blind.[8]

"Our Constitution is color-blind." Let those who now invoke Harlan's phrase ponder carefully the meaning he gave it.[9] He recognized and conceded the substantive social, economic, and political inequalities of race. He took white supremacy in those areas for granted. His colleagues in the majority had argued that "the object of the amendment was undoubtedly to enforce the absolute equality of the two races before the law, but in the nature of things it could not have been intended to abolish distinctions based upon color, or to enforce social, as distinguished from political equality."[10] Harlan did not disagree. His argument was that, when distinctions based on color are translated into legal categories, those categories are tainted by the discriminatory purpose of the categories themselves. The guarantee of "equality of the two races before the law" then becomes a pretense, a "thin disguise." The result of the decision, he predicted, would be "to render permanent peace impossible, and to keep alive a conflict of races, the continuance of which must do harm to all concerned."[11]

The lesson was clear. In a nation dedicated to constitutional democracy, "equal protection of the laws" was a minimal commitment. Whites could not have social peace on any other terms. But, correctly understood, the terms were good enough. To be sure, they deprived whites of legal recognition of white supremacy and of legal sanctions for enforcing it. The sixty years between *Plessy* and *Brown* measure the depth of white racism and the reluctance to abandon its public embodiment in the law. They measure a racial prejudice so deeply rooted that the courts would not even see the necessity for finding a "democratic" facade behind which to conceal it.

The courage of Harlan's dissent should not blind us to the moral and historical limitations of his argument. He argued against his colleagues that racial classifications in the law carry with them "the brand of servitude and degradation" with which they are socially tainted. But he did not imagine any more than his colleagues that the law should be a process for mediating between individual and social justice. He had tried to reassure his racist colleagues by arguing that white supremacy did not require the support of color-coded laws. The Constitution, he had suggested, could afford to be color-blind because the white race really is superior ("So, I doubt not, it will continue to be for all time").

Even some of Plessy's supporters had adopted this view in arguments presented to the Court. Thus, in a brief for Plessy filed by S. F. Phillips and F. D. McKenny, they wrote: "Sir Walter Scott reports *Rob Roy* as announcing proudly that *wherever he sate, was the head of the table*. Everybody must concede that this is true socially of the white man in this country, as a class. Nor does anybody complain of that. It is only when social usage is confirmed by statute that exception ought or legally can be taken thereto." [12] This position restricts the meaning of equality to the formal protection of civil rights where, as Harlan put it, "all citizens are equal before the law. The humblest is the peer of the most powerful." It would be grossly unfair as a historical judgment on Harlan, but it is nonetheless important for our own moral understanding to note that this is equivalent to saying that "even a nigger has a right to his day in court."

Harlan had seen that "separate but equal" is a "thin disguise" for legal inequality. His willingness to use a color-blind Constitution as a thin disguise for social inequality led him to seek, unsuccessfully, to convince his colleagues of the necessity for honor among thieves. He even proposed that only if the thieves were constitutionally honorable would the dishonor of their thievery go undetected and unopposed by their victims. This is not a moral judgment of Harlan. Men have a right to have their courage and their vision judged by their descendants only against the conventional wisdom as they found it. It suggests, however, how we should judge current efforts, in a different intellectual and moral climate, to invoke his color-blind principle.

Color-Blind Law in a Color-Conscious Society

In the state of race relations at the time, the constitutional principles of "separate but equal" and color-blindness appeared poles apart. But in an ironic way, the movement of historical change has created a situation in which Harlan's high-minded principle of color-blindness would impose barriers to achieving racial justice now that are similar to those imposed by the ignoble sophistry of his judicial colleagues in his own day.[13] The *Plessy* majority had left the question of social justice to white majorities and their legislatures: the law need not be color-blind; the Constitution requires only its equal application. Harlan's position—and later the impact of *Brown* and the decisions that followed—forced discrimination out of the law. What was left was its ultimate abode: the hearts and minds of men; the private realm (including the neighborhood, the workplace, and the schools) in which group prejudice hides as individual preference; and the unintentional discrimination resulting from the application of color-blind standards to individuals whose chances have been conditioned by their color. These, and the historical residue of meaner sorts of racism, define the battle line in the continuing and unfinished struggle for racial justice.

The Warren Court, virtually alone among the agencies of government, put the issue of racial justice on the nation's agenda. The progress for which the Court cannot be credited directly is largely attributable to the quickening moral and political effects of its decisions. A constitutional mandate of color-blindness would not only reverse this recent pattern of judicial leadership, it would make further effective public action by any public agency impossible. Broader social justice is not now an extension of a narrow interpretation of individual equality be-fore the law. Therefore, if individual justice is all that the Con-stitution requires or permits, the continued pursuit of social justice (which is, of course, a more real justice for individuals) by either courts or legislatures will be effectively halted. While the decision in *Plessy* decreed that the existing social inequalities of race could be freely translated into law by state legislatures and that the courts were powerless to intervene, a color-blind Constitution would now decree that social and economic injus-tice is beyond the reach of legislatures and courts alike. The *Plessy* Court left untouched the prevailing social inequalities en-shrined in the law; a color-blind position now would decree that similar inequities may never be touched through the law.

Whatever's Constitutional

An even more disturbing potential consequence of a color-blind Constitution emerges here. The *Plessy* decision did more than put a constitutional gloss on enforced segregation; it *promoted* it. Jim Crow—segregation in all areas of American life—grew rapidly in the years following 1896.[14] (During Woodrow Wil-son's administration even the federal civil service was segre-gated, with separate washrooms and drinking fountains, and a policy against a black ever having supervisory authority over a white employee.) The Court's decision in *Plessy* affected the political and social events that followed it. This is, moreover, a norm of American politics. The Supreme Court never simply announces what is constitutionally permissible and what is con-stitutionally proscribed; its decisions have a moral, as well as a legal, force.

"The greatness, but also the perplexity of laws in free societies," Hannah Arendt argued," is that they only tell what one should not, but never what one should do."[15] If Arendt is right, Americans often fall short of the required democratic at-titude toward the law, for it is one of their distinguishing charac-teristics, noted often by both foreign and native observers, to turn moral problems into legal and constitutional issues. This proclivity has sometimes been celebrated as the condition for social peace in a society as diverse and with as little binding consensus as ours. It is no doubt closely related both to the diversity of American culture and to the peculiar American institution of a written Constitution and a supreme judiciary as the final authority on its meaning.

But whatever its historical advantages, social peace among the races is unachievable without social justice. And the Constitution and the courts can assure us of neither. The Court that gave us *Brown* v. *Board of Education* had earlier given us *Scott* v. *Sandford* and *Plessy* v. *Ferguson.* [16] The tendency to substitute constitutional interpretation for moral debate meant, in each case, that public attitudes and public policies on essentially moral issues were shaped by judicial opinions.

The Court's interpretation of the Constitution defines what is publicly required of citizens, thus exhausting their public and social obligations. So, a decision that the law must be color-blind would tend to mean that *only* the law must be color-blind. Because such a decision reflects a blindness to invidious social uses of color, it would provide subtle, positive encouragement to racism. It may be objected that it would do nothing of the sort, that it tells us only what the Constitution forbids and not what justice in some larger sense requires. It might even be argued that, in decreeing that the Constitution is color-blind, our highest judges are instructing us that, as individuals, we should also be color-blind. But the Constitution is rooted in individualistic notions of natural right, and in a separation of the realms of society and the state, the public and the private. The Constitution, in a society like ours, committed to competitive, romantic individualism, becomes the only bracket that encloses our diversity. Thus constitutional doctrine tends to become the only court of public appeal.

For these reasons, the practical effect of a constitutional decision favorable to color-blindness would be to legitimize continued social and economic discrimination. A color-blind Constitution, in effect, defends an individual's constitutional right to prejudice. In these circumstances, individuals are encouraged to believe that they are publicly entitled to express whatever forms of social and economic discrimination are compatible with the formal requirement that the law itself must not embody racial classifications. But it is just these forms of discrimination that have kept color-blind laws from producing equality of results for nonwhites in America and that led to affirmative-action programs in the first place.

The effect, then, of making the Constitution color-blind would be to proclaim that there is no longer any public problem of racial injustice in America. The effect of such a proclamation would most likely be that racial injustice will be both prolonged and promoted. Like the *Plessy* decision, it would foster what it makes constitutionally permissible. And just as *Plessy* was followed by Jim Crow, we can anticipate that a color-blind ruling would be followed by increased discrimination in more subtle forms.

For these reasons, the Court's decision in *Bakke* (that quotas are illegal because they exclude individuals on the basis of race, but that race may be used as one factor among many) is likely to be an invitation not to use race at all. Justice Powell denied that future Courts would assume that the use of race as one factor would operate "as a cover for the functional equivalent of a quota system."[17] But the danger is that, using the Court's rejection of quotas as pretext, use of race as a factor will serve as the functional equivalent of business-as-usual. Continued white preference—not concealed quotas or preference for colored minorities—is the more likely result and the more plausible assumption.

The Rank of a Mere Citizen

Surprisingly, a plausible democratic foundation for the idea of a color-blind Constitution is found, not in Harlan's dissent in *Plessy*, but in a majority opinion of the same Court thirteen years earlier. The Reconstruction Congress had passed civil-rights acts with the express purpose of eliminating social inequalities based on race, and had initiated the Fourteenth Amendment to assure the constitutionality of its civil-rights measures. In the *Civil Rights Cases*, decided in 1883, again with Harlan in lone dissent, the Court declared the Civil Rights Act of 1875 unconstitutional by denying that the Fourteenth Amendment had empowered "Congress to pass laws for enforcing social equality between the races." But, in an aside, the majority opinion, presented by Justice Bradley, added the striking proposition that Congress had already accomplished that illicit purpose:

> When a man has emerged from slavery and by the aid of beneficent legislation has shaken off the inseparable concomitants of that state, there must be some stage in the progress of his elevation when he takes the rank of a mere citizen, and ceases to be the special favorite of the laws, and when his rights as a citizen, or a man, are to be protected in the ordinary modes by which other men's rights are to be protected.[18]

The Court granted, in that remarkable passage, what the main thrust of its opinion labored to deny: that a group suffering under social oppression and discrimination, and not yet able to take the rank of "mere citizen," may legitimately be made the "special favorite of the laws," that "beneficent legislation" may be invoked to change those social circumstances in which a person's "rights as a citizen, or a man" cannot be protected equally by the "ordinary modes" applicable to others.[19]

There is a striking parallel between Justice Bradley's dictum in the *Civil Rights Cases* and that portion of Justice Powell's opinion in *Bakke* that finds racial quotas to be unconstitutional. Powell too, finds that the "one pervading purpose" of the Fourteenth Amendment was "the security and firm establishment" of the freedom of "the newly-made freeman and citizen." He grants, by implication at least, that in 1868 this meant special and preferential treatment. Powell does not even argue, as Bradley did, that "beneficent legislation" had accomplished its purpose. Instead, he says—as we have seen in an earlier chapter— that the Fourteenth Amendment was scuttled by a "reactionary" Court before its purpose could be served. And now it is too late. Successive waves of immigrants have made us a "nation of minorities"—a "fact" that has been reflected in Court decisions "over the years," repudiating all "distinctions between citizens solely because of their ancestry." "It is far too late," Powell concludes, "to argue that the guarantee of equal protection to *all* persons permits the recognition of special wards entitled to a degree of protection greater than that accorded others." And, he adds, "The clock of our liberties cannot be turned back to 1868."[20] But the effect of Powell's argument here was precisely to turn "the clock of our liberties" back to Bradley's dictum in 1883.

The proponents of the civil-rights acts and the Fourteenth Amendment had argued strongly that a legitimate government and a binding Constitution require the social equality of the races. Bradley and his colleagues, perhaps because they were so close to the congressional debates on those measures, at least paid lip service to the principle of equality from which the arguments were drawn. It was, of course, only lip service. But similarly, it is only lip service to the principle of racial equality to invoke now the principle of color-blindness. However far we have come since 1883, it is still a deception to pretend that we have reached the stage at which "beneficent legislation" has finally enabled a black to take the rank of "mere citizen," or to pretend that blacks can be equally protected by the "ordinary modes" in which the rights of whites are protected.

Equal Protection: A Mask for Privilege

There is a striking historical irony in the parallel between the argument for a color-blind Constitution and the way in which the Court provided constitutional protection for the privileges of the new economic elite after the Civil War. The path the Court took to reach this end was simple and direct. By cloaking corporations with legal personality, the Court made them "persons" who could not be deprived of their "life, liberty, or property, without due process of law." Since this due process clause appears in both the Fifth and Fourteenth Amendments, corporations thus acquired protection against both national and state legislation. The courts then substituted a "substantive" for a "procedural" meaning of due process, the effect of which was to make "reasonableness" the criterion for judging the constitutionality of regulatory legislation.

Over a period of four decades (roughly from the 1890s to the late 1930s), the Court handed down a series of decisions that equated reasonableness with the doctrines of laissez-faire and freedom of contract. Efforts at both the state and national levels to control the new concentrations of economic power were invalidated as unreasonable infringements of the due process clause. The courts also invoked other constitutional provisions—especially limits on the taxing power—to accomplish the same purpose. Although the equal protection clause was seldom explicitly invoked to protect the new inequalities of wealth and power, the Court's use of the due process and taxing provisions implicitly embodied an interpretation of equal protection that confined its meaning within the limits of individual justice. The broader question of the social justice of expanding economic inequality was put beyond the reach of constitutional adjudication.

In 1895, for example, the Supreme Court struck down a 2 percent income tax, passed by Congress the year before, on the ostensible ground that it violated the provisions of Article I, Section 9 of the Constitution. These provisions state that Congress may levy "direct" taxes only in accordance with the rule of apportionment among the states on the basis of census enumeration or population. Justice Fuller, delivering the opinion of the Court in *Pollock* v. *Farmers' Loan and Trust Co.*, denied that the desirability of an income tax was at issue. He insisted that the Court was only deciding whether the income tax does or does not belong to the class of direct taxes.[21]

But behind this constitutional facade were deeper issues of equality before the law and social justice. Joseph H. Choate, counsel for Pollock, had argued to the Court that the tax is "communistic in its purposes and tendencies . . . socialistic . . . populistic."[22] Justice Field, in his concurring opinion, announced that "the legislation, in the discrimination it makes [the law exempted incomes below $4,000] is class legislation." Field

went on to state the general principle on which "class legislation" that discriminates against high incomes is to be voided:
"Whenever a distinction is made in the burdens a law imposes
or in the benefits it confers on any citizens by reason of their
birth, or wealth, or religion, it is class legislation and leads inevitably to oppression and abuses, and to general unrest and
disturbance in society."[23] And Justice Field warned that: "The
present assault upon capital is but the beginning. It will be but
the stepping stone to others, larger and more sweeping, till our
political contests will become a war of the poor against the rich; a
war constantly growing in intensity and bitterness."[24]

Justice Harlan noted in his dissenting opinion that "by
much eloquent speech this court has been urged to stand in the
breach for the protection of the just rights of property against
the advancing hosts of socialism." But Harlan granted that "if it
were true that the legislation, in its important aspects and in its
essence, discriminated against the rich, because of their wealth,
the court, in vindication of the equality of all before the law,
might well declare that the statute was not an exercise of the
power of taxation, but was repugnant to those principles of
natural right upon which our free institutions rest, and therefore was legislative spoliation, under the guise of taxation."[25]
Attorney James C. Carter had addressed this issue in his argument to the Court. The income tax law, he noted,

> is said to be class legislation, and to make a distinction be-
> tween the rich and the poor. It certainly does. It certainly is
> class legislation in that sense. That was its very object and
> purpose. This is a distinction which should always be looked
> to in the business of taxation. Unfortunately heretofore it has
> been observed in the wrong direction, . . . and the poorer
> classes prodigiously overburdened.[26]

But Carter's argument in defense of reverse discrimination
against the rich fell on deaf ears. The thrust of the Court's opinion was that the law must be "class-blind." Its effect was to
cover a preference for wealth in the mantle of equal protection.

Later, in 1936, in the dying gasp of a doctrine that had for
decades frustrated efforts to give preference to the poor through

taxation, the Supreme Court invalidated the Agricultural Adjustment Act. The word *tax*, the Court announced in *United States* v. *Butler*, "has never been thought to connote the expropriation of money from one group for the benefit of another."[27]

In other cases, the Court had used the due process clause to effectuate the same meaning of equal protection. In 1908, for example, the Court struck down a federal act that made it unlawful for railroad employers to discharge employees because of their union membership (*Adair* v. *United States*). The same Justice Harlan who had insisted that the Constitution is formally neutral in matters of color now issued for the Court a declaration of neutrality in the contractual relationship between employer and employee: "The employer and employee have equality of right, and any legislation which disturbs that equality is an arbitrary interference with the liberty of contract which no government can legally justify in a free land."[28]

A few years later, in *Adkins* v. *Children's Hospital*, the Court invalidated a law setting minimum wages for women and minors working in the District of Columbia. The ground for the decision was that the statute was an "unconstitutional interference with the freedom of contract included within the guarantees of the due process clause of the Fifth Amendment." In entering into contracts for employment, the Court said, "the parties have an equal right to obtain from each other the best terms they can as a result of private bargaining."[29] In the same way that the *Civil Rights Cases* and *Plessy* Courts had "emancipated" blacks by denying them favored treatment and giving them equal status under "equal laws," the Justices in *Adkins* saw themselves as according women "emancipation from the old doctrine that [women] must be given special protection or be subjected to special restraint in [their] contractual and civil relationships."[30]

In this and other cases, all that was required to protect the privileges of the wealthy and the powerful was for the Court to protect with a fine and impartial hand, the "equal" contractual rights of corporations and of unorganized workers, small farmers, women, and child laborers. The new economic inequalities required only a principle that offered equal protection to the wealthy and powerful and to the poor and the powerless alike. The corollary principle was that for the law to show partiality for the latter is no less evil than if it were partial to the former. The special protection of corporations and of the new elites that managed their affairs required only that the laws be neutral with regard to the claims of capitalists and individual workers, that the laws be "wealth-blind" and "class-blind," and that they leave distributive shares to the voluntary contractual agreements of the parties and the "free" operation of social and economic forces.

Justice Taft, in his dissenting opinion in *Adkins,* called attention to the basic flaw in the doctrine of equal contractual liberty. He noted that "employees, in the class receiving least pay, are not upon a full level of equality of choice with their employer and in their necessitous circumstances are prone to accept pretty much anything that is offered." "They are," he added, "peculiarly subject to the overreaching of the harsh and greedy employer."[31] So long as the Court required that the law be blind to differences of economic wealth and market power, it put the Constitution on the side of the wealthy and the powerful. Until 1937 the facade of equal laws and equal opportunity served to protect inequalities of both condition and opportunity against remedial legislation. After 1937, the Court finally "pierced the corporate veil" to discover the inequality of economic power to which Justice Taft had tried to call attention. Their decisions, in a series of cases that reversed their earlier rulings, rested squarely on the understanding that Alpheus T. Mason and William M. Beaney generalized in this way: "Liberty could be infringed by forces other than government, and infringement by those forces *may require the affirmative action of government for its protection.*"[32]

This altered view of the meaning of equality under the law enabled the New Deal to cement its governing coalition with programs of "beneficent legislation" that favored workers, small farmers, and—except for blacks—the disadvantaged generally. The effect of these programs was reverse discrimination against big business interests. Thus, the New Deal represented, in the most fundamental sense, an affirmative-action program for the victims of a legal equality that had sanctioned their poverty and powerlessness.

Colored minorities were excluded from that coalition and from the beneficent legislation that held it together. Affirmative action for them today involves the same liberal awakening to the fact that equal opportunity and equal protection can be effectively denied by a requirement of equal laws.

Middle-class whites, now in the backlash revolt against affirmative action, ought to know better. Their own experience, or that of their parents, should inform them of the pitfalls and fallacies of neutral laws, and of the necessity of legal partiality toward those who have been victimized by power and privilege under the banner of equal protection. Benevolent legislation, after all, is responsible for their being middle-class.

The question now is whether a requirement of color-blindness in the law is to be allowed to sanction and protect white supremacy in precisely the way the parallel principles of "wealth-blindness" and "class-blindness" protected business supremacy against the claims of disadvantaged whites in our earlier history. From the perspective of the future of a democratic society, the problem is that those who were the beneficiaries of the New Deal's preferential programs were a majority. The question now is whether those developments represented a liberal awakening to the reality of society—a stage in the education of the liberal conscience—or whether they were merely a revolt of the majority against a privileged minority for the sake of majority interests. If they were the latter, they only demonstrated the obvious truth that the political institutions of a democracy permit a majority to protect and advance its interests. But that, after all, has always been reckoned by political philosophers to be the danger, as well as a strength, of majority rule. A democratic society is tested by its ability to care for the rights of minorities. In Jefferson's well-remembered phrase, "An elective despotism was not the government we fought for." Philosophers of democracy have agreed that it is the danger of majority tyranny that is to be feared.

In our present circumstances, the possibility of escaping

this danger rests on two considerations. The first is whether the white majority can be convinced that its own present condition is the result of past preferential treatment justified by then-existing inequalities of conditions and opportunity, and hence applicable now to blacks. The second question is whether the Court, which for decades after the Civil War protected minority tyranny, will now invoke a similar rationale to protect majority tyranny from the parallel demands of justice for minorities. The answer to the first consideration will determine the ability of a majority to deal justly with the problem of poverty generally, as well as the problem of race. Whether a democracy can deal with poverty as a minority problem is, of course, the test of whether democracy can promise economic justice. The second consideration will determine whether the white majority, victimized for decades by court decisions, will now seek to protect their interests with the same judicial facade that guaranteed their own earlier oppression.

Race-Conscious Injuries
Require Race-Conscious Remedies

In law as in life, as Herbert Hill has said, "race-conscious injuries require race-conscious remedies."[33] Those who argue otherwise tend to base their case on a contrived distinction between law and life. They argue that the provision of equal individual justice exhausts the responsibilities and legitimate powers of government and the legitimate duties of its agents. It is not enough or, perhaps more accurately, it is too much too soon.

A color-blind Constitution now is not a valid principle because the valid ideal is a color-blind society in the future.[34] A color-blind society is, in fact, the necessary precondition for a color-blind Constitution. There must come a time, as Bradley asserted in his opinion in the *Civil Rights Cases*, when beneficent legislation that makes blacks the "special favorite of the laws" will have done its work and when, therefore, the Constitution can be made color-blind. That time must come; it has not yet. Until it does, color-blindness is not only premature; it postpones the time endlessly. The problem is to speed the time. But until the time comes, in Nat Hentoff's phrase, "it is both too late and too soon to be color-blind."[35]

9

It Is a Constitution
We Are Expounding

Affirmative action raises an even more fundamental constitutional question than those discussed in the preceding chapter. Racial injustice tests the legitimacy of the constitutional order itself. At issue are some of the most fundamental questions of political philosophy. What are the grounds for political authority? What terms are required to elicit a duty to obey? What is the source of political obligation and political legitimacy? How is equality—and, in particular, racial equality—related to a democratic Constitution? These are the questions pursued in this chapter.

Because Men Think Themselves Equal

The triumph of the elusive doctrine of equal opportunity, described in earlier chapters, has obliterated the meaning, if not the memory, of the pronouncement in the Declaration of Independence that "all men are created equal." We have in fact drained it of its most obvious meanings to make it mean almost its exact opposite. The common interpretation runs something like this: Everyone (that is, every modern, sensible person) knows that men are not equal by nature and that neither rhetoric nor legislation can make them so. Jefferson cannot have meant to deny it. Despite his reputation among his contemporaries for elegance and precision of expression, a reputation which had led to his selection to prepare the draft, Jefferson was too intelligent and too urbane to propose literally that men are naturally equal. (Besides, as every freshman knows, Jefferson kept slaves. Almost no freshman knows, however, that Jefferson confessed to trembling "when I reflect that God is just" or that slavery was the question that prompted his confession.) What Jefferson must have really meant is that all men are created *unequal* and are entitled to equal rights to realize their natural inequalities.

This interpretation, however, would be a distortion of Jefferson's intent, the effect of which is to confine the implications of equality to the elimination of the inequalities of a feudal past and to put the inequalities of an industrial capitalist present beyond the reach of critical examination.[1] But this kind of thinking has even more serious implications. It not only turns equality into a defense of existing institutions, it ignores the most significant characteristic of the Declaration itself. Jefferson and his colleagues were doing more than declaring and defending the grounds for the political independence of the colonists from England. They were, at the same time, creating a new political society and stating the principles on which it was to be formed. Natural human equality was set forth as the grounds for independence, but the Declaration was above all a statement of the necessary conditions on which a new and independent people could make a new government of their own. Its central premise in this regard was that men make governments by pledging their faith to one another, and that this pledge of mutual faith can only be undertaken by men who regard one another as equals. The principle of equality in the Declaration was intended to assert the premise on which a constitution could be built. No government could rest on the consent of the governed unless it was created by equals.[2]

The Declaration was written in the great age of constitution making, when men put to themselves Lowell's question of how legitimate rule is to be distinguished from robbery, and then returned to first principles for an answer. When they reflected on the character of a social contract that could induce men to leave the state of nature and join a society, it is remarkable how often they were led to the Declaration's radical principle of equality.

There were conservatives to be sure, like John Adams, who thought the principle of equality to be palpable and dangerous nonsense. "I believe," Adams wrote to John Taylor, "that none but Helvetius will affirm that all children are born with equal genius."[3] Actually, however, the belief in the natural equality of genius was a very common one in the eighteenth century. Helvetius himself had noted that "Quintilian, Locke and I say: Inequality among intellects is the result of a known cause and this cause is the difference in education."[4] Helvetius's claim was even more modest than it needed to be. It is striking that all three of the great philosophers of social contract theory—Hobbes, Locke, and Rousseau—found men to be naturally equal. Hobbes, though he reached undemocratic conclusions, believed that "the question of who is the better man, has no place in the condition of meer nature; where . . . all men are equall. The inequality that now is, has been introduced by the lawes civill." Rousseau was careful to distinguish the "equality which nature hath ordained between men" from "the inequality they have introduced." John Locke, "America's philosopher," held that there is "nothing more evident than that creatures of the same species and rank, promiscuously born to all the same advantages of nature and the use of the same faculties, should also be equal one amongst another without subordination or subjection." And John Taylor, philosopher of Jeffersonian democracy, declared: "The truth is that rare talents, like a natural aristocracy, are created by ignorance. . . . Ignorance . . . begets, and [knowledge] explodes the errour, 'that some men

are endowed with faculties, far exceeding the general standard.'"[5]

How are we to explain the prevalence among so many of
the philosophers who built the foundations of modern democratic thought of a conviction that John Adams—and most modern
Americans—regard as an affront to common sense? The answer
lies, I think, in understanding that their purpose was not so
much to describe human nature as it was to define the necessary
condition on which a government could be founded. They were
searching for the ground on which men might agree, as they
had in the Mayflower Compact, to pledge themselves to "enact,
constitute, and frame, such just and equal Laws, Ordinances,
Acts, Constitutions, and Offices, from time to time, as shall be
thought most meet and convenient for the general Good of the
Colony; unto which we promise all due Submission and Obedi-
ence." Only persons who recognize one another as equals, they
all believed, could engage themselves in such arrangements.

The purpose of a constitution, these men understood, is to
set out the terms of a social contract by which the members of a
political community could agree to be bound.[6] If it is to serve
that purpose, it must provide a plausible and persuasive answer
to Lowell's question of why men ought to obey. It must provide
the governmental agencies of coercion a legitimacy in the eyes of
those who will be coerced. This question of legitimacy is difficult
and complex. But a minimum prerequisite for democratic
legitimacy is the recognition of a fundamental human equality
that rules out prior group distinctions of superiority and inferiority. Who could be induced to agree voluntarily to a constitutional order that assigned him a position of inferior dignity and
worth on the basis of ascribed group characteristics; or one that
proposed to give him the equal protection of laws that are neutral toward his socially ascribed and enforced inferiority?[7]

Surprisingly, it is Thomas Hobbes, philosopher of political
absolutism, who gives us the clearest clue to the significance
and the rationale for the assumption of equality. It is a "Law of
Nature," Hobbes wrote, "that every man acknowledge another
for his equal by nature." Nature, herself, decrees man's natural
equality for the following reason: "If nature therefore have

made men equal, that equality is to be acknowledged: or if nature have made men unequal; yet because men that think themselves equal, will not enter into conditions of peace but upon equal terms, such equality must be admitted."[8]

So long as men "think themselves equal"—and, in the absence of some effective form of Plato's "Royal Lie," enforced by religion or tradition, men will "think themselves equal"—their equality is a necessary condition for their civil association. "In the beginning," said Locke, "all the world was America," and America took men back to the beginning. Without the aid of a binding belief that human inequality was the will of God or a tradition-encrusted system of social rank, men could not be induced to know their places in a hierarchical social order and fill them with good grace. A government could only be built on the consent of the governed; and consent would only be forthcoming from equals. In the circumstances, philosophers made a virtue of necessity. But it was, nonetheless, an ennobling and productive virtue. It led them inescapably to the great principle described by Henry Demarest Lloyd at the turn of the last century: "There is no true association except among equals. There is no true country where uniformity of right is violated by caste, privilege, or inequality."[9]

Just such a false association, however, was created by the Constitution, so far as nonwhites were concerned. For black and white alike there was no "true country." Whatever, in principle, the Declaration might have implied, in the realities of American life Stephen A. Douglas was correct in arguing that the principle "had no reference either to the Negro, the savage Indians, the Feejee, the Malay or any other inferior and degraded race."[10]

In Bondage to the Whole White Race

The central fact of American slavery was that it had been underwritten by racism—a distinctive characteristic not generally true of other nations in which slavery existed. In no other society was slavery so total a condition or so oppressive an institution.

Albion Tourgée, counsel to Vernon Plessy, accurately identified in his brief the nature and consequences of involuntary
servitude in America. The slave, he noted, *"was in bondage to the
whole white race* as well as to his master."* ("He could not resent
words or blows from any citizen. Only in the last extremity was
he permitted to defend his life. Impudent language from him
was held the equivalent of a blow from one of the dominant
class."[11] It was, of course, illegal to teach a slave to read and
write.)

Tourgée placed in clear focus the significance of this condition: "This bondage [of a slave 'to the whole white race'] was a
more important feature of American slavery than chattelism—
indeed it was the one feature which distinguished it from 'involuntary servitude' which is the chief element of chattelism." It
was this added burden of the badge of slavery, as Tourgée
suggested, that made emancipation less than a badge of equality. The social and moral heritage of "race bondage" survived
almost intact the end of chattelism. In order to make ex-slaves
equal citizens with equal rights and opportunities, to free blacks
from the special status of "bondage to the whole white race,"
nothing less was required than that they be made "the special
favorite of the laws" for however long was necessary for their
social emancipation.

To Save a White Man's Union

Our rhetoric has disguised the extent to which the making of the
American Constitution radically eviscerated the central principle
of the Declaration. Note what we have done, for example, with
the famous three-fifths compromise in the Constitution. We
treat it, in our history books, as a compromise over the slavery
issue; it wasn't. It was, instead, a compromise over the relative
political power to be wielded by northern whites and slave-
owning whites. It did not, as our history books have so often
pretended, define a black as three-fifths of a person; it did not
confer on a black three-fifths of a vote. It did not define blacks as

persons, but as property. The Constitution recognized the property interests of the white slave-owners by giving them three-fifths of an additional vote for every black they owned. So it had to be; no partial concession to the equal humanity of blacks could be made without compromising the integrity of a white Constitution predicated on the equality of its members. [12]

The racism inherent in the Constitution required a radical transformation of the principles on which the Declaration of Independence proposed that constitutions must be built. [13] As John P. Roche has noted, if the Declaration were translated into the theory that has, in fact, been applied in the United States, it would read this way:

> *All those who have been admitted to the political community are equal.* In other words, men achieve equality as a function of membership in the body politic—and this membership is not an inherent right, but a privilege which the majority accords on its own terms. [14]

Nor, despite the arguments of the Radical Republicans and the actions of the Reconstruction Congress, did the end of slavery mean inviting blacks to join the constitutional association. President Lincoln's description of the role of the "race question," in his 1862 reply to Horace Greeley's demand for emancipation, comes closer to describing the eventual impact of the Civil War on the constitutional status of blacks:

> My paramount object . . . is to save the Union. . . . If I could save the Union without freeing any slave, I would do it; and if I could save it by freeing all the slaves, I would do it; and if I could do it by freeing some and leaving others alone, I would also do that. What I do about slavery and the colored race, I do because I believe it helps to save the Union; and what I forbear, I forbear because I do not believe it would help to save the Union.

The Union that Lincoln fought successfully to save was still a white man's Union; Lincoln correctly understood that whites were unwilling to share their Constitution with blacks. In his Peoria speech in 1854, he had asked:

What then? Free them, and make them politically and socially our equals. My own feelings will not admit of this, and if mine would, we well know that those of the great mass of whites will not. Whether this feeling accords with justice and sound judgment is not the sole question, if indeed it is any part of it. . . . We cannot make them equals.

A Standard Maxim for a Free Society

Slavery was a clear violation of the Declaration's principles, but freed black men are not to be accorded the equality to make them parties to the Constitution. Within the narrow limits imposed by the racism of "the great mass of whites," Lincoln argued for easing the burden of black oppression. In his first debate with Douglas, he expressed the view that the Negro is "not my equal in many respects—certainly not in color, perhaps not in moral or intellectual endowment. But in the right to eat the bread, without leave of anybody else, which his own hand earns, he is my equal and the equal of Judge Douglas, and the equal of every living man." In other speeches he expressed the hope that the races might simply leave one another alone: "All I ask for the Negro is that if you do not like him, let him alone. If God gave him but little, that little let him enjoy." To seek this for the Negro is to ask substantially less than equality. It more nearly resembles, in fact, a plea in an antivivisectionist pamphlet than an appeal to human equality.

Lincoln wanted more than that. Unable to give constitutional status to the great principle of the Declaration, he nevertheless tried valiantly to hang on to it by challenging the arguments of Douglas and of Chief Justice Taney in the *Dred Scott* case. Taney had argued that, in Lincoln's words, "Negroes were no part of the people who made, or for whom was made, the Declaration of Independence, or the Constitution of the United States." Against this view, Lincoln insisted that the Declaration applied universally. The men who wrote it

> meant to set up a standard maxim for a free society, which should be familiar to all, and revered by all; constantly looked

> to, constantly labored for, and even though never perfectly
> attained, constantly spreading and deepening its influence
> and augmenting the happiness and value of life to all people of
> all colors everywhere.

Lincoln's case for the universal and continuing validity of the Declaration's assertion of equality is sound, but his effort to refute Taney's view of the Constitution did not fare so well. Indeed, he did not really argue that case, and by implication at least, he granted Taney's position. The authors of the Declaration, he conceded, did not mean "that they were about to confer [equality] immediately upon [blacks]. In fact, they had no power to confer such a boon. They meant simply to confer the right, so that enforcement of it might follow as fast as circumstances should permit."

"As fast as circumstances should permit." How fast that might be would depend on the extent to which the principle of equality in the Declaration came to be accepted as "a standard maxim for a free society, . . . revered by all; constantly looked to, constantly labored for." To say this is to grant that blacks stood, in Jefferson's day and in Lincoln's own, outside the Constitution; to hope that it would not always be so; to charge future generations with breathing new life into the Declaration; and so, one day, to make a Constitution that includes blacks.

The Sabotage of Beneficent Legislation

A glimmer of the light of that new day appeared briefly in the period immediately following the Civil War. In 1866, the Reconstruction Congress passed a broadly conceived civil-rights bill that reached beyond discrimination in the law to those forms of private and customary discrimination that denied blacks equal citizenship. They then proceeded to approve the Fourteenth Amendment in order "to render the constitutionality of the Civil Rights Bill free from doubt." Unfortunately, being aware of the racist consensus among whites that Lincoln had described, they feared to state their purpose baldly. They resorted, instead, to "vague and ambiguous phrases which, it was hoped, would accomplish the desired ends without too clearly indicating the purpose."[15] The purpose was clear enough: to create the conditions in which blacks could be parties to and not mere subjects of the Constitution. They followed out this great purpose in a series of civil-rights laws designed to put the power of the federal government behind equal political, social, and economic rights for blacks.

In the *Civil Rights Cases* of 1883, the Court wiped the Civil Rights Act of 1875 off the statute books by distinguishing between discriminatory laws—forbidden by the Fourteenth Amendment—and discrimination by private action and by custom, which may not be remedied by law. "It would be running the slavery argument into the ground," Justice Bradley said for the majority, "to make it apply to every act of discrimination which a person may see fit to make as to the guests he will entertain, or as to the people he will take into his coach or cab or car, or admit to his concert or theater, or deal with in matters of intercourse or business."[16]

As we saw in the preceding chapter, the Court was conscious of the effects of its decision on the constitutional status of blacks. It found it necessary, therefore, to pretend that the Reconstruction Congress had succeeded in making blacks equal citizens of a constitutional republic. "Beneficent legislation," Bradley interposed, which had made the black man "the special favorite of the laws," had succeeded in creating a situation in which "his rights as a citizen, or a man, are [now] to be protected in the ordinary modes by which other men's rights are to be protected."

Actually, of course, the claims of the black to "his rights as a citizen," and his need to have those rights protected "by the aid of beneficent legislation" had been recognized only in the very brief period of Radical Reconstruction. Both Congress and the president had abandoned blacks by 1877 in the settlement by which federal troops were withdrawn from the southern states. Congress, which had initiated three constitutional amendments and enacted several laws for the enforcement of the civil, economic, and political rights of blacks, abandoned its efforts and settled for reunion on the South's terms. The North did not find the price exorbitant for the simple reason that it "would be paid by the Negro." The price was a concession of "limited civil rights, but neither political nor social equality."[17]

The Court itself, contrary to Justice Bradley's assertion that blacks had risen to the rank of "mere citizen," had systematically sabotaged the beneficent legislation that had allegedly facilitated full black citizenship. When a mob attacked blacks who were trying to vote, the Courts in 1875 declared that the Fourteenth Amendment applied only to state and not to private interference with black rights. The Court held that it had not been shown that the white mob intended to prevent the blacks from voting "on account of their race." It would be only a supposition, the Court declared, "that 'race' was the cause of the hostilities." The Court had permitted a Kentucky election official to refuse to receive a black's vote on similar grounds. It had declared unconstitutional, as an interference with the exclusive power of Congress over interstate commerce, a Louisiana law forbidding discrimination in public transportation. It had overturned the conviction of members of a white Tennessee mob that had lynched four Negro prisoners on grounds that the Fourteenth Amendment did not give the national government authority to protect blacks against violence by individuals or mobs.

And now the same Court that had nullified the beneficent legislation that might have enabled blacks to take the rank of "mere citizen" could declare that it had happened! The time had come to repair to the legalistic doctrine of individual equality before the law. Enough of making blacks "special favorites"; enough reverse discrimination!

Justice Bradley, who authored those ideas for the Court, developed them further in his private correspondence. To friends he "noted that he was very disturbed by the alleged 'power of Congress to pass laws for enforcing social equality between the races. . . .' Bradley shared the common view that the white man had been discriminated against by the civil rights laws with unfortunate results. He demanded fair play for the white population."[18]

Do we hear echoes of the argument that again divides us in the crisis over affirmative action? The Court's presumption that white benevolence had made blacks full citizens, full members of the body politic, in 1883, tests our credulity. We now know that the Court's decision then led inevitably to Jim Crow, to continued racial oppression, and to the heaping of boundless indignities on black Americans. But we seem to be so taken by Harlan's appeal to color-blindness that we miss the deeper lesson of his lone dissent in *Plessy:* "The destinies of the two races in this country are indissolubly linked together, and the interests of both require that the common government of all shall not permit the seeds of race hate to be planted under the sanction of the law."[19]

Legalized segregation, Harlan understood, provides a soil in which race hate is nourished. We are now in a position to see that, where race hate exists, it may also be nourished by racially neutral laws. And, understanding that, we may recover the profound truth that race hate, however nourished, is incompatible with the "common government of all" required by a constitution.

A Common Government of All?

The willful failure of the Court to take these considerations into account was at the bottom of the monumental sophistry in their 1896 decision in *Plessy*. There they sanctioned the racism of their white countrymen under the mantle of color-blind equal protection. Recall Justice Brown's declaration for the majority, that "the object of the amendment was undoubtedly to enforce the absolute equality of the two races before the law, but in the nature of things it could not have been intended to abolish distinctions based upon color, or to enforce social, as distinguished from political equality."[20]

The Court could not have been more in error. When it said, "in the nature of things," the "things" it apparently had in mind were the same deep-seated, time-honored white prejudices that Lincoln too had accepted as a natural limit on what could be done. But, in the nature of a constitutional order of things, the object of the amendment had to be to eliminate the inequality that made blacks subjects of rather than parties to the Constitution. The Court chose to practice politics as "the art of the possible"; as is so often the case when that venerable proposition is made the basis of political action, the result was to make the necessary impossible.

Justice Brown revealed the constitutional inadequacy of the Court's position in these words: "If one race be inferior to the other socially, the Constitution of the United States cannot put them on the same plane." But "if one race be inferior to the other socially," the United States does not have a Constitution that can be applicable to the socially inferior race. If we are to create a Constitution, it must be one that puts nonwhites on the same plane. But the Court was content to interpret white racism as an absence of "mutual appreciation" on the parts of members of the two races, and to wait on a voluntary change of heart by individuals: "If the two races are to meet upon terms of social equality, it must be the result of natural affinities, a mutual appreciation of each other's merits and voluntary consent of individuals."[21]

The Court had forgotten Chief Justice Marshall's warning: "we must never forget that it is a *Constitution* we are expounding."[22] If they had remembered, they would have known that no Constitution can bind two races unless they "meet upon terms of social equality." Prejudice, to be sure, cannot be eliminated by law. But, unless the Fourteenth Amendment permits laws that redress those forms of discrimination that mark blacks as inferior members of the social order, whites can have no right to expect blacks to live among them as fellow citizens, bound to civil association through the terms of a constitution. No fundamental democratic document can provide the terms for organizing into one body politic, on the basis of consent, a dominant and a socially oppressed group. Our own most fundamental ideals declare it so. The Declaration's principle of equality, as Lincoln understood, sets out just those conditions of social inequality as grounds for the rights of revolution. Nor does the existence of formal equality before the law dissolve that right. Milton Mayer made this point eloquently in his description of the street politics of the late 1960s:

White "establishment" spokesmen sonorously proclaimed that "the United States is a society where [the] essential conditions [of liberty] prevail—certain inalienable rights are secure, the lawmakers represent the community, the courts and juries are free to interpret the laws without coercion, there are political means available to revise laws that are repressive or unjust." True, true—and black men, weary of crying out against the pretensions that underlay these truths, were at last in the streets exercising Locke's "right of revolution."[23]

The practical exigencies of Lincoln's own time—the racism of his white countrymen, and his own—seemed to him to dictate that the constitutional reunion of white northerners and white southerners on the basis of equality could only be achieved at the price of the continued social inequality of blacks. But he understood that the principle of the Declaration was the necessary basis of a constitution. He seems to have clearly understood that the future of a constitution that excluded blacks by excluding them from the Declaration was in grave peril. He offered the Declaration to future generations as the ground on which to save the Constitution by making it as universal as the Declaration's great principle of equality.

If Lincoln's hopes had been realized—if, for future generations, the Declaration had "set up a standard maxim for a free society," if it had been "revered by all; constantly looked to, constantly labored for"—we might now be justified in assuming that the Constitution could be color-blind. But the principle of equality has been, instead, subverted by misleading appeals to equal opportunity and equal laws. By assuming that the more fundamental equality of the Declaration has been achieved, these slogans relieve us of the responsibility for achieving it.

Thus, the argument that the Fourteenth Amendment must be interpreted in a racially neutral way is an unconstitutional doctrine in the most fundamental sense. It is incompatible with what must be done to make the document into a constitution with legitimate claims to universal allegiance.

10

Meritocracy, Efficiency, and Opportunity

In the *DeFunis* case, argued before the Supreme Court in the early 1970s but never decided, the same issues that were later posed by *Bakke* were raised in connection with law-school admissions. In his brief for DeFunis, constitutional scholar Alexander Bickel argued that whenever less qualified persons are employed or admitted to a school "solely on the basis of their race . . . a cost is paid in loss of efficiency and in injustice."[1] If the analysis above did not dispose of the charge of injustice, it seriously weakened it. At the very least, we are forced to conclude that under conditions of grossly unequal opportunity we are simply unable to say which candidates deserve the positions. But when we come to the question of efficiency, we approach the real basis for the claims of meritocracy.

A case against racial preference on grounds of the alleged social inefficiency of its consequences is a peculiar argument to be found in a constitutional brief. The Constitution does not say, "in order to found a more efficient union"; nor has efficiency ever appeared as a constitutional emendation of the meaning of "equal protection." How odd to find this claim in the arguments of those whose central contention is that the purity of the language of the Constitution must not be tainted by considerations of social realities like race.

Efficiency:
For What and for Whom?

Such inconsistencies aside, the case against racial quotas turns largely on their alleged inefficiency as obstructions to putting the gifts of the most meritorious individuals in the service of society. On this reckoning, in the case of medical school admissions, the rights of white males are not at issue so much as the rights of potential patients of minority doctors (who may be judged to be less qualified than rejected white applicants would have been). This question of efficiency, it should be noted, does not involve the question of incompetence, since we are entitled to assume that all those accepted by professional schools meet or surpass the minimum professional standards. (Even if one were to decline to make that assumption, the resulting problem of professional incompetence is of a quite different sort, not directly related to quotas. No professional school operating under a quota system professes to certify incompetents.)

The efficiency argument neglects the fact that society's stake in the provision of professional services encompasses more than the quality of its practitioners. Unless we propose to judge efficiency exclusively from a white perspective, we must start by recognizing that the socially efficient delivery of professional services is as much a matter of the equitable distribution of those services as it is of their quality. In 1970, only 2.1 percent of American doctors were black. Because America was still, in large measure, a racially segregated society, and because one-third of all blacks in the United States had family incomes in 1970 of less than $5,000 per year (the official "poverty line"), professional services were not equitably distributed among racial groups. There is, indeed, a desperate and unfilled need for doctors on the reservations and in the barrios and ghettoes of America.[2]

From the perspective of those who inhabit them, the claim of "efficiency" made by color-blind meritocracy is a hollow mockery.

Survival of the Unfit?

Even if we approach the question from a meritocratic stand-point, however, the question of efficiency is by no means easily answered. At the outset we need to consider whether quotas do, in fact, tend to favor persons who are relatively less qualified. Will the average standards of medical care, for example, be lower with affirmative-action quotas than they would be under the strict canons of meritocracy? Several considerations warn against an easy affirmative answer. The established criteria for admission may contain concealed racial bias, or they may be applied by persons with conscious or unconscious racial bias. More importantly, the criteria may not adequately reflect charac-teristics that have a significant influence on the quality of the service. Thus, the gatekeepers of medical school admissions have traditionally assumed that the practice of medicine was something that a professional expert, skilled in the science of disease, did to and for a patient. More recently, they have tended to view health care as involving a more active role for patients, as well as different skills—including social skills—of doctors. In light of these considerations, it may be reasonable to assert that those admitted under a quota are not necessarily less qualified to train for the profession.

But, in any event, from the perspective of social efficiency, rather than justice, it is irrelevant whether the qualifications for admission of quota applicants are relatively lower than those of whites who are excluded. The relevant question is whether rela-tively less qualified doctors will result. A positive answer to this question is by no means self-evident. It is quite possible that minority students, having demonstrated their ability to over-come the handicaps imposed by racial denigration, will develop their abilities more rapidly than whites.

But, beyond that possibility, a deeper issue is involved. The

117

meritocratic criteria that are ordinarily applied—past intellectual achievement and aptitude—are designed primarily to insure that meritocratic justice prevails, that individuals are rewarded on the basis of their individual merits. We then leap to the conclusion that if meritocratic justice is done for individuals, social efficiency will automatically be maximized.

Michael Kinsley has forcefully challenged this assumption:

> When the reward of merit is seen as something that serves the interest of society in general, rather than as something that is the *right* of the meritorious *individual,* it loses a lot of its moral force. It becomes harder to see why the principle of merit must never be sacrificed to other important social goals, such as integrating blacks and women into the high reaches of the economy. The principle has *no* force, except to the extent it actually does contribute to social efficiency. The traditional method of choosing among candidates for medical school, for example, clearly rewards the standard indices of merit— intelligence, determination, etc. But so what? The question is whether it produces the best doctors. Is each of the 100 students admitted to a class at the Davis Medical School going to be a better doctor than the 5000th candidate? The 500th? The 105th? In every common field of endeavor, the rhetoric of merit as moral worth disguises the crudeness of meritocratic principles as tools of social efficiency.[3]

Our infatuation with meritocratic justice also leads to a kind of escalation in our thinking about the requirements of a profession. Thus, the test of affirmative-action admissions to medical schools is typically formulated as the right of persons in need of serious and delicate operations to have them performed by the most skilled surgeons. But who would select a surgeon by examining his undergraduate GPA and aptitude test scores, or even his class standing at graduation? Would we rule out older surgeons who, a few decades ago, were likely to have been able to get into medical school with C+ averages?

And would we say, on reflection, that the criteria by which the best surgeons are selected are also the criteria by which we would select the best general practitioners? Whatever may be the case with medical specialties (in which standards are guarded by residency programs and board examinations), in providing family medical care, it does not follow that the applicant who scores highest on an aptitude test, or who makes the highest grades in college will necessarily be the best person to fill these needs. Nathaniel S. Colley, a black attorney and civil-rights leader, adds that "we are kidding ourselves if we think that only one with the mentality of an Einstein can guard the general health of the family. In fact, experience tells us that often such exceedingly superior intelligence, if it is not balanced with common sense and dedication, may well be an impediment to everyday performance with average people."[4]

Efficiency, moreover, is dependent on other qualities than those that can be measured by meritocratic tests. The quality of a professional service, for example, depends on a relationship of trust between professional and client: "Often, a patient or a client, more than anything else, needs a doctor or lawyer to whom he can relate, and in whom he has, for reasons relevant or irrelevant, complete trust and confidence."[5] Race in American society, however regrettably, continues to have an important relationship to the possibilities of trust. The very absence of minority doctors will continue to be deeply resented by non-whites and will further erode those possibilities of trust. Colley makes this point in the following observation:

> The missionaries were willing to minister unto us, but they lost interest when we insisted that we minister unto ourselves . . . and others. We no longer were satisfied at being protected. Now, we wanted to be the protectors. We no longer wanted to be merely loved, respected and treated fairly. Instead, we wanted to love, respect and treat ourselves and others fairly as well.

In a color-blind society, doctors would minister to patients; but in a color-conscious society, when white doctors minister to black patients, whites are ministering to blacks. Trust, in that situation, is clearly unlikely. For reasons that may or may not be valid, but are clearly relevant, black patients may understandably doubt whether white doctors weigh the seriousness of their symptoms and illnesses, or even the importance of their lives, on the same scale as they weigh the problems of white patients.[6]

The public purposes served by affirmative-action programs include redressing the damage done to the profession by the exclusion of nonwhites. Black patients who see that there are black as well as white doctors are more likely to be able to extend trust to white doctors. White doctors who have studied medicine with black fellow students, and who serve with them as colleagues, are more likely to deserve that trust.

But even on the assumption that some difference exists between the average performance levels of those selected under regular criteria and those who qualify under affirmative-action standards, the issue of efficiency is not resolved. The efficiency of the results of affirmative action must be judged over more than one generation. Meritocracy, for all its pretenses to the contrary, tends to reward individuals for qualities that are heavily influenced by the success of their parents. White males who presently occupy positions in the professions, for example, are themselves in large measure the beneficiaries of the advantages derived from their parents and grandparents. The fair test of affirmative action will be the children and grandchildren of those who benefit now.[7]

In summary, the charge that special admission leads to inefficiency completely neglects the damage done to the profession itself—to its white practitioners and to their ability to treat nonwhite patients—by the racial imbalance that established admissions criteria produce. Moreover, the continuation of the inequities of racial discrimination, unanswered by quotas, creates an inefficiency of its own that can be measured by the unrealized promise of nonwhite candidates. Every individual's unrealized potential represents a loss to a society's efficiency.

Remedying racial imbalance in the professions involves more than compensation for past injuries. "The need for more blacks in the professions," McGeorge Bundy argues, "relates to what our whole society requires, not just to what more blacks deserve." Its purpose, he adds, is "to improve our future, not just to overcome our past."[8]

Beyond those considerations, where the basic question of

racial equality is involved, efficiency cannot be achieved without justice. Justice has a higher claim, especially in a society that promises human equality. Only in a racially just society is the pursuit of efficiency justifiable as the highest good. And in a society that has not achieved racial equality, the effect of pursuing efficiency will be to reinforce existing racial inequality. To see why this is the case, a brief historical excursion will be helpful.

Social Darwinism and Plessy v. Ferguson

It is no historical accident that the American world of *Plessy* v. *Ferguson* was the world of Social Darwinism. The same Henry Billings Brown who, as Supreme Court Justice, wrote the opinion in *Plessy*, could say in a public address in 1893:

> While enthusiasts may picture to us an ideal state of society where neither riches nor poverty shall exist, . . . such a utopia is utterly inconsistent with human character as at present constituted; and it is at least doubtful whether upon the whole it would conduce as much to the general happiness and contentment of the community which excites the emulation and stimulates the energies, even if it also awakens the envy, of the less prosperous. Rich men are essential even to the well-being of the poor. . . . One has but to consider for a moment the immediate consequence of the abolition of large private fortunes to appreciate the danger which lurks in any radical disturbance of the present social system. [9]

Brown's colleague in the *Plessy* majority, Justice David J. Brewer, echoed this Darwinian view, and offered his testimony to the fitness of the winners:

> The great majority of men are unwilling to endure that long self-denial and saving which makes accumulation possible; they have not the business tact and sagacity which bring about large combinations and great financial results; and hence it always has been, and until human nature has been remodeled always will be true, that the wealth of a nation is in the hands of a few, while the many subsist upon the proceeds of their daily toil. [10]

For Social Darwinists like Justices Brown and Brewer, racial equality must have appeared as an especially dangerous doctrine. It threatened to popularize once again the radical egalitarianism of the Declaration and, by unleashing the frenzies of the mob, to lead toward a radical disturbance of the Darwinist inequalities of the present social system. Men who were so satisfied that the fittest were surviving and that their triumphs were socially benevolent, even for the losers, could not be expected to worry much about blacks, any more than they worried about the condition of the poor generally. Even if they had believed that the condition of blacks was the result of discrimination, even if they had been morally disturbed by white racism—which most of them were not—they could hardly be expected to act out of that concern. The poor and the blacks, they believed, were better off in their poverty than they could otherwise be. Social Darwinists could hardly be expected to mount a campaign for racial equality that would arm the time bomb of the Declaration by popularizing the contagious and dangerous idea of human equality, and so risk a social upheaval of poor whites and blacks alike.

From Social Darwinism to Meritocracy

It is no accident that the current reaction against affirmative action—the demand for color-blind laws, the insensitivity to social racism, the charges of reverse discrimination—occurs in the context of meritocracy. Until this point I have used the term *meritocracy* as if it were synonym for "equality of opportunity." But meritocracy is actually a special version of that older ideal. The ideological credentials of meritocracy are found, not in the ideas of Jeffersonians or Jacksonians, but in the doctrine of Social Darwinism, with which it shares its assumptions and its attitudes toward the problem of racial justice.

Meritocracy describes the meaning of equality of opportunity in a posttechnological, bureaucratized, corporate, consumption-oriented society. As Daniel Bell has argued, "Post-industrial society, in its logic, is a meritocracy."[11] The roles required for the efficient operation of the social and economic machinery require natural gifts cultivated through higher education. Individuals will be motivated to develop their skills only if they are rewarded by "differential status and differential income." IQ becomes the basis of qualification for entrance into the elites, and education becomes the certifying agency. Success reflects natural intellectual superiority developed through effort and measured by technical competence.

Much earlier, the original agrarian contours of opportunity had given way gradually to the new opportunities of business and industry. More recently, as Seymour Martin Lipset has described it, "opportunity, as measured by the chances of success in building up a major enterprise of one's own, has given way to opportunity measured by advancement in the bureaucratic elites."[12]

Both the objective conditions that distinguish meritocracy from earlier patterns of inequality, and its formulation as a democratic norm, mark a sharp break with the liberal past. Historically, the liberal emphasis on opportunity had framed its promises in universal terms. Abundance, as David Potter has argued, was the key; the unlimited opportunities made success universally available, in keeping with the Declaration's promise of equality.[13] Meritocracy breaks, sharply and openly, with that tradition. It builds its case instead on Julian Huxley's argument that "our new idea-system must jettison the democratic myth of equality: human beings are not born equal in gifts or potentialities, and human progress stems largely from their inequality."[14] The older idea of equality promised that everybody could be somebody. Meritocracy rests, instead, on the assumption that, as Mark Hanan has put it, "when everybody is somebody, nobody is anybody."[15] In place of boundless opportunity for all in an unstratified social order, meritocracy makes room at the top for the most talented few. For the idea of the unlimited capacity for development of every individual, meritocracy substitutes the proposition that efficiency and progress depend on insuring that the mediocre mass is governed by the talented few.

These doctrines were, of course, not new. They had, however, been outside the ideological mainstream. They were the assumptions underlying Alexander Hamilton's efforts to put a new social and economic aristocracy beyond the reach of popular meddling. They found expression in John C. Calhoun's proposition that "it is, indeed, this inequality of condition between the front and rear ranks, in the march of progress which gives so strong an impulse to the former to maintain their position, and to the latter to press forward into their files."[16]

The theory of elitism, given a certain democratic plausibility by the stipulation that elite status was to be achieved rather than ascribed, was finally fully developed (though not widely accepted) in the philosophy of Social Darwinism toward the turn of the last century. But meritocracy did not become the accepted creed of America until the economic and organizational transformation dictated the need for a highly trained technical and intellectual elite whose skills were needed to sustain the efficiency of the bureaucracies on which economic growth appeared to depend. More importantly, from the perspective of the chances for popular acceptance, meritocracy could not win its way in the hearts and minds of the masses until rising standards of living of the great middle class had given people a real stake in economic growth and in the efficient operation of the dominant bureaucracies.

Meritocracy in its modern form inherits all of the ambiguity and antiegalitarian tendencies of Social Darwinism. It is, in fact, cut from the same intellectual cloth, tailored to fit changed economic circumstances. Social Darwinism and meritocracy stand on the same ground:

- In their assumption of a radical, natural inequality among men.
- In their belief in a "trickle-down process" through which the superior talents of a few make possible a bearable life for the many.
- In their faith that the going system consistently matches real merit with social position, wealth, and power.
- In their commitment to efficiency and economic growth as the highest social goods.

- In their addiction to law and order as the basis for the social stability required by efficiency.
- In their belief that equality is a thin veil for the malignant envy of the masses, and their fear of equality as a major threat to the stability of the system.

Elitism and Equal Opportunity

The radical way Social Darwinism altered the meaning of equal opportunity is clearly revealed in the writings of George Harris, a Congregational minister, the president of Amherst College, and an intellectual partisan of Social Darwinism. In his *Inequality and Progress*, published in 1897, Harris launched an all-out attack on the idea of equality in all of its forms.[17] His first target was the idea of a "mechanical equality," which he accused Edward Bellamy of having fostered in his widely read *Equality*. Those radical, leveling ideas, he argued, are incompatible with human nature and would, if acted upon, destroy incentive and result in economic and social decline.

But Harris's real quarrel was with those more dangerous social reformers who invoked the seductive slogan of "equality of opportunity." Harris was responding here, too, to Bellamy's radical analysis of equal opportunity. "Economic equality," Bellamy had argued, is the necessary prerequisite for genuine equality of opportunity. In order that "the competitive struggle . . . might be called, without mockery, a fair test of the qualities of the contestants" it would be necessary "to equalize their educational equipment, early advantages, and economic or money backing."[18] So long as economic inequality of condition exists, it is impossible to know whether the social hierarchy reflects natural differences or artificial advantages. Only economic equality could provide "the even floor" on which all men might stand in order that their natural inequalities might be fairly measured. By exposing the contradiction inherent in equality of opportunity, Bellamy had given the idea a radical cutting edge. Harris met the challenge head-on; "equality of opportunity," he argued, "is both impossible and undesirable."

Harris's argument rests on a distinction between the valid idea of "careers open to talents" and the false and dangerous idea of "equality of opportunity," which claims to give everyone the same opportunities for all pursuits. The "prime necessity," if society is to be governed by the most able, is "inequality of opportunity in agreement with inequality of individuals." The necessity for unequal opportunity is most clearly evident, he argues, in education. In allocating educational opportunity, no "external discrimination" (discrimination based on "class, means, and family") should be made. Unequal opportunities should correspond not with arbitrary social advantages but with the individual abilities of unequal persons.

At the same time, however, it is a dangerous fallacy to believe that the actual inequalities of opportunity rooted in "class, means, and family" can or should be remedied by law or social action. Nor need they be in order to insure that careers are open to talents and that social efficiency is maximized. Exceptionally talented and ambitious individuals will find their way: "With rare exceptions they find or create opportunities, and by the very effort necessary for making their way, are developed in character and talent as they might not be if the doors of opportunity were held open for them, and they were kindly pushed along the line of least resistance rather than obliged to push themselves along the line of greatest resistance."

Harris does not argue that, in the actual conditions of society, "everyone has a suitable opportunity." His claim is, rather, that "external opportunity has but a small part in the conditions of success, and that, on the whole, persons of character, ability, and energy do find or make opportunities by which they rise to their proper level in the economic, professional, and social scale." And that, he maintains, is enough. Anything more—any effort to equalize opportunities—encourages the dangerous idea of human equality. Even the notion that every man deserves a fair chance to succeed threatens the rule of merit because *fair* is so easily translated into *equal*. Properly understood, however, *fair* means "just, right, and fitting" in the sense of proportioning opportunities to individual abilities. A born businessman,

126

lawyer, scholar, or statesman deserves a fair chance to occupy a corresponding social status; a born shoemaker deserves a fair chance to become a good shoemaker. Echoing Aristotle's doctrine of "proportional equality," Harris advanced the basic rule that "so far as men are equal," opportunities should be in proportion to their merits. To accomplish this, equal chances are not necessary; some chance is enough. The effort to establish equal chances, even for the equally meritorious, is positively dangerous.

The touchstone of Harris's philosophy is "the rule of the best"—the acknowledgment and enthronement of "the aristocracy of merit, . . . the few who by intellectual superiority and unbounded energy are the born leaders, teachers, judges, rulers, and benefactors—the genuine aristocracy" on whose natural gifts the welfare, culture, and progress of society depend. Harris recognized, as his modern counterparts are more reluctant to do, that equalizing opportunities to provide for a fair race would require a large degree of equality of condition and would thus undermine elite rule. The commitment to elitism, Harris recognized, is safe only when no more is required than that careers be open to talents—not that they be open on the same terms for everyone. He recognized further that meritocracy is threatened when the ideal of equal opportunity, with its Jeffersonian undertones, is taken seriously. Modern meritocrats, recognizing that equal opportunity is no longer taken seriously, have been able to appropriate the ideal to their own uses. They nonetheless share with Harris the view that social efficiency and progress depend on rule by the elite of merit. They also share with him the belief that all other social values, including individual, racial, or sexual justice—equal opportunity itself—must give ground wherever those values threaten meritocratic rule.

The meritocratic assumption that efficiency (and civilization itself) depends on inequality means that it is more important that human affairs be in the hands of an energetic, capable, skilled elite than that every person has an equal chance to rise into its ranks. In a racist society, in which the opportunities to rise depend significantly on skin color, this assumption leads to a new version of the "white man's burden."

The Cult of Efficiency

As Harris understood, the old Jeffersonian dream, even as it had been adapted to new economic conditions by the Jacksonians, potentially had a radical cutting edge. Genuine equality of economic, social, and cultural opportunity implied at least rough equality of condition. At the same time, the gross inequalities of power and wealth that accompanied the growth of industrial capitalism after the Civil War were clearly incompatible with the equal start in life promised by "the dream." Elitism and genuinely equal opportunity were always contradictory.

The Jeffersonian ideal was built on the notion that if genuinely equal opportunities were offered, actual equality of results would be approximated. Harris realized that this expectation led to the conclusion that where great differences of circumstance exist among social classes, they must be the result of arbitrary preference and political and legal advantage. Judged on traditional egalitarian standards, the very existence of an elite was evidence that its members had been cheating—that they had acquired their wealth and power as a result of unequal opportunities. Success means greater opportunity for the sons and daughters of the elite; both success and failure tend to be hereditary. Harris was correct in assuming that the idea of equal opportunity is incompatible with Social Darwinism, meritocracy, or elitism in any form. His own assumptions led him to the view that the end of elitism is the end of civilization and progress; hence, his fear of the idea of equal opportunity.

A similar fear must lead any modern believer in meritocracy to be suspicious of all deliberate efforts to equalize opportunities, beyond removing formal and legal barriers. Unlike Harris, however, modern apostles of meritocracy are content to allow the rhetoric of equal opportunity to win the day, provided it can be limited to a rhetorical victory. Unlike Harris, they do not feel compelled to take the doctrine of equal opportunity seriously.

The Elite of Intellect

In two respects, each having some significance, meritocracy parts company with its Darwinist antecedents. The first involves a difference in the natural talents selected for recognition and reward; the second lies in the mechanisms through which the fittest are selected.

In its definition of merit, meritocracy substitutes brain power (IQ) for what Justice Brewer called "business tact and sagacity." This shift in emphasis reflects the increasingly technical tasks of organized bureaucracies. But it has further implications. So long as money-making was the measure of success, its acquisition seemed to be open to all—especially in a relatively simple, rapidly expanding economy characterized by rising values. The skills appropriate to economic success were ill defined. It was, in fact, precisely because the skills of money-making were so ill defined that Social Darwinism was able to conceal its elitism in the more egalitarian rhetoric of abundant opportunity for all.

Meritocracy, by contrast, locates the ground of merit clearly and narrowly in intellectual aptitude. Indeed, in the totality of human efforts to define and judge the human potential, modern meritocracy sets a record for narrowness of vision. Meritocracy is the most limited of man's historic efforts to identify the qualities appropriate to a ruling class. While Plato's guardians monopolized the human capacity to know the true and the good, Plato never imagined that technical experts could run a society. The qualities measured by modern IQ tests are a long way from defining the qualities Plato thought necessary for ruling. Indeed, in its traditional meaning of defining public goals and purposes—of "history-making," in C. Wright Mills's phrase—the function of rulership disappears altogether in modern meritocratic society. The technocratic elite is judged by its ability to keep the existing machinery of power running smoothly and efficiently and by its ability to deliver on its promise of increasing material affluence. Persons recruited into the elite for intellectual talents appropriate to this task are not expected to judge the desirability of the goals for which their energies are expended. Thus, while Plato left unsolved the question of who will stand guard over the guardians, meritocracy solves the problem by eliminating guardianship.

Meritocracy is rule by "the best and the brightest," where *best* has no meaning other than *brightest*. [19] The meritocratic elite, because of the conditions of its recruitment and advancement up the ranks, is unable to view the system in which it functions critically. Jeb Stuart Magruder, reflecting on his ruined career after pleading guilty to an indictment for conspiracy to obstruct justice and other Watergate-related crimes, recognized that he had never really examined his goals and motivations. "The last twenty years," he acknowledged, "all I've done is kept moving up the ladder, working very hard to make sure I was going up that ladder." If Magruder's reflection on his experience is unusual, the experience he speaks of is not. The rewards offered in the meritocratic race determine the goals of the competitors. The prizes go to those who are willing to surrender at the starting line the right to judge the uses to which their skills will be put. And if, by chance, some urge to moral autonomy remains, ambition may be counted on to blunt or divert it. "Spiritually," Lionel Gelber has written, "if he knows on which side his bread is buttered, organizational man must devalue himself." Magruder made the same point in a more homely fashion: "You've got to do what the hierarchy wants, that's why you're here." This subversion of self, Magruder added, continues "on a daily basis." Success in the power structure is continuously at odds with setting one's own standards; the result is "a question of slippage." [20]

There is yet another significant consequence of the meritocracy's identification of the best with the brightest. An earlier faith in natural human equality rested on the claim that natural differences among men are slight, and that even those natural differences are leveled out when each man is averaged for his degrees of excellence in the myriad characteristics that contribute to social life. But the averaging of talents for socially necessary skills, and for individual virtues, weaknesses, and vices, is no longer possible where intellect becomes the sole criterion of social reward.

When the social worth of persons, and the social rewards to which they are entitled, are defined by the single standard of technical intelligence, the tenuous historical links between elitism and equality of opportunity are completely severed. Meritocracy, unlike previous forms of elitism, cannot masquerade as a new version of abundant opportunity for all to develop their diverse and infinite potentials. Meritocracy means opportunity for the intellectually gifted few. Because it implies a disproportionate allocation of society's resources to the educational cultivation of the talents of the few, its commitment to inequality is readily apparent. It is, in short, a bald doctrine of "every man in his place," where, moreover, the places are determined by a single human characteristic outside the control of individuals. Michael Young makes this last point forcefully in his brilliant satirical novel of the future, *The Rise of the Meritocracy*, by imagining the development of a technique for predicting IQ in the fetal stage.[21]

Various characteristics of meritocracy fly too flagrantly in the face of the old egalitarian myths to permit the obfuscations by which earlier forms of elitism have flourished. These include:

- The isolation of a single standard for allocating status, wealth, power, and benefits.
- A standard that is ascribed rather than achieved, and that, therefore, has little connection with effort.
- The allocation of limited social resources to the recruitment and training of those meritorious few who meet the prescribed standard.

Meritocratic equality is no more than equality of opportunity to be born bright—a proposition no less inane than the traditional invitation to be born to aristocratic parents. Meritocracy is so blatantly elitist, and its premises so clearly incompat-

131

ible with any intelligible meaning of equality of opportunity, that the old American game of packaging the elites in populist rhetoric is over. As a nation we shall now have to face openly the choice between elitism and populism. If we make the populist choice, equality may once again become a threat and a challenge—rather than a solace—to the rich and powerful. The other alternative is that, for the sake of an efficient social machine that produces an expanding consumer affluence for the majority, we will embrace inequality without needing a saving egalitarian myth.

From Natural Laws to IQ Tests

The second major difference between Social Darwinism and meritocracy involves the processes by which elites are selected. Whereas Social Darwinists imagined that the fittest individuals would be selected through the natural economic law of competition, modern meritocracy has to make its way in a world that has lost its capacity to believe in natural law. In the modern meritocracy, the process of selection is made not by nature (or by Adam Smith's "invisible hand"), but by admissions and personnel officers who apply cultural standards to applicants for admission, appointment, and promotion.

Institutional processes through which individuals are selected and certified have replaced what the Social Darwinists claimed to be impersonal, natural mechanisms. The appeal of Social Darwinists to the laws of nature was crucial to their case. Without it, their argument was open to the charge of circularity.[22] The fitness of the survivors is proved by their survival; their survival proves their fitness. We are left with the unenlightening proposition that the survivors survive. "Natural selection," through an impersonal "law of competition," provided a way out of the circularity by positing that the fittest are selected by nature herself.

Meritocracy, in contrast, makes no claim that the meritorious are selected by natural laws or by autonomous market processes. Its elites are self-chosen, having been co-opted into elite status by the previously existing elites. The criteria that define merit are not nature's judgments; they reflect social values. If the case for meritocracy is not to be an empty, circular argument, the question then becomes: How is the definition of merit to be justified as serving the interests of society? The meritocratic answer is efficiency. But efficiency turns out to mean simply the effective conduct of business-as-usual through the dominant bureaucracies. The efficient operation of the existing machinery, in turn, guarantees that the rich will preserve their wealth, the privileged their advantages, and the influential their power. And insofar as wealth, privilege, and power are disproportionately in the hands of whites, they will stay that way.

Meritocracy does not seek to justify the inequities of the existing order; it simply overlooks them. It ignores the inequalities of opportunity that lead to economic inequalities, just as it neglects the heritage of injustice that handicaps racial minorities.

11

Social Darwinism Revisited

Meritocracy or "Effortocracy"?

Meritocracy, I have argued, has attached itself, fraudulently and without historical justification, to the traditional American ideal of equal opportunity. In sharp contrast to the idea of meritocracy, the older version of equal opportunity may be described as "effortocracy." Until very recently, this was the dominant version of the idea of equality in America. The American creed opted for effort, as opposed to natural endowment, as the basis for social rewards and the path to individual success. Indeed, it was not until the development of Social Darwinism toward the turn of the last century that there was in America a significant and widely shared apologia for inequality that rested on the legitimacy of rewarding assumed natural differences in talent.

The earlier emphasis on effort had reflected the then-dominant interpretation of the meaning of equality. It was a radical interpretation in which success was available to all, dependent only on individual exertion. The accumulation of property, for example, was viewed as an important avenue to success, but property rights were defined in a way that emphasized the role of effort in the acquisition of property and insured its widespread distribution. Here, as elsewhere, young America took its cue from the English philosopher John Locke. Central to Locke's defense of private property was the assumption that men's chances to acquire it will depend more on "their willingness to apply a capacity for industry with which they are all equally endowed" than on differences in natural talents or rational capacities. As Sanford Lakoff has concluded, "If the diversity of social advantages or of natural talents counted as much as sheer industriousness, the ethical justification of property erected by Locke would be gravely undermined."[1]

Early liberal democrats had no intention of dismantling the regime of inherited and legal privilege only to enthrone a new system of achieved inequality and hierarchy. Their assumption of the natural equality of men meant that differences in achievement were entirely the result of will and effort. In an agrarian republic of equal laws, men would be involved, in the Puritan sense, in the cultivation of their divine, God-given, and relatively equal talents and in a "competition in virtue." Jeffersonians never developed a doctrine of equality of opportunity in the competitive sense because they saw interpersonal rivalry for status, wealth, or power as incompatible with both equality and individuality.[2] In their agrarian outlook, the Jeffersonians thought they had found a formula in which the individual struggle against nature replaced rivalry for position and power, so that man's natural equality would not be overridden by artificial legal or social advantages.

Industry, Economy, and Virtue

When, in the Jacksonian period, this agrarian utopia was forced to come to terms with the facts of rapidly developing commercial competition, liberals failed to face the problem squarely. The ambiguities and contradictions in their position resulted in a confused and highly sentimental acceptance of the new capitalist order. But in all its romantic vagueness, the liberal response insisted on clinging to the notion that effort, not natural endowment, should be rewarded. They sought thereby to salvage the basic belief in equality, since they supposed that making an effort was equally within the capacity of everyone. The idea of an elite of merit, even one selected on the basis of equal opportunity, was incompatible with their belief in equality and their commitment to a society of equals.

Success, argued Robert Rantoul, Jr., who was one of the most influential of the Jacksonian philosophers, depends more on virtue than on talent, and virtue can be produced in every man by "moral science," which it is the function of a universal education to inculcate. Uncounted numbers of "self-made men," he wrote, "have risen, not by strength of talents, but by an unexceptional course of direct and upright dealing in all their concerns."[3] Marvin Myers summarizes Rantoul's defense of a "liberal" theory of enterprise as resting on three prerequisites: "a wide dispersion of wealth and land"; "circulation of fortune and power"; and "the keying of success to industry, economy, and virtue." Andrew Jackson, in his presidential veto of a national bank, expressed these sentiments when he declared that the farmers, mechanics, and laborers who were "the bone and sinew of the country" were able to prosper only in a climate in which "success depends upon their own industry and economy."

Unfortunately, the Jacksonians, like subsequent generations, failed to assess accurately the threat to their ideals of new economic conditions. The dream of the agrarian utopia—a power-free society of independent and equal citizens—obscured the implications of an interdependent commercial and industrial system. Jacksonians believed that economic laissez-faire would approximate the conditions of agrarian utopia in producing opportunity for all and a rough equality of condition, as well as leaving every man entirely in his own power. As Myers describes their predicament: "The republican yeoman on his hundred acres, building his farm and his character together and taking his reward in self-sufficient independence, populates the speeches of Jacksonian Democrats but not the countryside that observers viewed." The decisive element in this self-deception was a continued insistence on the proposition that industriousness, effort, and will are the key elements in individual success.

The True System

As social and economic reality diverged further and further from the agrarian dream, many Americans relied on rhetoric to salvage the dream. Thus, in his New Haven speech on March 6, 1860, Lincoln presented an altered version of the dream, but one still in keeping with its egalitarian spirit:

> When one starts poor, as most do in the race of life, free society is such that he knows he can better his condition; he knows that there is no fixed condition of labor for his whole life. . . . I want every man to have a chance—and I believe a black man is entitled to it—in which he can better his condition—when he can look forward and hope to be a hired laborer this year and the next, work for himself afterwards, and finally hire men to work for him. That is the true system.

The central characteristic of Lincoln's version of the success myth is that the conditions for achieving it are not only open, but are actually possible for all. Although Lincoln uses the metaphor of "the race of life," he does not see success as a prize held out only to the swiftest competitors. His view of life is not a winnowing, sorting process for selecting the fittest; success does not measure the superiority of winners over losers. His interpretation of the American success story is not reflected in the career of a captain of industry, a merchant prince, or a political hero; it is, potentially, *every* man's biography.

The essence of the dream is as old as the Republic. To be sure, Lincoln's is not exactly the language of the old Jeffersonian, anticapitalist vision—yeoman farmers inhabiting an agrarian republic, in which the moral and intellectual independence of each is made possible by the economic independence of all, and in which the destructive human vices of avarice and ambition are not inflamed by the habits of commercial life. Lincoln, like countless others, sought to save the essential features of the older, agrarian ideal by adapting it to the conditions of a new industrial society. It was, he imagined, a small-scale industrialism, which he hoped would not produce social or economic hierarchies or great inequalities of material condition. There was, of course, more hope than truth in a vision which looked back to the old egalitarian dream and ignored the emerging industrial reality.

This faith in a universal system of opportunity to build one's own enterprise was rapidly undermined by the development of giant industrial corporations and the emergence of new "captains of industry" like the Carnegies, Fiskes, Vanderbilts, and Rockefellers. But, while the impact of these changes on the meaning of *opportunity* was striking, the capacity of the old myth for adaptation and survival was even more remarkable.

The Moral Economy of Pluck

The intellectual defense of the new industrial capitalism was undertaken by the Social Darwinists. As social theory, Darwinism at least had the virtue of faithfully describing the economic realities it set out to defend and legitimize. Social Darwinists did not seek out old egalitarian virtues in the realities of industrial concentration. They saw, and rationalized, a system of competition in which success meant the elimination of rivals and the conquest of power and wealth. The outcome of competition, they argued, is governed by the natural law of the survival of the fittest; the survivors are nature's own elite. In intellectual circles, from the lecterns of academia and in the columns of sophisticated periodicals, these ideas won the day.

There were intellectual critics, of course, who rested their cases on a radical or socialist version of the idea of equality. But, in any event, Social Darwinism was not the message that captivated the popular mind. The explicitly elitist analyses of intellectual Darwinists like Herbert Spencer and William Graham

Sumner were too clearly at odds with the old egalitarianism to be palatable to a public that still dreamed the dreams of the Jeffersonians, the Jacksonians, and those for whom Lincoln had spoken. A new formula for self-deception—one that would keep the dream alive—was necessary, and it was supplied by those romanticized versions of Darwinism described as the "gospel of wealth."

The gospel of wealth was a fundamentally un-Darwinian interpretation of the American scene. In the theory of Social Darwinism, the inevitable outcome of Nature's "law of competition" is the triumph of the fittest that is also, happily, the only path to future improvement in society. But in the gospel of wealth (developed in the voluminous "success" literature that became staple reading for American youth) the winners are not Nature's fittest, but young "everyman." Success depends not on superior natural gifts, but on self-improvement, achievable through industriousness and education. Everyone can win. Horatio Alger's heroes are not Darwinian survivors or a natural elite of any sort, but rather youths who caught the fever of ambition and persevered to success through honesty, tenacity, frugality, and enterprise. The term then in vogue was *pluck*, and pluck was thought to be within the reach of all.

Nor did the popularized transformation of Social Darwinism into the gospel of success endorse the great wealth or glorify the careers of the captains of industry. Alger's heroes rise from poverty and obscurity—bootblacks and newsboys were favorite starting places—but do not attain great fortunes or positions of power. Alger calls the conditions of their success "fame and fortune," but he describes a condition of middle-class respectability of exactly the sort that was imagined to be within the grasp of all poor boys.[4] Thus the gospel of wealth heralded not the triumph of the meritorious few, but the message to all that was contained in Horace Greeley's advice to young men: "I would have you believe that success in life is within the reach of every one who will truly and nobly seek it."

A similar message was contained in the approach to failure. Where Social Darwinism taught that poverty was Nature's verdict on the unfit, the message that captivated American minds was that poverty, where it existed, was a temporary condition, remediable through individual effort and will. Opportunities were felt to be abundant. All that was necessary, William Makepeace Thayer argued, was that the poor boy "should watch and improve his opportunities; that he should be industrious, upright, faithful, and prompt; that he should task his talents, whether one or ten, to the utmost; that he should waste neither time nor money; that duty, and not pleasure or ease, should be his watchword."[5]

The sermons of the popular preachers of the gospel of wealth echoed the same theme: Poverty is not part of Nature's plan; it springs, rather, "from laziness, lack of thrift, vice, and sometimes misfortune." There is not a word in these sermons that suggests a natural distribution of talent as a significant determinant of worldly success. Wealth is assumed to be potentially available on equal terms to all who make the effort and practice the appropriate virtues. Not only is poverty never described as a badge of natural inferiority, it is typically even seen as a blessing in disguise. Thus Andrew Carnegie presumed to "congratulate poor young men upon being born to that ancient and honorable degree which renders it necessary that they should devote themselves to hard work."

Both these ideas and the medium through which they were popularized have a long history in America. "Success literature" had long been a means for the cultivation of the desired moral qualities in American youth. And the message had always been the same: egalitarian and antimeritocratic. Even apparent exceptions turn out not to be such. Thus, Louisa C. Tuthill, one of Alger's leading predecessors in self-help literature for children, writing in the period from 1830 to 1850, seems at first glance to be publicizing a case for meritocracy. In a society without hereditary titles, she says, "there can be no higher distinction than that which belongs to moral worth, intellectual superiority, and refined politeness." But her belief in the central role of "intellectual superiority" in producing success does not mark her, as some interpreters have concluded, as a believer in the "ideal of natural aristocracy." She later makes her meaning clear: "Those glorious institutions of New England, common schools, afford to every boy the opportunity to acquire that intelligence and taste, and his associates there are from every class of society. There is no insurmountable obstacle in any boy's way; his position in society must depend mainly upon himself."[6] Thus, even when intellectual superiority is stressed, intelligence is viewed as an acquired characteristic, the development of which depends mainly on individual will and effort.

In most of the other success literature that predated Alger, intellectual superiority, or any other so-called natural basis for social hierarchy, is missing altogether. The ingredients of success in these stories, from the 1830s onward, parallel those that later account for the rise of Alger's heroes. The virtues that led to success included cultivation of the moral qualities of gentility, frugality, piety, and temperance, as well as industry and determination. Often, virtue was rewarded by a chance encounter with a wealthy and benevolent man or his fair daughter, leading to a fortunate marriage and a junior partnership.

The Obsession with Luck

The role of luck in social ascent is a pervasive theme in American success literature. One of Alger's heroes, Raggedy Dick, speaks for all of them when he says, "I was lucky. I found some good friends who helped me along." So prominent is this theme that one observer has concluded that "Alger was obsessed with luck." John G. Cawelti explains this obsession as a literary device that both compensates for "sloppiness and inadequacies in plotting and motivation" and provides an easy means of maintaining suspense. Cawelti also sees luck as a clue to the dominant role in Alger's and his audience's assumptions of a Divine Providence that "acts to reward the deserving, punish the evil, and convert the doubting."[7] No doubt both those functions help explain the central role of luck in success literature. But luck plays another, ideological, role. Pluck had been the great equalizer that brought the dream within the reach of all. As the actual conditions of economic life made universal success increasingly unrealistic and unbelievable, luck was brought in to accomplish what pluck could not.

The appearance of luck as a legitimate lever of opportunity

ran directly counter to the Puritan ethic, although Alger obscured that fact by taking care to insure that only the righteous got lucky. In any of its forms, luck appears to be in flagrant contradiction with a creed that links success to individual achievement. Yet, luck was accepted early on, in the form of rising values of land and other assets, fortunate marriage, or inheritance.

Later, the stock market became an honorable and legitimate form of gambling for the already affluent; numbers games served as an accepted safety valve for failure among the urban masses. In a peculiar way, luck reaffirms equality in a competitive order; luck thumbs its nose at the aristocracy of merit. Everyone has an equal chance to get lucky. Irish Sweepstakes winners make the front page, and television giveaway shows get high Nielsen ratings because in the blink of an eye the poor and humble are randomly selected to share the wealth and status of the successful. It is the instinct to equality, not mere envy, that attracts large audiences to witness and approve the instant success of random chance.[8]

Chance reaffirms equality by challenging merit. For chance, along with effort, determines success in those kinds of games that provide real, as well as formal, equality of opportunity to succeed. But beyond that, there may be in the American fascination with luck the suspicion that effort itself may not be an ideal criterion for an egalitarian game.[9] People may vary, through no fault of their own, in the degree to which they are able to make an effort or to persevere. Thus, luck appears to compensate partially for the arbitrariness inherent even in the moral economy of pluck.

Pluck and Luck

Pluck and luck are the levers of opportunity in the gospel of wealth as it was popularly preached. At the same time, they provide solid evidence of how far Americans were from a willingness to accept a Social Darwinist jungle in which the survival of the fittest meant the triumph of a natural aristocracy. Like the

Jeffersonians before them, and the Jacksonians and Lincoln, "the ideologists of success refused to believe that some individuals were inherently more fit than others." As John G. Cawelti has put it, "Reasserting the traditional maxim 'where there's a will there's a way' they insisted that there were more opportunities than ever for a man who was determined to get ahead. Failure, they insisted, was largely caused by defects in the individual's character and will."

How was everyone to have an equal chance, or even a fair chance, if nature had decided the outcome ahead of time? Success and failure themselves must depend on qualities within each individual's control if a competitive order is to meet the demands of American individualism and optimism, if success is to be available to all, and if individuals are to be rewarded for their success and punished for their failure. For this reason, determination, perseverance, and "true grit" have always occupied the central place among individualist virtues. And what pluck failed to accomplish, luck might complete. This view of the world was, of course, out of date even when it was preached and written. It was, in fact, a view of a simpler, more egalitarian world of the open frontier and of small commercial undertakings, which was already being replaced by corporate giantism. As Cawelti describes it:

> Alger's favorite reward is a junior partnership in a respectable mercantile house. This emphasis is a throwback to the economic life of an earlier period, when American business was still dominated by merchants whose economic behavior in retrospect seemed refined and benevolent in comparison to the devastating strategies of transcontinental railroad builders, iron and steel manufacturers, and other corporate giants. Alger's version of success is, in effect, a reassertion of the values of a bygone era in an age of dramatic change and expansion.

The reassertion of those older values is a revealing phenomenon. The new industrial order—with its accompanying concentrations of great fortunes and power and the sharp increases in the range of wealth and poverty—found its logical defense in the theory of Social Darwinism and the survival of the fittest. But those ideas required a belief in natural inequality and interpersonal struggle for social and economic superiority, which Americans were not willing to embrace. The new system of economic and social inequality could only be legitimized if it could be disguised as the old equality. It had to appear as if there were unlimited opportunities for everyman. A meritocracy had to masquerade as an effortocracy.

From Character to Personality

By the 1920s, the image of the self-made man in America had taken on some new characteristics. This new image was more appropriate to the changed conditions of success in the organizational world of corporate capitalism, with its developing emphasis on consumerism. The nature of these changes is reflected in the language of the new high priests of the cult of success.[10] Andrew Carnegie *(Triumphant Democracy)* was replaced by Dale Carnegie *(How to Win Friends and Influence People)*; Elbert Hubbard *(A Message to Garcia)* gave way to Norman Vincent Peale *(The Power of Positive Thinking)*; the moral lessons of Horatio Alger's stories were transformed into Bruce Barton's homilies on "What to Do If You Want to Sit at the Boss's Desk." The old Puritan idea of man as a "moral athlete," obligated to undergo strict training to overcome the temptations of the flesh, was eroded by what David Riesman later described as "other-direction" and the regime of "antagonistic cooperation." The movement was from improvement of character to the cultivation of personality as the key to success; from individual conquest over both one's own internal nature and the objective natural world to mastery of the techniques of "human engineering" and manipulation of others; from carrying "a message to Garcia" to the art of "putting your best foot forward."

Bruce Barton, in his own career, was symbolic of the changes that were occurring. The influential editor of *American Mercury*, the lay preacher who, in *The Man Nobody Knows*, managed to make Christ into "a good Rotarian," was also a pioneer in the development of the techniques of the new profession of "public relations." A founding partner of one of the first great Madison Avenue firms, Batton, Barton, Durstine and Osborne, he was intent, in Rousseau's phrase, on turning "the arts of pleasing into a system." (The result, Rousseau had accurately predicted, would be that "the question is no longer whether a man is honest, but only whether he is clever.") When, some three decades later, one of the great national political parties for the first time turned the management of its campaign for the presidency over to the professional manipulators of mass attitudes, the choice was Batton, Barton, Durstine and Osborne. Eisenhower was packaged and merchandised, successfully, like corn flakes and the newest Detroit cars.

The gulf is wide between the qualities exhibited by Raggedy Dick and those cultivated in the newer schools of personality development. But one central characteristic of success is maintained—the fiction that the game is open on equal terms to all, and that eligibility to compete does not depend on any form of "natural" certification. "A hard-hitting mediocrity," Barton insisted, "is almost certain to score over genius." Again, the egalitarian myth was preserved in the face of new and rapidly expanding inequalities.

Through Free and Universal Education

As hierarchy and bureaucracy came increasingly to characterize organizational life, and as the skills appropriate to its efficient operation became increasingly technical and specialized, the gulf widened between the dream of abundant opportunity for all and the reality of room at the top for only the talented few. A new formula for concealing the contradiction was required if the dream was to serve an increasingly inconsistent reality. The responsibility for this fell on education.

In Herbert Hoover's praise of equal opportunity, quoted in an earlier chapter, he went on to describe further what he saw as the distinctively American version of this ideal: "It is as if we set a race. We, through free and universal education, provide the training of the runners; we give to them an equal start; we provide in the government the umpire of fairness in the race. The winner is he who shows the most conscientious training, the greatest ability, and the greatest character."

With Hoover, Darwinism had won a partial victory. Social life had become a racetrack, success had come to mean competitive triumph over others, and the result of the race ushered in gross inequalities of condition. But in "free and universal education" Hoover found the key to reconciling the values of an agrarian past with those of an industrial present. If the race inevitably produces more losers than winners, education can at least provide a genuinely equal start. The qualities that determine the outcome include ability, as well as "conscientious training" and "character." But there is the old implicit faith that effort and character, which every person can cultivate, can counterbalance deficiencies in natural ability.

The magic of "free and universal education" conjures away the unequal starting lines encountered by the children of winners and losers. But, if this is still the American creed, it is not the American reality. In a fundamental sense it never was. "Free and universal education" never did successfully bring all the runners equally to the starting line. But that venerable proposition did have more validity in earlier times than it now has under the conditions of meritocracy. In the 1920s, it was still true—true enough, at least, to get by—that the education needed by an individual to succeed was the functional literacy represented by a high school diploma, or less. Education could, therefore, be viewed as a "free and universal" ladder to success.

Cawelti has provided an admirable description of this transformation:

> The increasingly technical and specialized character of modern work made formal education a much more essential part of the normal career line. Both the apprenticeship system and individual entrepreneurship, major success strategies of the nineteenth century, had been largely superseded by formal education. Today's self-made man does not rise from the ranks; he is hired as an executive trainee on the basis of a college degree in business administration, engineering, or economics. The office boy of Horatio Alger's day might have

had some hope of rising to a partnership, although he was probably mistaken if he thought that diligence and punctuality in filing correspondence would help him to do so. Today's office boy knows that a year at Harvard Business School will do more for his career than a lifetime of industry, economy, temperance, and piety.

The elites in a meritocratic society are credentialed, and educational institutions are the major "credentialing" agencies. Colleges and professional schools certify the merit of their graduates, as well as the lack of merit of those to whom they deny admission or fail. This is a far cry, indeed, from a "free and universal education" that opens the doors of opportunity equally to all.

Vast changes in the social and economic order underlie the changed role of education in determining who gets ahead, and on what terms. Under the conditions of meritocracy, education is both more necessary for social ascent and less accessible to all. The sort of education required for success is now neither free nor universal. Instead of being available to any person who seeks it, education has become the ladder leading to and defining success. Where it once symbolized opportunity for all, it now represents a reward for the demonstrated merit of an elite. From kindergarten on, there is a scramble for place and position in the progressively more rarified atmosphere of the higher learning, and relentless competition for grade point averages and recommendations that will admit one to the next higher and more exclusive rank of the meritocracy.

Those who lose out at the lower levels are, for all practical purposes, out of the race altogether. This is because education ceased to fulfill Hoover's ideal of universal opportunity to develop the "ability and character" necessary to carve for oneself a "position in life." It became, rather, a "position in life" that one earned by demonstrating "ability and character." Once an opportunity, open to all, education (of the sort that leads to elite status) has come to be a reward bestowed on the few. The system of equal opportunity then proceeds as it has always done—but now mainly through education (which was once the safety valve against just this sort of inequality of opportunity)—to reward rewards. And thus meritocracy becomes, in the wisdom of Archie Bunker, a new version of "the survival of the fattest."

Silencing the Forces of Populist Equality

From the perspective of the meritocracy, as Clark Kerr put it in *The Uses of the University,*

> the great university is of necessity elitist, the elite of merit. It operates in an environment dedicated to an egalitarian philosophy. How may the contribution of the elite be made clear to the egalitarians, and how may an aristocracy of intellect justify itself to a democracy of all men? It was equality of opportunity, not equality per se, that animated the Founding Fathers and the progress of the American system, but the forces of populist equality have never been silent, the battle between Jeffersonianism and Jacksonianism never finally settled. [11]

While Kerr's statement of the issue—elitism, resting on "equality of opportunity," versus "the forces of populist equality"—is accurate, his definition of the philosophic and historical terms of the conflict is distorted and misleading. The battle has not been between Jeffersonianism and Jacksonianism. If the Jeffersonians had taken the position Kerr imputes to them, they would have been Hamiltonians. Hamilton, himself a paragon of the self-made man in a climate of "equal opportunity," is the founding father of the theory of "democratic elitism." The battle between Jeffersonianism and Hamiltonianism has never been settled. By identifying Jefferson with the elitist ideal, Kerr seeks to disarm those who question whether "an aristocracy of intellect [can] justify itself to a democracy of all men."

The historical link between an aristocracy of intellect and a democracy of all men is not found in Jefferson but, as Kerr recognizes, in "equality of opportunity." Although this was not, as Kerr claims, the ideal that "animated the Founding Fathers," it has been the magic formula through which an increasingly elitist reality has been made to seem consistent with the traditions of a populist equality. "The forces of populist equality," as Kerr maintains, "have never been silent." But most often they have spoken in the curious and self-defeating dialect of equal opportunity, formulating the claims of "equality per se" in language that obscures the issues at stake, playing tailor to the emperor, winning rhetorical victories while the forces of elitism have their way in the world.

In a meritocracy, where education means opportunity and opportunity is for the meritorious, it would appear that the elastic limits of the concept of equal opportunity are finally reached. The meritocratic society, after all, promises an equality of educational opportunity in which the game is fixed beforehand in the genes of the competitors. Its purpose is not the release of the creative energies of all its citizens, or any of them, but is simply "to mobilize needed skills" in the service of efficiency. Yet the capacity of the old myth to obscure and distort, to put an egalitarian gloss on an elitist reality, is apparently not exhausted.

The Domestication of Equality

The version of equal opportunity we have been examining is a uniquely American phenomenon, with uniquely American consequences. Americans never accepted the idea of a social hierarchy based on natural inequalities. As a result, the necessary condition for the stable exercise of elite power in the United States was always a successful effort to maintain that it did not exist. As ideology, Social Darwinism never captured the popular mind. As economic reality, the Carnegies, the Vanderbilts, and the Rockefellers triumphed when they were transformed in the public imagination into Raggedy Dick. The social and economic hierarchy always had to be concealed in a rhetoric of equal opportunity for all; the talents of money-making had to be disguised as pluck and luck; the educational mill for producing the new meritocracy had to wear the mask of free and universal education; and a social pyramid with finite room at the top had to seem a plateau of abundant opportunity for all.

In Europe, by contrast, the dominant version of equal opportunity was always meritocratic. The implications of the liberal revolution there were limited to providing moral approval to the new inequalities of industrial society under the slogan of "careers open to talents." In their approach to the new regime of competitive inequality, European liberals rarely went beyond John Stuart Mill's complaint that "accident has so much more to do than merit with enabling men to rise in the world."

Because the dominant European version of equal opportunity was openly and explicitly meritocratic, it was never able to exhaust the meaning of equality or to preempt the moral ground of debate over its meaning. This is, no doubt, a major factor in any plausible explanation of the vitality of European socialism and the absence of a vital socialist or radical movement in America. In the face of the new inequalities of a rapidly developing corporate capitalism, European radicals had not been ideologically disarmed. The weapon of equality had not been preempted for them as it had been for their American counterparts.

When it was proposed that poverty was attributable to the moral faults of the poor, or that the elites deserved their wealth and power because they had proved their fitness in a competitive struggle, European radicals could consistently, though not always successfully, repair to Babeuf's telling question whether it is an individual's fault "that he did not receive at birth more fortunate dispositions? Should he on that account enjoy fewer advantages?" [12] They could challenge, with Jeremy Taylor, the very idea of compensating extraordinary natural ability with wealth or power: "If a man be exalted by any excellence in his soul, he may please to remember that all souls are equal, and their differing operations are because their instrument is in better tune, their body is more healthful or better tempered; which is no more praise to him than it is that he was born in Italy." [13]

Europeans were thus saved, in a way that Americans were not, from the possibility of believing that individual self-help could somehow level out the institutionalized inequalities of a regime of competitive inequality. In America, this romantic and sentimental premise was so deeply ingrained that even a devastating encounter with reality in the Great Depression meant only a temporary weakening of the faith. As recently as the early 1970s, Christopher Jencks and his associates ran into a storm of criticism when they announced that their research had confirmed a conclusion that, after all, should have surprised no one:

> The reforms of the 1960's were misdirected because they focused only on equalizing opportunity to "succeed" (or "fail") rather than on reducing the economic and social distance between those who succeeded and those who failed. The evidence we have reviewed suggests that equalizing opportunity will not do very much to equalize results, and hence that it will not do much to reduce poverty.[14]

The War on Poverty of the 1960s was built on the twin pillars of individual self-help and governmental assistance. Its goal was to enable the poor to organize themselves to participate effectively in the pluralist process of group power and bargaining. It was never an assault on the structure or rationale of inequality.

A society in which the ideal of equality had not been so thoroughly compromised might have approached racial oppression as a betrayal of the universal principle of the Declaration and as a denial of inalienable rights. But in America, racial oppression was viewed as a limit on the upward mobility of the brightest minority individuals, and as a cost in social efficiency from the failure to use their superior talents.

Beyond Affirmative Action

The most frightening aspect of our current predicament is that the flexible doctrine of equal opportunity has so crippled the capacity for critical thought that Americans now generally accept competitive elitism as a definition of democracy and regard meritocracy as a synonym for equality. The ancient Greek, Menander, accurately formulated the alternatives in one of his maxims: "Choose equality," he advised, "and flee greed."[15] The universality of greed in a meritocratic, consumption-oriented society places tremendous pressure on the broad middle classes to jockey for position on the growth-powered escalator of American life, and to rationalize the process in the name of its traditional ideals.

This possibility is less frightening than it would otherwise be because the public that accepts it does not understand what it is doing. We still think we are embracing the old ideal of full and equal opportunity for all to develop individual potential. Vitality still abides in that dream, if it can be made to serve the purpose dreams are meant for—to criticize and change social reality. If we are to be saved, perhaps the agents of our liberation will be the meritocrats themselves. For in their fear of populist rhetoric, they appear not to be content with winning practical victories; they want a rhetorical victory as well. Not satisfied to accept the capacity of populist liberals to fool themselves, they want the ideological triumph of an explicit acknowledgment that excellence, progress, and civilization itself depend on the ministrations of a meritocratic elite. Their efforts may yet bring the populists back to their senses and rescue the idea of equality from the perverse logic of a meritocratic "animal farm." An approach to racial justice might then be grounded in the historic promise of America. We might then, in the vision of black poet Langston Hughes, "let America be America again—the land that has never been yet—and yet must be."[16]

But, in the meantime, we have only a second-best alternative—to squeeze out of the old ideal of equality of opportunity a little more equality, and to breathe enough of its old life back into that tired slogan to make it a vehicle for reducing the economic effects of racism. That purpose defines both the goals and the limits of affirmative action. If the potential effects of affirmative action are limited, its inestimable advantage over any practicable alternative is that it commits us publicly to the position that racial inequality is an intolerable evil. And, indirectly, it prompts us to turn our backs on elitism, so that we face the right direction—toward trust, confidence, and a renewed encounter with the principle of equality.

12

Meritocracy and Racism

Affirmative action is necessary because American society is meritocratic. Meritocracy is racist and, left to its own devices, unlikely to effect any significant improvement in the relative status of racial minorities. This is true for both ideological and social reasons. As ideology, meritocratic doctrine rests on assumptions that have racist consequences. As a set of institutional practices and relationships, meritocracy tends to create an elite whose members are indifferent to racial injustice and a middle class that may even psychologically require it. This chapter seeks to defend and amplify these assertions.

Meritocracy: Inequality as Principle

Ironically, the successes of the civil-rights movement in the 1960s deepened the racial crisis in America. Since legal equality had been achieved and race was no longer a legal barrier to individual achievement, it became possible to believe that the

153

competition was fair enough to make success available to minority individuals who have it in them and make the effort.

Historically, even before the achievement of legal equality in the 1960s, the slogan of equal opportunity had been ambiguous enough to provide many Americans with a painless escape from the dilemma of reconciling racism with the Declaration of Independence. Even in the period of "separate and unequal," most whites welcomed Booker T. Washington's self-help doctrine as a vindication of the myth of equal opportunity and a denial of the injustice of racist practices.

On its face, equality of opportunity to rise in the world is an individualistic doctrine, which appears to rule out discrimination based on group characteristics of any sort. But, paradoxically, it is precisely because of its individualistic bias that equal opportunity is able to conceal the existence of group prejudice. Individualism, in its materialistic and status-seeking sense, successfully conceals group prejudice under the banner of "individual preference." Social prejudice against groups can be dismissed as the chance result of individual choice because competitive individualism posits a false distinction between the private and the public, and because competitive individualism does not imply any public standard of universal human worth.

This capacity for self-deception increases as a society moves closer to the requirements of meritocracy. As legally sanctioned inequalities of opportunity to demonstrate merit are eliminated, and as effort and luck play a diminished role in determining life chances, it becomes easier to imagine that privately enforced group prejudice is inconsequential. Thus, group disadvantage rooted in racism can be made to appear as individual moral failure. And a no longer respectable belief in innate racial differences can masquerade as "the individual failings of blacks as a group." As some nonwhites are recruited into the meritocratic elite, it becomes possible to rationalize that the disproportionate number of nonwhites who remain poor have simply failed, as individuals, to meet the meritocratic test. Thus the myth of equal opportunity operates to conceal our racism, even from ourselves; the closer we move toward meritocracy, the easier this self-deception becomes.

At just that point in our history when a developing meritocracy has most severely and obviously limited opportunity for social ascent, the old myth of abundant opportunity for all is revived and offered as an invitation to nonwhites to join the mainstream and to demonstrate for whites that white racism no longer exists. Having eliminated legal barriers, we can blame individuals for a condition that can only be explained by our racism. And we can encourage the victims of our prejudice to try harder, when our very attitudes toward their failure contribute powerfully to making it permanent.

The problem is not simply the oft-noted fact that those without boots have extraordinary difficulty lifting themselves by their bootstraps. It is more deeply rooted in the idea that an endless series of individual demonstrations of merit will at some point add up to white recognition of the equal worth of members of minority groups. Even if this were likely, it would be manifestly unfair. There is no moral reason why blacks, for example, should be required to demonstrate their worth, or to earn a secure sense of self-esteem, on different terms than whites. But even if it were not grossly unfair, it is not likely to happen. Judgments of individual merit are judgments about individuals; they do not cumulate in judgments of group worth.

What is involved here is a reversal of the private and public realms. Invidious judgments of groups, inherently social in their nature and impact, are relegated to the private realm of individual conscience. At the same time, judgments of the relative worth of individuals, made on the basis of their imputed intellectual value to society, become public. The genius of the Declaration of Independence was to make the universal equality of human worth a public principle. Even when that principle was translated into equality of opportunity, it was kept alive as long as success was linked to effort and thus made to seem within the potential reach of all.

But meritocracy completes the process through which the ideal of equality has been sabotaged and eroded. On its terms, properly private judgments of the merits of others are elevated into a public standard for judging their relative worth, and the properly public standard of equal human worth dissolves into individual preference. Inequality becomes the public principle. Minorities, and the underclass generally, are deprived of any possibility of appeal to a public standard of equality in light of which their condition might be recognized as unjust.

Meritocracy: Cultural Determinism and Racism

Meritocracy, in its infatuation with efficiency, is dubious about any effort to tamper with existing social prejudices. "Benign neglect" is an accurate description of the meritocratic attitude toward the problem of race. Modern meritocrats tend to share with William Graham Sumner, preeminent philosopher of Social Darwinism, the conclusion that: "Serious study of society shows us that we can never do anything but use and develop the opportunities which are offered to us by the conditions and conjunctures of the moment."[1] Reformers, Sumner believed, fail to understand the limits of human intervention in social and historical processes. His response to their misguided zeal was to quote Daniel Webster: "A strong conviction that something must be done is the parent of many bad measures."

The theory of meritocracy, like Social Darwinism, accepts the social structure as a given, and takes the growth of economic concentration in its stride. The growth of corporate giantism and concentrated control, seen in the earlier view as evidence of sharp-dealing and conspiracy, are regarded as the result of autonomous historical forces and as the necessary condition for economic and social efficiency.

Sumner also argued that those who talk about the "power of ideas" indulge in "a relic of the sympathetic magic of savage men." It is no coincidence that those who speak for meritocracy in our day tend to be those who a few years ago heralded "the end of ideology." Like mass society itself, meritocracy offers a tolerant creed, capable of easy adjustment to the "mores and folkways" that happen to prevail. Having repudiated all other standards than the efficient operation of the existing social machinery, and viewing the development of consumerism and managerial autonomy in the postindustrial society as a hospitable environment for rule by a meritocratic elite, a meritocracy confuses *more* with *better*. Its intolerance is reserved for those ideologues and reformers who imagine that the system is subject to moral judgment and human control. The issue of racial injustice, beyond all others, activates the reformist conviction that something must be done. It becomes, therefore, the major threat to a stable meritocratic order.

Sumner's position on the "race question" reflected his deterministic assumptions. His attitude was one of sympathetic but detached resignation. He noted that the status of a black man prevents him from realizing "the powers which he may possess." But he noted it without passion. Racism was not a wrong to be righted—not even a violation of equal opportunity to be corrected—but a given fact of the prevailing mores. It might even be lamented, but not too loudly or passionately, lest the reformers' zeal be activated. With a refined and scholarly objectivity, Sumner described the condition of blacks three years after the "separate but equal" decision in *Plessy:* "For thirty years the Negro has been in fashion. He has had political value and has been petted. Now we have made friends with the Southerners. They and we are hugging each other. We are all united. The Negro's day is over. He is out of fashion."

For the same reasons, modern meritocracy accommodates itself to racism, even as it accounts racism as an evil. Doubting that social practices are open to social reform, and seeing efforts at reform as threats to efficiency, the meritocratic perspective can contemplate with equanimity the fact that the Negro is, once again, "out of fashion."

Meritocracy: The Fear of Populism

Contemporary meritocrats worry more about white backlash and the potential for racial conflict than about racial injustice. Their central value is a social efficiency that requires a stability and order that are seen to be threatened more by affirmative action than by racism.

For meritocrats, as for Social Darwinists, the central threat is equality, and the populist spirit it animates. Populism is the enemy of merit, and meritocrats see it everywhere—in affirmative action, in open admissions, in mass culture, and in the women's movement. Minorities and women can be admitted to the game—the logic of meritocracy requires that they be—but only within the limits of the conditions of public opinion and within the rules of individual demonstration of merit. To change the rules in order to compensate for group disadvantage involves invoking a more radical ideal of human equality that threatens to trigger and legitimize the envy of the poor and the unmeritorious. The meritocratic response to the demand for racial justice is the offer to accommodate the victims of discrimination into the system at a pace consistent with the rigorous selection of an aristocracy of intellect. That pace is unlikely to meet the test of even the most cautious interpretation of "all deliberate speed." But a speedier alternative would threaten the rule of merit itself, and then we are all undone. Whatever may be said for this view of the world, it is a long way from any intelligible meaning of equal opportunity, and further still from the vision of a society dedicated to the fullest development of the possibilities of all its members.

The Elite of Merit:
Whiz Kids as Moral Cripples

The ideological outlook of meritocracy toward racism is reinforced by its social consequences for elite and nonelite alike. In traditional versions of the success philosophy, it was assumed that consistent exercise of moral virtue is the primary requisite for success. This heroic assumption not only that virtue is its own reward, but that it pays off in the currency of wealth and power, was always a dubious proposition. It becomes absurd in a society that carefully separates scientific knowledge and technical skill from moral insight and wisdom, and deliberately identifies rationality and education with the former.

The result is the creation of a singularly arrogant and unlovely elite. It is arrogant because its members have been encouraged to believe in the highly questionable proposition that exceptional natural talent is morally entitled to the rewards of wealth and power. And it is unlovely because it is insensitive to John Hammond's insight that "anyone who wants gratitude from or credit for a talent that already exists is a pain in the ass."[2]

The process of recruitment and training of the meritorious, and the ensuing scramble for bureaucratic place, produce an elite that is unlikely to sympathize with the plight of the failures or of those who were denied admission to the race. Here again, the confessions of Jeb Stuart Magruder are enlightening. After having reported that the most disturbing thing to him about all the Watergate revelations was that his own conversations with superiors in the White House had been taped without his knowledge, Magruder was asked how this could have affected him more strongly than the secret bombing of Cambodia. His reply is worth pondering for what it tells us of the way the meritocracy dehumanizes its own elite, and of the hapless plight of the nonelite: "I'm disturbed by that, the lying and so on. It's inexcusable. And the bombing of the civilian population. But the taping is so personal. Most of us are affected by what we can directly relate to. It's natural. If I were in a village in Cambodia, I'd be more concerned about the bombing."[3]

The meritocratic elites are not Cambodian villagers; neither are they black, brown, female, or poor. The assumption that compassion and sympathetic involvement in the injustices suffered by others is somehow less "natural" than egoism reflects the meritocratic loss of faith in human equality. It reflects the way in which an elite is likely to lose track of what it means to be equally human. Such an elite is encouraged to believe that social worth is measured by intellectual ability, and that its own superior worth is assured by its success in climbing the meritocratic ladder. This erosion of the capacity for compassion—the psychological prerequisite for a sense of justice—is reinforced by the imperatives of careerism. Protest resignations, for example, are almost unknown among the elite technicians of the bureaucratic order in America.

The consequences for the victims of social injustice are clear enough. The meritocratic elite is capable of yielding to pressure for the sake of reducing friction that threatens the efficiency of the administrative machinery, but not of responding to moral argument for the sake of justice.

The Nonelite: Fear of Equality

In a game in which the results are alleged to measure relative individual worth and in which the stakes are income, status, and power, the losers will always confront a critical problem of self-image. The problem is how to avoid the conclusion that one's failure is due to some inadequacy within oneself—to find a way to avoid blaming, and thus hating, oneself for one's failure.

In the past, those who are white and losers have partially resolved this crisis of self-worth in two ways. The first protective response has been to appeal to the very inequalities of opportunity that have conditioned their chances (family background; luck; "it's who you know, not what you know, that counts") to conclude that their positions in life do not accurately reflect who they are. The second defense has been to look down on those below them ("the welfare class"; colored minorities) as evidence of their own relative success and worth.

From Robert E. Lane's classic study of American attitudes toward equality, he concluded that the greater society's emphasis on equal opportunity, the greater both the need and the difficulty for its members to find a comforting rationalization for their own statuses. Self-esteem, he found, is maintained, insofar as it is, through the ambivalent devices of finding those of higher status to be not really better than oneself, and those of lower status to be really worse. When Americans survey those above them, they find that the higher statuses of those on top are justified by their education and their responsibilities. They rationalize their own relative position in terms of luck, the failure of their parents to encourage their education, or their own youthful lack of foresight. The relative failure of those below them, on the other hand, is attributed to "not caring." Success, when they are considering their own in relation to their status inferiors, is viewed as "a triumph of the will and a reflection of ability. Poverty is for lazy people." The greater the emphasis on equal opportunity, the greater the strain on individual self-esteem, and "the greater the tendency of those of marginal status to denigrate those lower than themselves."[4]

There is in these attitudes, as Lane points out, not much envy and not much compassion. Individuals defend the existing order of things because it is the source of any self-respect its victims can salvage. These particular dignity-saving rationalizations, it is important to notice, reflect the assumptions of older versions of the gospel of equal opportunity. They are made possible by *inequalities* of opportunity (the luck and the family circumstances of the successful), and by the assumption that effort and not native genius is the key to success ("poverty is for lazy people").

Significantly, Lane found education to be the key concept by which Americans reconcile the conflicting myths of equal opportunity and equality. As he says, education "provides a rationale for success and failure which does minimum damage to the souls of those who did not go to college." But this rationalization will work only so long as education is seen to rest more on effort than on native ability, and insofar as there are real inequalities of educational opportunity. As Lane says, "In this and other ways, education serves as a peg on which to hang status; and, like 'blood,' whether a person got the education or not is not his 'fault,' or at least it is only the fault of an irresponsible youth, not a grown man."

By promising to eliminate inequalities of opportunity and by keying success to native intellectual ability, meritocracy undermines those rationalizations. The first—blaming the unfairness of competitive conditions—is possible only so long as the race is patently unfair.

Michael Young, in his satirical fable of the rise of a strict meritocracy, provides a portrait of a society in which all arbitrary restrictions on the rule of individual merit (defined as "natural" intelligence) have been eliminated. No longer do the extraneous advantages of family background, nepotism, luck, race, religion, sex, skin color, and so on, condition any individual's chances. Individual merit, and only individual merit, determines success or failure. In such a society, he tells us, the psychological insecurity of the lower classes will be greater than ever, there being no way for anyone to blame failure on luck or circumstance. Education, of course, is the sorting mechanism and the ladder to elite status in this hypothetical society. And the elimination of inequalities of educational opportunity will deprive the losers of sources of self-esteem; it may even destroy the idea of human equality altogether. "Educational injustice," Young's man of the future proclaims, "enabled people to preserve their illusions. Inequality of opportunity fostered the myth of human equality."[5]

From the point of view of a genuinely humane society, the worst thing that could happen is for opportunities in a meritocratic setting to be made really equal. Society, then, would be divided more sharply between the winners and the losers. The losers would be more systematically deprived of a sense of their own dignity and worth, and the winners would be more arrogant in their assurance of entitlement to their advantages. In a secular society like ours, these results would be even more marked and devastating. The saving graces of religious belief are no longer available: the succor losers have obtained in the past by reflecting that in some significant sense we are all equal in the sight of God; the humility the winners might experience from a divine obligation to charity and compassion.

To recognize the dehumanizing consequences of the movement toward meritocracy, however, is not to argue against affirmative action. Such programs, it is true, function within a meritocratic framework; by reducing the arbitrary handicaps of race and sex, they render the society more consistently meritocratic. But racial justice is the most fateful issue in our culture. Justice for nonwhites cannot wait on whites to come to their democratic senses and to reaffirm a more radical ideal of equality. If affirmative action is the flawed and partial justice of meritocracy, it is after all the sort of justice whites demand for themselves, and therefore the only justice they are currently in a position to offer others.

162

The dehumanizing consequences of meritocracy do, however, help to explain the resistance to affirmative action, as well as to define the limits of its effectiveness. In principle, the doctrine of equal opportunity was always incompatible with racism. But historically and psychologically racism was a necessary, or at least a useful, instrument for making the game tolerable for white losers.

James Baldwin has argued that whites have often maintained a precarious hold on their own self-esteem by depriving colored minorities of theirs:

> One cannot afford to lose status on this particular ladder, for the prevailing notion of American life seems to involve a kind of rung-by-rung ascension to some hideously desirable state. If this is one's concept of life, obviously one cannot afford to slip back one rung. When one slips, one slips back not a rung but into chaos and no longer knows who he is. And this reason, this fear, suggests to me one of the real reasons for the status of the Negro in this country. In a way, the Negro tells us where the bottom is: *because he is there,* and *where* he is, beneath us, we know where the limits are and how far we must not fall. We must not fall beneath him. We must never allow ourselves to fall that low, and I am not trying to be cynical or sardonic.[6]

The psychological need that racism helps to fill is magnified, for reasons discussed above, as a society moves toward meritocracy. As overt expressions of racism have become less respectable and less socially permissible, the "welfare class" has come in for a greater share of contempt and abuse—often as a socially acceptable synonym for nonwhite minorities.

As compared with earlier versions of equal opportunity, meritocracy produces more envy but even less compassion. Resentment toward an elite whose wealth and power are based exclusively on the "natural" gift of brain power is likely, because the consoling belief is no longer available that one's inferior condition does not really evidence one's inferior worth. But, deprived of this consolation, the only remaining source of self-esteem is an enhanced conviction, in relation to those on lower rungs of the social ladder, that their relatively inferior position does indeed evidence their inferior worth. In these circumstances, increased upward mobility on the part of those below—which affirmative action produces—is a serious psychological and economic threat.

For these reasons, the middle classes are likely to share the reluctance of the elite to carry the principles of meritocracy to their logical conclusions. They are likely to settle for the elimination of legal barriers to opportunity as a satisfactory approximation of equal opportunity. Admitting minorities to the game on formally equal, but socially unequal, terms does more to aggravate their problem of dignity and self-esteem than it does to improve their real chances for success. Without touching the historical and social causes that condemn minorities to relative failure, eliminating legal barriers removes the overt inequalities of opportunity that they could invoke in their efforts to salvage a sense of self-worth.

The elimination of legal disabilities has given nonwhites a chance, which is all that many Americans have come to expect or demand. For whites to expect that for themselves is to seek much less than their own humanity demands. For them to imagine that nonwhites should find the same consolation in a legal equality that perpetuates the effects of racial denigration is both presumptuous and obtuse.

The Meritocratic Limits
of Affirmative Action

The same ambiguities in the doctrine of equal opportunity and the same inherent characteristics of meritocracy that make affirmative action necessary also impose important limits on its success. Specifically, affirmative-action programs are not likely to affect significantly the conditions or the chances of lower-class nonwhites. Nor are affirmative-action programs likely to eliminate racial tension; they may even increase it.

The National Advisory Commission on Civil Disorder

noted in its 1968 report that "a rapidly enlarging Negro middle class" would not "open up an escape hatch from the ghetto." The modest but significant successes of the affirmative-action approach provide support for this proposition. Thus, while black family income was in 1977 still significantly below that of whites, some 44 percent of black families earned incomes of $10,000 per year or more. But the evidence indicates that the rising proportion of black families with incomes greater than $10,000 was related to the shrinking number of those with incomes between $5,500 and $10,000. Almost one-third of all black families in 1977, however, continued to live on incomes less than $5,500 (the official poverty line then for an urban family of four), and this proportion was not shrinking appreciably. The implications of this growing gulf between an expanding black middle class and ghetto blacks have been clearly defined by James W. Compton of the Chicago Urban League: "But, as the gulf between haves and have-nots widens, as the comforts of the well-off stand out in sharpening contrast to the discomforts of the poor, the threat of social disorder and disruption grows."[7]

The bottom third of black families who live outside the system constitutes a major part of a new underclass residing in urban ghettoes, without hope of contact with the American Dream, and unreachable by affirmative-action programs in a meritocratic setting. Thus, as *Time* magazine recently put it, "the new opportunities have splintered the non-white population." As middle-class blacks have moved up, the underclass has been left "farther and farther behind—and more and more angry."[8]

The underclass, of course, is not all black (and not all those who are poor may be characterized as underclass). But, as *Time* reported, while a third of black families were below the poverty line in 1977, only 8.9 percent of white families were in that condition. This result is clearly the consequence of our racist history and our continuing racism. A solution to these inequities is unreachable by affirmative-action programs, much less by equal-opportunity programs that operate within the assumptions of meritocracy. This point was dramatically made by David L. Evans, a Harvard admissions officer, in his letter to the *New York Times*, written the day after the *Bakke* decision:

> It is strange that on the day of the famous Bakke decision ABC televised a frightening documentary, "Youth Terror: A View from Behind the Gun," about the millions of bitter and hopelessly lost members of minorities in the urban centers of this country.
>
> If that documentary accurately reflects the existence of these young people (I have no reason to think it does not), then debating the correctness of the Supreme Court's Bakke decision is like arguing over sun-chairs on the Titanic.[9]

Those who experience the reduced opportunities that result from the combination of poverty and race are not likely to benefit from the effort to screen out and cultivate the meritocratic elite. They are more likely to be left to their own devices, which, in American politics, means to their own efforts to organize effective pressure groups. The politics of organized group pressure does not work effectively for nonwhites (for reasons described in the next chapter). Nor does it work for the underclass generally, in which nonwhites, for reasons of white racism, are disproportionately represented.

But if meritocracy imposes significant limitations on the effectiveness of affirmative-action programs, consider the consequences of ending such programs in these circumstances. Latent white racism and the continuing effects of past racism rob blacks of the opportunity to compete on equal terms. The hard-won sense of racial pride achieved by blacks—even in the face of a cultural conspiracy to make it impossible—would be threatened. And with it would go the increased self-confidence and self-regard that made achievement more likely.

In the "equal-opportunity society," group pride requires results, role models, and ultimately proportional group success. In the absence of the opportunities for expression opened up by affirmative-action programs, black pride will be eroded by failure, and its erosion will produce more failure—and more alienation, more bitterness, more of the black rage that erupted in the cities in the 1960s. This vicious cycle can lead nowhere but to increased consciousness of race and the escalation of racial hostility.

Thus, affirmative action is necessary because it is the closest approximation to justice that meritocracy permits. But it is inadequate because meritocracy permits far too little. A society based on the pure application of the merit principle would be an unlivable society, without any vestige of loyalty or community. We are already so far down that road that affirmative action may mean no more than a willingness of whites to share their affluent loneliness fairly with nonwhites. But perhaps the willingness to offer fair shares of even shoddy goods will reawaken that egalitarian conscience that alone can set us on the road to the restoration of trust and mutuality.

13

Toward an Ethnic Feudalism?

A common criticism of affirmative action is that, by giving preference to some ethnic groups, it would encourage all ethnic groups to make similar demands. The ultimate result, it is claimed, would be the balkanization of American politics. "A new kind of feudal system," as one such critic has called it, would make ethnic groups the basic political units. The result would be social polarization and, ultimately, the destruction of democratic values.

Although this argument has been most commonly advanced by partisans of the meritocratic viewpoint, its more interesting and challenging advocates have been egalitarians. Eliot Marshall, for example, argued in a recent essay that affirmative action presents a choice between two general positions. The first endorses governmental enforcement of "the ethnic allocation principle": Affirmative action would create "a new kind of feudal system in which the nation's wealth would be allocated according to affinity groups." The second would insist on a government that is "race-blind, as it is supposed to be," but one that would embark on a program of guaranteed minimum income, guaranteed jobs, and radical income redistribution. Such a race-blind government

> would still outlaw discrimination. But in order to contribute positively to the well-being of the disadvantaged (of whatever race), it . . . could redistribute wealth from the upper half of the scale to the lower half more vigorously than it does today. For example, it could stipulate that the poorest man's income would be no less than one-half as large as the richest man's. That would accomplish the same end as affirmative action, but it would do so without provoking the deadly passions of racial enmity.[1]

Marshall's conclusion is compelling, on egalitarian grounds. The proposed reallocation of wealth will appeal to those of us who are already convinced. But it will not seem to be an allocation "along more sensible lines" to those who identify the rule of merit with the welfare of society; nor to those who, like Lane's respondents, believe that "equality, at least equality of income, would deprive people of the goals of life."

The difficulty with Marshall's conclusion is not that it is wrong but that, in order to implement it, a radical transformation of values is required. And, however necessary or desirable this transformation is, the grounds he offers for it are inadequate. His argument is essentially that a more egalitarian distribution of income is a good idea because the alternative—affirmative action—is such a bad idea. He feels that affirmative action is a bad idea because it turns ethnic categories into political categories and it distributes limited resources in statistical proportion to their memberships. It therefore stimulates ethnic-group organization and an individual scramble for group identification. "This is," as Marshall calls it, "the ethnic porkbarrel."

An argument that relies on a description of affirmative-action programs as a new ethnic-group feudalism is inadequate and inaccurate in two respects. First, if it were accurate to describe affirmative action as a program for allocating resources on the basis of group affinity, that would be an old, and not a new, phenomenon in American politics. It would be, indeed, politics as usual. But, in the second place, "ethnic-group feudalism" is an inaccurate description of the character, intent, or effect of affirmative-action programs. Explication of these two points may shed some light on broader issues, as well as those immediately at hand.

Race and the Politics
of Interest-Group Pluralism

Group feudalism is not new in American politics. It is an accurate description of liberal pluralism, the essence of which is that the nation's wealth should be allocated in accordance with the negotiation, accommodation, and compromise of the claims of politically organized groups. Whether or not they have found the results pleasing, most American political scientists have agreed for the past several decades that interest-group conflict and compromise is what American politics is all about.[2]

The theory and the practice of interest-group liberalism violate the norms of an older theory of liberal democracy. Historically, political liberalism represented a commitment to a politics of conscience and principle and to the method of reasoned persuasion. The liberal answer to Lowell's question of how to distinguish majority rule from robbery was contained in Jefferson's proposition that "the will of the majority is in all cases to prevail, but that will, to be rightful, must be reasonable." That is, the will of the majority must both reflect and be amenable to appeals to reason. The key to liberal majoritarianism was a public to which reasoned appeals could be made and a public interest, defined by reasoned argument, that contained principles of justice by which to judge the validity of the claims of organized private interests. Public opinion was a court in which individuals and groups who felt oppressed could appeal the justice of their cause. This system demanded of citizens and politicians alike that, in their public offices (and voting was assumed to be a public office), their behavior be informed, principled, and altruistic. As a pluralist critic of this model of liberal democracy has noted, "the political community had some of the characteristics of an Oxford debating society, policy emerging from endless argument, with reason presiding in the speaker's chair."[3]

This is the model of a democratic polity that was challenged by both the practice and the theory of interest-group pluralism. The pluralist theorists found its demands on the political system, and on the citizens who operated it, to be ridiculously optimistic and ruinously utopian. In its place they proposed to put more realistic requirements—those, indeed, that appeared to characterize the political process as it had actually developed. Interested groups replaced disinterested citizens; majority rule was replaced not by minority rule but by *minorities* rule; the "majority" was only a convenient way of describing the governing coalition of minority interests; compromise took the place of principle; the important interests in society were recognized as veto groups, with the power to block any policy that threatened their core interests; the public interest was exposed as the fraud it was held to have always been and became no more than "a tremendously useful promotional device," the very vacuity of which permits the freer play of private interests. Citizens whose first and last political question is, "What's in it for me?" became the heroes of the new political order, their countervailing egotism the basis of the system's stability. The broker politician who is able, in T. V. Smith's phrase, to rise above principle to serve the higher principle of compromise became the democratic ideal.

These are the characteristics of the "new feudalism." If affirmative action introduces any novelty into these arrangements, it is not by introducing ethnic identification as a basis for group treatment, but by making ethnic-group membership for the first time an advantage rather than a liability for nonwhites.

Nowhere is the interest-group pluralism of American politics more evident than in the history of the political treatment of colored minorities. In the new feudalism of interest-group politics, minorities were the serfs among the feudal baronies of power. Time after time, efforts to put the issue of racial justice on the political agenda were bogged down in group pressure and bargaining. Appeals to principle were treated by the political power brokers as the demands of private interests. And, because the groups whose interests were at stake were relatively powerless, they came away relatively empty-handed.

White ethnics fared better in this process than their nonwhite counterparts. Whatever the prejudices against white minority immigrants, they were exempt from the more fundamentally invidious stigma of color. This—and the fact that they were useful to the boss-ridden political machines in the big cities that became ethnic enclaves for new European immigrants—made possible their gradual accommodation into the political game. The device of ethnic "ticket-balancing" developed to express this mutual dependence. At the same time, the established, powerful, legitimate groups, and the political parties themselves, became increasingly accessible to white ethnic membership.

The same pluralist processes, operating in a racist climate, were responsible for decades of frustration and defeat for the cause of civil rights for nonwhites. Consider, for example, the civil-rights records of two presidents, Woodrow Wilson and Franklin D. Roosevelt, both with reputations as active, progressive, liberal leaders. During Wilson's 1912 campaign for the presidency, he had promised that Negroes could "count on me for absolute fair dealing and for everything by which I could assist in advancing the interests of their race." On the strength of such campaign pledges many black voters, including influential leaders, broke away from their traditional allegiance to the Republican party to vote for the first time for a Democratic candidate. Yet the early months of the Wilson administration saw the rapid development of racial segregation, including segregation of physical facilities within federal employment, reversing a fifty-year history of an integrated federal civil service.[4] Desks of Negro employees were curtained off; separate bathrooms and separate tables in cafeterias were established. As Justice Marshall noted in his opinion in *Bakke*, even the galleries of the Congress were segregated. Blacks soon discovered that, despite Wilson's promises and the justice of their cause, their lack of bargaining power was the key to their inability to halt this process.

The newly organized National Association for the Advancement of Colored People (NAACP) lodged official protests, and both black and white liberals mounted a public campaign for social justice. Letters and editorials poured into Washington. Wilson's attitude, as reported by one of his cabinet members, was that while he wished "to do them justice," his main desire was to see "the matter adjusted in a way to make the least friction." Weighing the claims of justice against the necessity of managing friction meant treating appeals to justice as pressures to be coped with, to be balanced against other pressures in the system. In this case, coping with the pressures for Negro rights meant weighing them against the strength of the segregationist southern forces entrenched in the Congress. In response to the argument of crusading journalist Oswald Garrison Villard that the issue was one of "right and wrong," the president was willing to grant only that "in several instances the thing has been managed in a way that was not sufficiently thoughtful of their [Negroes'] feelings." Wilson's final response to Villard's arguments is singularly revealing. While declining altogether to respond to Villard's efforts at argument and persuasion, he expressed the hope "that by the slow pressure of argument and persuasion the situation may be changed and a great many things done eventually which now seem impossible." He then appealed to Villard to assist in "holding things at a just and cool equipoise until I can discover whether it is possible to work anything out or not."

The implicit premise in Wilson's appeal to the reformers to cool off their demands until "argument and persuasion" have had time to work was that politics is not a forum for argument and persuasion. The politician's role, instead, is to seek to adjust things "in a way to make the least friction." Politically, this means rejecting argument and persuasion in order to placate the sources of friction in the system. The southern leaders in Congress had the power to create friction that could block Wilson's progressive program. The reformers, lacking institutionalized power and not yet organized for militant or obstructionist tactics, could create very little friction. The lesson was clear: coping with a situation by minimizing friction means placating the powerful. The rights of the powerless and the arguments of reformers are, in effect, irrelevant. Having made it clear that power, not reason or morality, moves politics, Wilson added the final touch by insisting that the reformers put their faith in a process of argument and persuasion, the political efficacy of which he had just dramatically disproved.

Some twenty years later, in 1935, another liberal president, Franklin Delano Roosevelt, reacted in the same way to the arguments of civil-rights proponents. Here again, the problem is dramatized by the fact that the particular demand at issue was not even a plea for the extension of Negro rights; it was essentially a defensive measure. Where the earlier effort had been to prevent segregation of the federal service in 1913, the issue in 1935 was passage of a federal antilynching law. (Official U.S. Census Bureau statistics show that over 3,000 Negroes were lynched between 1882 and 1935. These figures do not include legal lynchings in the form of "kangaroo court" verdicts or unresolved or unreported murders.)

Roosevelt advised Walter White, the secretary of the NAACP, that "the Southerners by reason of the seniority rule in Congress are chairmen or occupy strategic places on most of the Senate and House committees. If I come out for the antilynching bill now, they will block every bill I ask Congress to pass to keep America from collapsing. I just can't take that risk."[5]

Wilson had given civil-rights advocates a lesson in the political realities of pluralism; Roosevelt drove the lesson home. The nature of the politics of group pressure meant that blacks who did not share significantly in the system through land ownership, investment, industry, or trade were excluded from the gains in economic welfare and security achieved by other groups through the New Deal social programs. When government responded to the pressures of business, finance, industry, farmers, and trade unions for favorable treatment, nearly everyone got something (though not equal amounts).

The benefits of New Deal programs reached into every community in the country, rural or urban. Some of those benefits filtered down to blacks, especially the emergency measures designed to alleviate the effects of the Depression. But the effect was incidental, not deliberate. Blacks benefited because they were, in disproportionate numbers, unemployed and hungry. Thus, in the largest New Deal relief program, the Works Progress Administration (WPA), Negroes made up 14 percent of WPA workers in 1939, 16 percent in 1941, and 20 percent in 1942.[6] The increasing percentage reflects the fact that even with the war, unemployed blacks did not enter the labor force until the manpower shortage had absorbed the white unemployed. When the war ended, black workers were hit first and hardest. The limits of governmental response to the civil-rights movement were set by the basic racial values of the white South. As Morroe Berger has noted of this New Deal period: "The balance of interests enabled the federal government to help the urban and rural needy in the South but not to upset white domination."

The only significant action taken directly by Roosevelt to protect the civil rights of blacks was his 1941 executive order forbidding discrimination in defense industries, which was hardly a moral initiative. It was issued only after the pleas of A. Philip Randolph, a black civil-rights and labor leader, had been rejected, and Randolph had threatened a massive march and demonstration of more than 100,000 Negroes on Washington.

There is nothing in the record to suggest that pluralist politics can rise above group interests to give weight to the moral authority of the case for racial equality. In the default of the political agencies of government, the Supreme Court gave voice to those considerations, but the Court had to mask its moral leadership under the veil of constitutional authority. Aside from Court decisions, Eric F. Goldman noted, virtually every advance blacks made toward equality came in response to the "pressure they have been able to exert alone or with allied movements."[7] Daniel Berman, the leading student of civil-rights legislation, added that "it is a sad commentary on the American system of government that the Negro had to go into the streets before anything even approximating serious attention was paid to his legitimate grievances."[8] This result was implied in the positions of Wilson and Roosevelt. They would have understood the reactions of Presidents Kennedy and Johnson, and the congressional leadership in 1964, when they reached the conclusion, described by Berman, that "only a strong civil rights bill could possibly prevent widespread racial bloodshed and utter catastrophe for the nation." It might be argued that the system showed it could respond. But no amount of response to pressure can heal political conflicts over fundamental human rights. Blacks are not likely "to concede the good faith of the white political elite merely on the basis of a law whose enactment has been compelled by marching feet."

By the 1960s, blacks had learned the lessons taught by the liberal practitioners of interest-group politics. The black-power movement was a direct reaction to the two characteristics of American politics that had governed the behavior of presidents and congressmen: its ethnic basis, and its power-oriented nature. "Middle-class America," Stokely Carmichael and Charles V. Hamilton asserted in their *Black Power* manifesto, "is without a viable conscience as regards humanity."[9] Because interests replace conscience in American politics, no appeal to justice is possible; the only alternative is power through organization.

Because the exclusion of blacks from the bargaining process is historically rooted in racism, Carmichael and Hamilton argued that black admission to the pluralist game would require a resort to violence and to the politics of mass disruption. "A nonviolent approach to civil rights," they added, "is an approach black people cannot afford and a luxury white people do not deserve." Even these tactics, however, do not really violate the principles underlying group competition for power. In a pluralist system, the boundaries of political morality tend to be set by those restraints on political warfare that guarantee established groups against effective assault on their privilege. The restraints are, therefore, incompatible with the invitation to new groups to pull up a chair at the bargaining table. Such groups (organized labor, for example) have usually discovered that it is necessary to kick down the door first. When that happens, the reaction of spokesmen for the entrenched coalition is predictable: no one is to be allowed to shoot their way to the bargaining table. But if the interchange gave evidence of power to cause continuing friction, the offender is offered a chair—at the far end of the table, and a long way from a microphone.

An Ethnic Pork Barrel?

The creation of an "ethnic pork barrel," even if that were the effect of affirmative action, would not represent a radical alteration in American politics. Ethnic identification has been an important source of group power—of access to the pork barrel—or the lack of it. As a national committee of influential black ministers put it in a 1966 statement on black power, published in the *New York Times:*

> We must not apologize for the existence of this form of group power, for we have been oppressed as a group and not as individuals. We will not find our way out of that oppression until both we and America accept the need for Negro Americans, as well as for Jews, Italians, Poles, and white Anglo-Saxon Protestants, among others, to have and to wield group power.

Resistance to the creation of an ethnic pork barrel, by those who accept the operation of pork-barrel politics for other groups, reflects a general tendency in pluralist politics for successful groups to change the rules to protect their gains from new competitors. As Sethard Fisher has put it, "As given interest groups achieve specific goals, they frequently so alter the rules that further achievements are facilitated. Potential competitors are increasingly encumbered as the successful ones maneuver and manipulate from a vantage point of power."[10] From this perspective, the complaint against an ethnic pork barrel is merely a defense of the advantages whites have secured from the operation of a color-blind pork barrel that has, in practice, excluded nonwhites. It amounts to an effort to change the rules of the game just when nonwhites threaten to become able to organize themselves to play.

The expansion of the process to include previously impotent groups based directly on ethnic affiliation may, of course, introduce into the system divisive and unwelcome forces, and even some ludicrous results. The HUD agency for regulating mobile homes, for example, has a twelve-member advisory panel, whose "balanced" membership represents "female, minority, regional, raw-material, supplier, industrial, regulatory, consumerist, and political" interests.[11] If group representation has produced an absurd result in this example, it is not because racial and female groups are included, but because it is absurd to assume that justice, or a public interest of any sort, will emerge automatically from the compromises and accommodations of private interests. In the long run, the proliferation of interests may even make the system unmanageable. Alan Fox, I believe, is correct in his warning that if we "continue trying to combine the enthronement of competitive, acquisitive, self-seeking, and socially divisive values with the present massive inequalities of distribution, the growing tendency toward group self-determination and self-assertion through power could introduce gathering social and economic instabilities from which privileged and unprivileged alike may eventually seek protection" through totalitarian practices.[12]

If the effective organization of new interest groups threatens the system's stability, that tells us simply that the system works only when a few dominant interests share the loot. And if the inclusion of previously excluded ethnic groups has destabilizing consequences, that tells us only that the system is inherently racist—that group representation of white interests has depended for its stability on the exclusion of effectively represented nonwhite interests.

Ethnic-group feudalism, in short, is an accurate description of the historical political experience of blacks in America. Even if affirmative action is interpreted—incorrectly—to be an extension of interest-group pluralism to include groups based on ethnic affiliation, we could not conclude that something novel or subversive has been introduced into the political process. We could merely conclude that groups that previously lacked effective organization for the pursuit of their interests have learned the rules of the game—that they have, at last, taken the advice

the philosophers of pluralism give to all disadvantaged groups
—to organize.

In any event, equality of group results cannot be achieved
or even effectively pursued within the limits of interest-group
politics. Insofar as the civil-rights movement has been forced to
operate as a colored "lobby," it has been foredoomed to seek
only marginal and incremental change within the consensus
shared by established groups. It has been forced to define its
core interest as legal, rather than social, equality. And it has had
to accept as its fair share whatever side-payments the more
powerful participants in the established coalition have been willing to make. No black pressure group, whose potential membership is 12 percent of the population and whose political will is
sapped by its relative poverty and powerlessness, could ever
hope to negotiate equality of group results.

The underlying reason for this is rooted in the basic premises of a pluralist system. Pluralism involves, after all, simply
the application to politics of the principle of equality of opportunity. It substitutes the idea of equal opportunity for groups to
compete for political influence for the traditional ideal of equality of political power for individual citizens. Whereas political
equality had been a weapon to challenge all inequalities of
power, equality of political opportunity provides an ethical justification for the existing inequalities of political power (provided only that opportunity to become more powerful is not
legally denied to any group). This new formulation of the democratic ideal suffers, of course, from the same contradictions
examined in earlier chapters:

- Real opportunities to acquire political power vary
  because power is unequally distributed.
- Those who *have* more have greater opportunity to
  acquire more, and to protect what they have from
  new claimants.
- The opportunities of those who have less are crippled by their powerlessness.

Thus pluralism saddles colored minorities with exactly the same handicaps in political competition that they experience in the economic sphere.[13]

The fact that affirmative action cannot be understood as a response to group pressure in a pluralist system has not prevented it from being viewed in that way. Indeed, this is the basis of the common charge that affirmative-action programs, once instituted, will become permanent. Thus, Paul Seabury, using India as an example, argues that "the beneficiaries of quotas or other forms of compensatory treatment come to look upon them as prescriptive rights."[14] This happens, he adds, for the same reasons that Texas oil-depletion allowances prove resistant to change. Certainly his basic premise is correct: all political and economic advantages tend to be self-perpetuating. But that does more to explain why affirmative action is so difficult to initiate than why it would be difficult to terminate. In the absence of quotas, white advantage *is* likely to perpetuate itself. Moreover, the elimination of the existing preferential advantages of white males is both the goal and the limit of affirmative-action programs.

It is, therefore, a misperception of American political history to view affirmative-action programs, in the words of Leonard Fine, as efforts to "treat collectively" individuals "for whom merit did not work" in the past.[15] Nonwhites are, rather, individuals for whom the collective treatment of interest-group politics did not work in the past. They are individuals who, because they were treated collectively (under the guise of individual white preference), were denied access to those political processes that allocate resources to groups, collectively. For most Americans, group membership was the means to inclusion in the politics of the pork barrel; for nonwhites, imputed group identification was the criterion for exclusion.

The Politics of a Confused Principle

The second deficiency in the argument under consideration lies in its contention that ethnic-group feudalism describes the intent and the effect of affirmative-action programs. It does neither. Affirmative action does not represent or reflect the politics of an ethnic-group feudalism. It is, in fact, the failure of group feudalism to work effectively for nonwhites that has made appeal to the principle of equality of group results necessary.

Justice Powell, in his opinion in *Bakke,* got this point backward. Citing pluralist political scientists as authority, Powell asserted that political judgments on affirmative action "are the product of rough compromise struck by contending groups within the democratic process." That being so, he argues, it becomes the responsibility of the courts to protect the rights of individuals by "constitutional standards [that] may be applied consistently."[16] Taken literally, this is a blank check for judicial policy making. Since political judgments, in his definition, are not consciously directed to rights or justice, a moral vacuum is created that the courts are obligated to fill. If Powell is correct, it becomes the role of the courts not simply to correct occasional lapses from constitutional safeguards, but to provide the *only* source of justice in the system. The circumstances in the *Bakke* case, however, do not square with his analysis. The admissions program designed by the university rested clearly on a conception of rights and justice. In contrast, Justice Powell's effort to reconcile a prohibition against quotas with a ruling that race may be used as one factor in future decisions more nearly resembled a rough compromise among contending groups, engineered by a master political broker.

The most effective phase of the civil-rights movement, under the leadership of Martin Luther King, Jr., involved an attempt to change the basic nature of the neofeudal political system through an appeal to conscience and to the principle of equality. Affirmative action is solidly within that same tradition. It seeks to apply the old politics of principle to victims of the group struggle for power. It proposes, in the name of justice, to redistribute relative advantage among racial groups. True, it invokes the principle of equality in its meritocratic, rather than in any more radical, form. And its goal of "equal group results" is simply the demand that nonwhites suffer (or enjoy) the same inequalities of opportunity as everyone else. Still, affirmative action rests on an appeal to conscience. It asks the white majority to put racial justice ahead of their interests. Far from reflecting the politics of an ethnic feudalism, it is the politics of principle.

Putting the Emphasis on Equal

If the meaning of the principle underlying affirmative action is an ambiguous triumph for the cause of equality, by emphasizing the "equal" side of the formula, it may at least keep that broader ideal alive. And, given adequate public discussion of the issues, it may lead to an increased commitment to racial equality and, more generally, human equality.

Affirmative action rescues a public standard of racial equality from the morass of private group interests to which pluralism has consigned it. It puts clearly on record the public nature of the "private" and "personal" prejudices of whites. It also erects a public standard of equality to which those prejudices can be referred.

Affirmative action does not propose, as is commonly claimed, to relocate the meaning of rights in groups rather than individuals. Of course, rights inhere in individuals; and power inheres in groups. The problem is how to secure equality of individual rights where there are gross inequalities in the power of groups. How is this possible in a meritocratic climate other than by treating as members of groups those individuals who are denied equal individual rights on grounds of invidious group identification?

Affirmative action goes further. Its insistence on equality of group results demands that whites recognize that their own advantages are, in significant measure, group benefits rather than individual achievements, and that their own success has been, in part, a matter of their own superior group opportunities, purchased at the expense of opportunities for nonwhites. Affirmative action asks whites to recognize that group power supports the favored positions of the members of an affluent white majority, while the rhetoric of individual rights has informed their approach to the claims of the disadvantaged. Affirmative action calls on whites to agree that this has been an unfair game, in which the rules are rigged.

The questions raised by affirmative action may even threaten the whole edifice of equal opportunity in its meritocratic form. As both Social Darwinists and meritocrats have feared, the demand that opportunities be made more genuinely equal may lead to critical examination of the inequalities themselves, thus triggering the latent populism in the American experience. For, if blacks as a group are entitled to equal results with whites, then why not also the poor as a group? The logic of equal opportunity, where the "equal" is given practical meaning, requires a leveling of wealth and a sharing of power radically at odds with our present arrangements.

Ethnic-Group Feudalism:
Without Affirmative Action

The common argument that affirmative action would usher in ethnic-group feudalism misses the mark. The elimination of affirmative-action programs—not their effective implementation—would produce that result. It would leave the processes of American politics just what they were before affirmative action was instituted: neofeudal, group-based, and ethnically biased.

Nor would the creation of a race-blind government be new. There is no more color-blind government than one powered by the free play of group interests. Just as most Americans are probably not consciously racist—only preoccupied with their own interests and therefore oblivious of or indifferent to the racist consequences of the institutions in which they live—the normal American political process is not overtly racist, but merely indifferent. The politician, as an honest power broker, is conscientiously sworn to the proposition that the interests of competing groups are equally legitimate and equally worthy. He seeks a winning coalition of groups, and if his coalition excludes nonwhites or does not adequately weigh their interests, that is because the pursuit of his own political career requires him to take them into color-blind account, not on the basis of his own prior valuations of the merit of their claims, but on the basis of their relative power. "We both know," Thucydides tells us the Athenian representatives said to the Melian Council, "that in matters of this kind the strong exact what they can, and the weak yield what they must." The mediator in the bargaining process is not prejudiced against the weaker party. He is merely, as an honest broker must, recording its relative weakness. This is not, of course, a very comforting truth for nonwhites. But it describes the circumstances in which, without affirmative action, a race-blind government would leave them.

If the attack on affirmative action is not generally characterized by a sense of the inadequacy of existing pluralist processes for dealing with the just claims of minorities, neither is it informed by a concern for broader questions of equality. Its impulse is explicitly meritocratic and inegalitarian, and implicitly racist. The color-blind government it would establish would be hardly likely to embark upon a reallocation of wealth along more sensible lines. So, the issue to which affirmative action is a response is not—however much some of us wish it were—the equity and justice of the general distribution of wealth along meritocratic lines. It is, rather, the narrower issue of whether nonwhites and women are to share fairly in the results of meritocratic distribution.

The practical effect, then, of an argument for making the government race-blind is to insure the existing distribution of wealth against any deliberate effort to reallocate it. And, if it succeeds, it will promote the politics of ethnic-group feudalism, since it will leave nonwhites with no recourse but to an intensification of the struggle for group power. Blacks, once again, will be forced to appeal in the court of power, and with the justified conviction that middle-class America is "without a viable conscience as regards humanity." It is likely, in that event, that nonwhites will see no alternative but a return to the politics of confrontation and disruption. White backlash is also predictable. Thus, the choice of a race-blind government is no more likely to still "the deadly passions of racial enmity" than it is to promote racial justice.

The Necessity for
Putting First Things Second

The effort to achieve equality of group results may not, of course, lead to heightened sensitivity to the more general inequities of income, power, and status in America. It may even make the inequalities of a meritocratic order more palatable by making them appear to be more legitimate. But even that would not be valid ground for abandoning the effort to achieve equality of group results. Those who share the nobler egalitarian dream of Martin Luther King, Jr., are obligated to share also his understanding of why blacks "can't wait." We have no moral right to hold nonwhites hostage in that broader struggle.

14

The Crisis of Democratic Legitimacy

Historically, the liberal spirit in America was animated by the idea of equality. Eric Goldman describes it as "a way of thinking and reacting, a receptivity to change, a sensitivity to the man in trouble, an assumption that the mighty are not necessarily right." Liberalism was also, Goldman adds, "a program, the nub of which was to use governmental powers to increase—gradually and without violence—the economic and social opportunities of lower-middle and bottom income groups."[1]

In our earlier history, because the disadvantaged and the powerless were a majority, this liberal impulse seemed to be compatible with the majority principle. Neither workers nor farmers were organized; only the new giant businesses had effectively marshaled their forces for political combat. In these circumstances, a political coalition of disadvantaged groups could be justified in the name of equality and social justice. Interest-group liberalism triumphed because it was able to combine self-interest with the claims of justice and to implement both through the majority principle. But, in the process of extending the benefits of group power to enough group interests to constitute a majority, the "new liberalism" destroyed the political order itself as a process for meeting the demands of social justice or the needs of those still unorganized.

As a result, we are back to the question posed in the 1830s by de Tocqueville: "When an individual [we should now say, a group] is wronged in the United States, to whom can he [they] apply for redress?" To public opinion? The legislature? The executive? Public opinion, in any meaningful or relevant sense, no longer exists. The legislature and the executive have been political midwives at the birth of the compromises that reflect the prevailing balance of group interests. They are not, therefore, in a position to challenge the terms of those settlements. The governing majority is simply all of the groups whose interests have been effectively represented, and its program is merely whatever the next round of bargaining and compromise will produce. (A "silent majority," meanwhile, sits menacingly in wait for those who challenge the underlying consensus on which the system rests.) In these circumstances, the economic underclass and the racial minorities are deprived of any court of political appeal.

The Passion of Compassion

At issue here is more than the fact that some persons are excluded from the coalition that constitutes the governing majority. The question involves the means by which those who are left out can get their claims recognized and legitimized. The answer, in a system of interest-group pluralism is raw power. Traditional democratic theory assumed that an appeal to justice is the means to power, and that the appeal to justice is made possible by compassion. The basis of our current predicament is the fact that the motive force of justice, rooted in the capacity for compassion, has been eroded and almost obliterated by the modern version of equal opportunity.

"Justice will be secure," Solon advised his fellow Greeks, "only when those who are not injured are as indignant about injustice as those who are." Compassion—in Rousseau's words, an "innate repugnance at seeing a fellow creature suffer"—is the master political virtue, especially in a democracy. It is, finally, the only barrier to majority tyranny. It furnishes the only answer to Lowell's question, the only ground for a political process in which majority rule can be distinguished from robbery.

An important difference, but one difficult to formulate, distinguishes compassion from pity. They are in some ways very similar attitudes. Both reflect sorrow over the suffering of others, and suggest an obligation to relieve the suffering. But where pity implies suffering "over" or "about," compassion means suffering "with." Pity is controlled; benevolent, but arrogant; deliberately and selectively extended; conditional. Compassion is, by contrast, an unconditional sharing. Pity, Arendt has said, "does not look upon both fortune and misfortune, the strong and the weak, with an equal eye; without the presence of misfortune, pity could not exist."[2] Pity is the feeling of the fortunate for the unfortunate, the strong for the weak. And while it looks toward relief of the suffering, it does not contemplate eliminating or reducing the gulf between fortune and misfortune, between the strong and the weak. It is immune to imputations of guilt. It led masters to treat their servants well, and led many Americans to seek to ease the burden of oppression on blacks. Pity is the master political virtue of inegalitarian societies.

Compassion, since it implies the ability to put oneself in the position of another—to think and feel from another's standpoint —requires the belief that the others are in the most fundamental sense, one's equals. Compassion suggests humility: why another, and not oneself? Compassion fosters a commitment, beyond easing another's suffering, to eliminating the social and remediable causes of the suffering. Compassion is the master political virtue in a democratic society.

Sheldon Wolin has argued that the bonds of political community are not in the shared pursuit of pleasure, for pleasure, because it rests on the gratification of individual desires, cannot be shared, at least politically. Community, Wolin adds, must be built on a shared recognition of our human frailty.[3] Pain, not pleasure—tragedy, not triumph—is the common condition that makes it possible for people to form a genuine political community. As Rousseau understood,

> We become attached to our fellows less because we respond to their pleasures than because we respond to their pains. . . . All men are born poor and naked. All are liable to the sorrows of life, its ills, its needs, its sufferings of every kind; and all are condemned at length to die. This is what it really means to be a man, this is what no mortal can escape.

Compassion—not the passions, and especially not the passions for distinction and wealth—is the source of both equality and community. In the final analysis, Wolin may even be right—I believe he is—that "to communicate is to commiserate." Our common needs "unite us by interest"; but, as Rousseau understood, "our common miseries unite us by affection." A society organized to employ science and technology for the purpose of conquering unhappiness by satisfying desires is thus unable to tap the sources of human compassion.

Even conservatives, who have insisted on the virtues of a stratified society, have understood the social need for compassion and the role of equality in making it possible. Thus Edmund Burke noted the ties of sympathy that bound and nourished men who shared membership as equals in a particular class or caste. He then went on to argue that when equality extends the range of men's affection, it dilutes the intensity of their sympathetic feelings. A people who are charged to give their sympathetic loyalties to all mankind, he argued, will be able to give them to none. De Tocqueville echoed Burke's argument that the doctrine of equality, spread throughout society as a solvent to dissolve ties of class and caste, would so dilute the human capacity for sympathy that every man would be left alone, stripped naked before the pressures of society.[4]

Conservatives like Burke and de Tocqueville were right in understanding that only compassion makes the human condition bearable. Their error lay in assuming that it was the radical idea of equality that threatened to dissolve human ties of sympathy and fellowship, when what was actually involved was a new doctrine of natural inequality, disguised as equality of opportunity. The results they feared did not develop from some alleged limit on mankind's capacity for compassion, but rather from a society built on competitive inequality. Like the radical idea of human equality, individualistic competitive inequality destroys the basis of class and caste loyalties but, unlike the radical idea, it does not provide a more inclusive loyalty. It speaks in the name of a self-interest that dissolves all loyalties and makes impossible any larger loyalty, except one based on national chauvinism. The "mission of America" in the age of American imperialism was thus rooted in free enterprise, not only because of the need for markets and raw materials, but primarily because it provided the only available outlet for the expression at home of a fraternity that equal opportunity, in a market society, made otherwise impossible.

Only the highly self-conscious act of sympathetic imagination permits one person to empathize with the feelings of another. Capitalism on the economic side, and the division of power, checks and balances, and liberal pluralism on the political side, provided an organization of society uniquely hospitable to the rise of equality of opportunity as a protective cover for egoism. Indeed, an understanding of those characteristics of our contemporary society that does not see them as mechanisms for making human compassion unnecessary is inadequate.

Compassion and the Capitalist Ethic

The unique characteristic of capitalism as an ideology and a way of life was that, for the first time in recorded human history, it set out to build a society on the premise that men are exclusively creatures of self-interest. It did not, of course, reveal for the first time that avarice and ambition are human characteristics. Indeed, the rise of conscious social philosophy has involved the effort to examine how avarice and ambition were to be reconciled with the need for community and for a common moral meaning in experience. "Ambition and avarice," Aristotle noted, "are exactly the motives which lead men to commit nearly all intentional crimes."[5] Unless effective safeguards were provided, the state would be increasingly imbued with "a spirit of avarice" that, by substituting private interest for the good of the polis, would threaten its very nature.

What distinguishes capitalism as an ideology is that its assumption of an essentially egoistic nature is accompanied by the proposal that men are morally entitled—indeed, obligated—to be self-interested, ambitious, and aggrandizing and unlovely, and that this self-centeredness need not be tempered by a concern for justice or by compassion. This remarkable proposition that men can best serve their common purposes by pursuing their private interests was built on the assumption of natural laws of competition operating in free markets. The law of supply and demand, in particular, was assumed to do what egoistic man is incapable of doing consciously and rationally: to provide distributive justice by allocating rewards to individuals in precise proportion to their social contributions, to maximize the wealth of the nation, and to realize a public interest that men are incapable of consciously knowing or preferring.

While men are creatures of private vice, in the competitive society vices, properly understood, are virtues in disguise. The laws of the marketplace transform private vices into public virtues, and they do so automatically and impersonally. All that is required is that men refrain from trying to be publicly virtuous, from the temptation to substitute their own conceptions of justice for the impersonal justice the market automatically provides. For, human nature decrees that when a man says *we*, he really means *me*; when he says *justice*, he means only to dress up his own greed in the language of moral justification; and when he says *public interest*, he is merely putting a moral gloss on his private interests.

Thus, the dream of a laissez-faire society has always been an ignoble utopia. It rests at bottom on Adam Smith's assumption of an "invisible hand." It is based on the proposition that man has a moral right to be selfish because his very selfishness promotes "a good which is no part of his intention," and does this more certainly than his good intentions could. It proposes, in short, that the road to heaven is paved with bad intentions.

So long as the implications of capitalism were confined to the economic realm, politics remained a realm in which altruism might have some sway, and in which compassion could limit the effects of a rampant egoism in economic affairs. But what capitalism legitimized and universalized in economic affairs, the new liberal pluralism completed in the political sphere.

Perhaps it was inevitable, once men were led to believe that the free pursuit of their economic interests was legitimate and need not answer to principles of justice or the common good, that politics would come to be seen as a fair and profitable arena for the pursuit of those interests. The movement from the principle of equal laws, with no special privilege for anyone, to the principle of equality of opportunity for all organized groups to seek special privilege was a perfectly natural and inevitable development. The assumptions underlying economic free enterprise, once they were accepted as authoritative, led inevitably to the politics of group interests.

From Capitalism to Interest-Group Liberalism

The link between capitalism as economic theory and pluralism as political theory lies in their concurrence on the proposition that materialistic self-interest is the mainspring of human behavior. Both derive whatever democratic legitimacy they have from the idea of equality of opportunity for egoism to express itself. Long before either capitalism or pluralism had triumphed, one Jeffersonian philosopher had seen their affinity, and predicted that the triumph of capitalism would inevitably produce the triumph of pluralism. John Taylor had described capitalism as "a system of paper and patronage." Wherever economic power prevails, he argued, it will be translated into political power. The legislature "will be governed by that interest and legislate in its favor."[6] This corruption of the political order to serve the interests of the new men of power inevitably leads to an even greater evil.

The process begins with the manipulation and control of legislatures, executives, and courts by the bourgeoisie with the objective of inducing or pressuring them to "deed away a nation . . . by privileges, charters, loans, banks, and all the variety of incorporations." The masses of men, making their livelihoods in "honest property" and committed to the ideal of equality, may still be capable of "publick indignation." Common men might still "disdain to serve under their banners or to become the dupe of their frauds." But as the pecuniary and acquisitive spirit spreads through all classes, it threatens to corrupt the whole country.

Taylor saw politics as the most important casualty of this corruption. Initially, the economic power of the capitalists would be translated into exclusive privilege through their conquest of politics. But then, "on account of the necessity of extending corruption to defend a fraud," the principle of equal opportunity would be invoked to open the door to special privilege for all social classes. Politics would cease to be a forum for "moral liberty" and would become, instead, an arena of conflict for private advantage. Taylor even foresaw a day, like our own, in which "no dishonesty" would be attached to the unfettered pursuit of interest in politics. The result, he predicted, would be that "parties are converted into mere ladders of power, and election is restricted to the barren right of saying which ladder shall be mounted." The interests will pretend to champion public purposes, but no mere name can "infuse republican principles into unrestrained parties of interest, of ins and outs, struggling for wealth and power."

Liberal pluralism, as Taylor so perceptively saw long before it developed, is "political capitalism." It is the democratization of capitalistic vice. It represents not so much the ascendancy of capitalists as a class as the triumph of the spirit of capitalism over the spirit of democracy and equality. This ultimate corruption of the political order could only occur when men no longer conceived of themselves as rational, choosing, public-spirited—and therefore political—beings.

It Might Happen to You

In the society Taylor described, no disadvantaged group could look to the compassion of the more powerful for aid and comfort. The closest such a society can come to compassion is the informed, long-range selfishness reflected in the advice that one ought to care about the injustices suffered by others because "it might happen to you." The possibility of compassion comes to rest entirely on the egoistic calculations described by Rousseau. "Why is it," Rousseau asked, "that kings have no pity on their subjects? Because they never expect to be men themselves." And, "why are the rich so hard on the poor? Because they have no fear of becoming poor. Why do the nobles have so much contempt for the people? Because the aristocrat knows he will never be a commoner."[7]

So long as a regime of competitive inequality was thought to rest primarily on effort and luck, the self-interested basis of compassion could be expected to operate. Rags to riches, and back to rags, was always seen as a possibility. Both the rise of meritocracy and the group basis of politics undermine that condition. As success comes to depend more and more on "natural" intellectual qualities, educational certification of individuals as bona fide applicants for elite status tends to be a permanent imprimatur. Moreover, the cardinal ground rule of the game of pluralist politics is that no established, respectable group ever loses anything that threatens its core interests. Under these conditions, the intellectual aristocracy and those whose relative affluence and power is protected by a footing on the escalator of success, find less and less reason to sympathize with the plight of those beneath them in the economic and social hierarchy. And they have no grounds at all for compassion for the underclass of those who are powerless.

The Death of Sympathy

Racial minorities, of course, have always been excluded from a compassion rooted in self-interest. No white ever had occasion to imagine the possibility of waking up one morning to find a black or brown face in his mirror. Nor, with a safely guaranteed white majority, need he ever worry that the racial hierarchy might be reversed.[8] It was always a vision of human equality—never a foreboding of threatened self-interest—that made sympathy for the plight of oppressed nonwhites possible. When it existed, sympathy for oppressed minorities was always a moral duty rather than a mere hedge against future personal discomfort.

The triumph of self-interest and the ascendancy of pluralist politics have deprived the poor, as well as nonwhites, of the prospect of compassionate understanding of their plight. Those whose interests are protected in the group process no more expect to be poor tomorrow than they expect to be black. The much-publicized taxpayer revolt reflects the absence of compassion of the middle classes for the less affluent and the poor, when they see their relative affluence or their expectations of greater affluence to be threatened.

This has now become the cultural framework in which the new meritocratic elite functions. And this elite, no less than the masses whose interests it manages, suffers from the inability to feel, think, and speak from the standpoint of those who are victimized by the system. This makes it possible for the elites, including the politicians and the bureaucrats, to pursue their careers with neither a passion for justice nor the compassion that must underlie it.

The springs of compassion have been so thoroughly eroded by an economically capitalist and politically pluralist society that, in recent years, even the human possibility of compassion has been denied. ("You can't know what it is to be . . . black . . . a woman . . . poor.") It is true, of course, in one sense that the immediate experience of one person can never be totally accessible to another in its immediacy. But in another sense, while the pleasures of dominion cannot be sympathetically shared by those over whom it is exercised, the suffering of anyone demands the compassion of all others who see their own humanity in the sufferer. Equal-opportunity liberalism offers the false promise of a society based on shared pleasure. At the same time, it robs us of the capacity for compassionate suffering that reveals inequities and demands remedies for them.

So it is that, insofar as prospects for justice have come to depend on "enlightened self-interest," we have come to the end of the line. The interests of the white majority never provided either sustenance or hope for nonwhites. And now the interests of a majority grown affluent and longing for greater affluence no longer respond to the needs and claims of the oppressed, the weak, and the neglected.

Compassion has always been the fruit of equality, the basis of democratic morals, and the only hope for reconciling majority rule with justice for minorities. It is, at the same time, the last word on the fallacy of meritocracy. As E. E. Schattschneider put it: "Only the compassionate are capable of understanding this truth about people. That is why there are no experts in morals: an incompassionate expert is as obtuse as an antisocial thug."[9]

Compassionate elites are neither inconceivable nor unknown to history. America, in the great tradition of the Declaration, has had more than its share. But they are always elites who grow out of and whose roots continue to be nourished by the soil of equality. It is more than coincidence that the meritocratic elites whose credentials lie in their natural superiority have come to resemble more and more, in Vietnam and Watergate, the "antisocial thug." We will not be saved, in any event, by elites—or brought to disaster by them—but by the yearnings of our own hearts, the cultivation of our own compassionate imaginations, and the rekindling of the spirit of equality that makes compassion for the victims of injustice a universal duty.

The Rediscovery of Sympathy

The sabotage of the Declaration's pronouncement of equality, and the erosion of the capacity for compassion that accompanied it, were implicit in what the revolutionaries left unsaid. For all their sensitivity and insight, the Jeffersonians made a fatal blunder. At the time they made their revolution, roughly one of every four or five persons living in the colonies was a Negro. Yet the Negro was, in the terms of the Declaration of Independence, "completely overlooked."[10]

Only a few whites were aware of "the primordial crime upon which the fabric of American society rested," and "trembled" with Jefferson when they thought that "God is just." And most of those who were, were motivated by the incompatibility of freedom (for whites) with slavery, and not by the "passion of compassion." Most of them did not regard blacks as equal sharers in the natural rights of mankind. On the question of the incompatibility of freedom and slavery, they were correct as far as they went—but it was not far enough. Their understanding did not reach to Tourgée's insight into the distinctive character of American slavery. Nowhere is there evidence that whites understood the implications of a reality in which blacks were "in bondage to the whole white race" and in which all whites became masters and beneficiaries, even if they were not slaveowners. They were thus able to imagine that, in the interest of union, slavery could be left off their agenda.

Their commitment to a radical vision of equality, in which liberty is safe only so long as its promises are equally shared had forced on them the alternative of attacking slavery head-on by declaring blacks full and equal citizens, or of reading blacks out of the human race altogether. Most of them tried to avoid making the choice. But refusal to choose is itself a choice.

Their silence contributed powerfully to the development of full-blown racism in the antebellum South. It paved the way for the shift from a view of slavery as a necessary evil to its celebration as a positive good and even a divine command. This view made the Negro a separate species, and placed him altogether outside the fraternal bonds of compassion and, therefore, the claims of justice. The position of spokesmen for the South was their answer to the Jeffersonian dilemma: African slavery, they argued, need not be seen as a threat to freedom or equality because no white man need fear that he might become a slave. Having ruled blacks out of the human race, the argument for equal rights ceased to be grounded in the inherent dignity and ultimate worth of all, and came instead to rest on the egoistic calculation that "it might happen to you." The result was the denial to slaves of any of the rights due men—and the continued denial, after the end of slavery, of rights to emancipated blacks. For if no white needed to fear he might become a slave, neither did he need to fear he might become black.

Those who wrote the Declaration were silent on the issues of racism and slavery at their peril—and ours. Liberalism belatedly rejected the teaching of the proslavery philosophers that freedom and slavery were compatible, but it had abandoned by then the principles that would have entitled freed slaves to the compassion of whites. Thus whites were able to imagine that they could have both equality and white supremacy through the muddled principle of equal opportunity within a framework of legal equality.[11] They achieved only legal equality, and in the process corrupted the idea of equality itself and deprived themselves of its blessings.

The process worked two ways. The equal opportunity that was alleged to follow automatically from equal laws served as a rationale for keeping the Negro in his place. At the same time, its use for that purpose fastened it more securely on whites as a limit on the meaning of equality. The principles that falsely legitimized white supremacy were equally serviceable, and were being effectively used, as a rationale for a new Darwinist elite. By the time of the Civil War, as Richard Parker points out, "One could propose to give the Blacks freedom, but one could not propose to give them equality in any broad, meaningful sense because already . . . to have released the issue of equality into the American political mainstream would have laid bare too many other inequalities and unleashed too many volatile political debates."[12]

How could "equal laws" be thought to provide genuinely equal opportunity to those so recently victimized by unequal laws? If Americans had not been so thoroughly racist and so intent on preserving their racism, the transparent sophistry of the proposition that equal rights insure equal opportunities for blacks would have been obvious enough to lead to a reexamination of the validity of the formula itself—and its application to economic inequalities. Instead, the formula continued to protect both white supremacy and the emerging extremes of poverty and great wealth. In both cases, in R. H. Tawney's words, "the fact of the equality of legal rights could be cited as a reason why any other kind of equality was unnecessary or dangerous."[13]

This experience demonstrates that justice is of a piece. The duty of compassion is owed to all who suffer unjustly, or its connection with justice is severed. The Jeffersonians, although they clearly understood that equality and social justice are rooted in sympathy, still were able, mainly by their silence, to exclude blacks from its benefits. Blacks were the immediate victims of this deceit, but those who thought they were creating the conditions for the emergence of a "new man" also paid dearly for this fatal compromise of their ideals. The exclusion of blacks undermined the universality of those ideals and paved the way for the triumph of a version of equal opportunity that would eventually universalize the principle of self-interest and deny universally the claims of compassion.

The underlying problem of our time is to reverse that process. And perhaps the place to start is the point at which the erosion of our humanity began—with the denial of the equal humanity of nonwhites. Justice for nonwhites demands it. But in addition, the rediscovery of the capacity for compassion may even make it possible for whites to extend it to one another.

15

The Land of Equality

As recently as the 1890s, Lord Bryce, observing us from a European perspective, could say that "the United States are deemed all the world over to be preeminently the land of equality." Bryce, of course, like the Americans he observed, was inclined to overlook completely the conditions of blacks. But even judging the condition of whites, his observations led him to qualify the traditional view of America as "the land of equality." He did so by distinguishing between "legal equality" on one hand, and on the other, "equality of material conditions, that is of wealth and all that wealth gives; . . . education and intelligence; social status or rank; . . . the equality of estimation, i.e. of the value which men set upon one another." And he found that America was characterized by legal equality, but not

> as regards material conditions. Sixty years ago there were no great fortunes in America, few large fortunes, no poverty. Now there is some poverty (though only in a few places can it be called pauperism), many large fortunes, and a greater number of gigantic fortunes than in any other country of the world. [1]

Bryce's analysis led him to predict that "the equality of material conditions, almost universal in the last century, still general sixty years ago, will more and more diminish by the growth of a very rich class at one end of the line, and of a very poor class at the other end."

Bryce's perceptions were acute, but his prediction was in error. America became not a land of tramps and millionaires, but a middle-class society. Poverty still existed, gigantic fortunes multiplied, and wealth and power were increasingly concentrated. The rich did get richer, but so did the poor. And even though the rich got richer faster, a rapid rise in the general standard of living produced a society in which most people were pleased to describe themselves as middle-class. Since their own conditions were improving, the relatively poor could accept the widening gap between themselves and the rich. The citizens of "the land of equality" accommodated themselves to the new inequalities more readily than the people of any other industrial nation.

Formal Equality and Unlimited Liberty

Equality of opportunity and equality before the law (governmental neutrality toward social and economic inequality) furnished the ideological rationale for the widening gap between rich and poor. This formula reconciled the claims of liberty and equality in precisely the sense necessary to furnish moral credentials for a competitive, industrial, free-enterprise society.

Because the form of those "principles" was retained while their substance was being altered, C. Wright Mills could speak, accurately, of "the rhetorical victory and the intellectual and political collapse of American liberalism," the effect of which was to make liberalism "painless to the rich and the powerful."[2] The serviceability of equal opportunity for that purpose depended on an increasing insensitivity to the "equal" part of the slogan. The demands of equality, even of opportunities, had to be minimized. Thus, almost alone among industrial democracies, we make do with an incomes system that rewards individuals with no regard for the consequences for the opportunities of their children. All the others have adopted one scheme or another of family income supplements. This is not because other peoples are less concerned about individual opportunities, but because they have been concerned about making those opportunities more equal. Without that emphasis on equality, opportunity easily degenerates into the right of every person to anything he can come by.

Nor can our attitudes be explained as a mere preference for liberty over equality. True, we have valued liberty, but only in the sense necessary to make it compatible with competitive inequality. The meaning we have tended to profess is the liberty of individuals to act as they please without external restraint. In a competitive order, liberty thus defined comes to mean the absence of restraints on avarice and ambition. And in a hierarchical order, one individual's successful pursuit of wealth and power imposes external restraints on the similar freedom of others.

The American version of liberty and equal opportunity required that the meaning and scope of equality be restricted to the formal provision of equal liberty before the law. The inevitable result was that the criterion for judging the actual conditions of the competitive race shifted from equal chances, to a fair chance, to some chance. Liberty came to mean not much more than a license for the winners to maintain control of the market. Equality, which had been the watchword of the Revolution, became the watchdog of the status quo.

Some of the philosophers of the Revolution were aware of the danger that their ideal of equality, disguised as equal opportunity, could be subverted into its opposite. In a society that regards life as a competitive racetrack, they warned, the vices of avarice and ambition will be legitimized and fostered. (In their more pessimistic moods they doubted that the egalitarian ideal would survive the Revolution itself. Thus Jefferson worried that, "from the conclusion of this war we shall be going downhill. . . . The people . . . will forget themselves but in the sole faculty of making money."[3] And General Warren, writing to John Adams in 1786, lamented what he saw to be "a total change in principles and manners—interest is the great object, the only pursuit, and riches only respected.")

Equality as a Revolutionary Ideal

If the idea of equality has now lost its sting, it was not always so. Indeed, the older, more radical, idea of equality was so widely shared and deeply rooted that it was necessary to subvert it from within, rather than to challenge it directly. Had it not been so, the new system of inequality could have been recognized for what it was.

The nature of that older, radical egalitarianism is suggested by Tom Paine's description of the significance of the Revolution: "The Independence of America, considered merely as a separation from England would have been a matter of but little importance had it not been accompanied by a Revolution in the principles and practice of governments."[4] The doctrine that made it a revolution, and not merely a revolt against British rule, was the novel and shocking doctrine of the natural equality of all men. The assertion that all men are born equal was not calculated simply to strike terror in the hearts of European monarchs and feudal aristocrats. It did, of course, call into question all of those inherited inequalities of birth and rank on which the old order had rested. But in America, where those social and political institutions had never taken root, an attack on the trappings of feudalism would hardly qualify as a movement "fraught with truly revolutionary implications."

Nor was the Revolution intended as merely a justification of the principles of Whig ascendancy in England. Paine became "Citizen Tom" in the French Revolution, and Joel Barlow, the "poet laureate" of the American Revolution, lived with a warrant for his arrest in England after the publication of his *Advice to the Privileged Orders of Europe*.[5] The men who forged the new and bracing idea of equality had no intention of furnishing credentials for what they described as a new "aristocracy of paper and patronage" based on competitive inequality in a market economy. They intended, on the contrary, to eliminate most inequalities, and to put those that remained on the defensive. Nor did the implications of their commitment to equality begin to be exhausted by the Napoleonic doctrine of "careers open to talents." They did not intend to eliminate merely the old, arbitrary restraints on the ability of men to rise in an established social hierarchy. Their aim was, rather, full opportunity for every man to develop his talents free of the restraints imposed by social, political, or economic hierarchy.

The closest thing to the modern concept of equal opportunity to be found in the writings of the Jeffersonians is the concept of a natural aristocracy. Those who seek to find in Jefferson a doctrine of competitive inequality are fond of quoting his now familiar statement: "The natural aristocracy I consider as the most precious gift of nature, for the instruction, the trusts, and government of society." And they cite further his acceptance, in an exchange of letters with John Adams, of the latter's distinction between a natural and an artificial aristocracy. But they neglect the conclusion Jefferson drew from the distinction: "I think the best remedy is exactly that provided by all our constitutions, to leave to the citizens the free election and separation of the *aristoi* from the pseudo-*aristoi*, of the wheat from the chaff."[6] This is emphatically not a defense of an aristocracy of merit chosen by the "natural" competitive processes of a free market or co-opted by the already established elite. It is a vision of men as political and moral equals conferring temporary and conditional authority on some of their fellows. Its significance grows out of the necessity, as Hannah Arendt put it, of choosing men of "genius and virtue" for roles of leadership in public life.

The Aristocracy of Paper and Patronage

The antipathy of the Jeffersonians for what later came to be called "equality of opportunity" is revealed most clearly in the writings of John Taylor. A "natural aristocracy" of talent, Taylor argued, is the one form of elitism still to be feared.[7] The bases of older aristocratic types had been effectively undermined. Insofar as they rested on superstition, they had been exploded by knowledge. Feudal relations had been destroyed by alienation of land titles. (*Alienation* refers to the elimination of legal limitations—primogeniture and entail—on the transfer of land ownership.) But there were no similar barriers yet built to the growth of a new system of commercial and industrial aristocracy. "The Americans," Taylor commented, "devoted their effectual precautions to the obsolete [aristocratic] modes of title and hierarchy, erected several barriers against the army mode, and utterly disregarded the mode of paper and patronage."

What made the new aristocracy especially dangerous was that it had an insidious appeal to a free and democratic people. Masquerading as a form of equality under the deceptive formula of equal opportunity, the Hamiltonian program proposed to underwrite the new system by creating "a mountain of dollars exposed to be scrambled for by a nation." The underlying principle, Taylor observed, was the same as in the case of "a handful of guineas thrown among a mob." And it would have the same consequences: the decline of "good order" and of "respect for the rights of others." It would evoke the worst elements in human nature, dampening man's capacity for public-spirited behavior and promoting his egoistic impulses. Men are capable of embracing the ethic of equality, but "where avarice and ambition beat up for recruits, too many are prone to enlist."

The spirit of the new aristocracy is one of "insatiable avarice," and unlike earlier aristocracies, it holds out an invitation for the entire nation to join its ranks and share its vices. But, while everyone would come to share equally the moral corruption of the system, they would share very unequally in its benefits. Still, Taylor foresaw, "a greater portion of a nation will receive a share" than under other aristocratic systems. The result will be "a spur to labor and industry . . . [since] the efforts of twelve millions of persons would be more vigorously excited by the enrichment of fifty thousand than of one hundred and fifty individuals." But just there, paradoxically, lies the danger. If the wealth of the few is to be justified, the many must be brought into the game of greed. Taylor's insight here offers a startling prevision of the terms on which corporate capitalism won popular allegiance in the early decades of this century. As the abundant opportunities of the frontier were exhausted, the new corporate elites began to see the necessity of reforms to produce a wider sharing of the benefits. As James Weinstein describes it: "Radical critics of the new centralized and manipulated system of social control were disarmed by the corporate liberals who allowed potential opponents to participate, even if not as equals, in a process of adjustment, concession, and amelioration that seemed to promise a gradual advance toward the good society for all citizens."[8] It is worth pondering Taylor's explanation of the reasons for the transformation of American capitalism from a ladder into an escalator. It had to happen, he predicted, "on account of the necessity of extending corruption to cover a fraud."

Regardless of its size, Taylor added, the "natural aristocracy" that would result from the free pursuit of "avarice and ambition" would be "neither conspicuous for virtue or knowledge." (Nor, we might now add, is a meritocracy of knowledge likely to be conspicuous for virtue.) And, finally, Taylor clinched the case against meritocracy of any sort in this powerful and telling advice to his countrymen:

> Oh people! do not be deluded to pay away your liberty for talents and merit. By rewarding them with great power, or great wealth, or long duration in office, you will lose the power of rewarding them at all; and these rewards, by destroying your liberty, will destroy publick merits and talents, and put an end to the objects of your bounty. It is only by withholding rewards, destructive both of the power and the objects of rewards, that nations will be able to evince their gratitude to benefactors.

It should not be surprising to find these ideas in the writings of revolutionaries. After all, as Arendt has pointed out, "no revolutionary ever thought it his task to introduce mankind to [status seeking] or teach the underprivileged the rules of the game."[9] American revolutionaries sought to teach, rather, the rules of a radically new game of equality.

A Pleasing Uniformity of Decent Competence

These revolutionaries set forth the principle of the natural equality of man, even proclaiming as a truth that was "self-evident" a proposition that seemed to later generations to contradict universal human experience. But it did not contradict their own experience. Their faith in natural equality seemed to them to be reinforced by the actual equality of condition in America. More importantly, the fact of relative material equality seemed to constitute a fair test of man's nature. Men lived for the first time in history in a new world, as John de Crevecoeur in his *Letters from an American Farmer* put it, with "no aristocratical families, no courts, no kings, no bishops, no ecclesiastical dominion, no invisible power giving to a few a very visible domination, no great manufacturers employing thousands, no great refinements of luxury." [10] The sheer physical space and natural resources, "scattered over an immense territory," also helped to produce a "new man" who was "animated with the spirit of an industry which is unfettered and unrestrained, because each person works for himself."

"In the beginning," as Locke had said, "all the world was America"; America was, therefore, the only real testing ground for the question of what man was "in the beginning." As early Americans observed what the "natural" conditions of America had wrought, they found a "pleasing equality . . . a pleasing uniformity of decent competence," in the sense of both ability and reward, revealed "throughout our habitations," as well as in other aspects of life. Were these new men not made of the same material—indeed, were they not, in many cases, the same men—as those who had dwelled in "meanness, smoke, and indigence" in the miserable hovels of Europe, accepting their conditions as a "natural" fate? Here was physical proof that men are roughly equal in their natural endowments, and that the gross inequalities of other societies were the result of artificial and adventitious circumstances. Where the contest was fair, where men competed with nature and not for mastery over others, where opportunities were in fact equal, experience itself seemed to them to settle the question in favor of natural equality.

The conclusions early Americans drew from this experience were influenced, as are all such conclusions, by the value judgments they made. De Crevecoeur found the "uniformity of decent competence" that he observed to be a "pleasing" phenomenon. So also did Benjamin Franklin, in his "information" for potential immigrants, in which he described the absence of both poverty and great wealth in America as "a general happy mediocrity" of condition.[11] There are in America, he advised, "few people so miserable as the poor of Europe," and "there are also very few that in Europe would be called rich." William Penn had echoed this point in his description of America as "a good poor man's country." These evaluations tell us a great deal about the meaning that generation of Americans gave to the idea of equality. Men who found pleasing the evidence of a "uniformity of decent competence" were obviously not impressed by the notion that social stability or progress depends on a natural hierarchy of human talents. They rejected the idea that the mass of mankind depends for its sustenance and progress on the ministrations of a natural elite—an idea flirted with by conservatives like John Adams, embraced by elitists like Hamilton, later elaborated into a way of life by Social Darwinism, and still later fashioned into the theory of meritocracy. They were ready to put their faith in the abilities of average men to live lives of fruitful independence and productive cooperation.

Those who believed that the "general mediocrity" of economic circumstances was a "happy condition" and who celebrated a "uniformity of decent competence" shared little in common with those who believed that "the fertile and beneficent inequality of men" constitutes a "natural" verdict on how society is to be organized.[12] Thus, the "moral conclusion" to be drawn from the early experience of equality was categorically opposed to the idea of opportunity to compete for scarce prizes. It was an affirmation of fraternity and human solidarity, as well as of individual moral autonomy, not a celebration of a society that offers the main chance to the man on the make. Walt Whitman drew the conclusion clearly: "By God! I will accept nothing which all men cannot have the counterpart of on the same terms."[13]

Are Men Equal?

The old argument raged on. There were men—like de Crevecoeur, Franklin, Taylor, and Jefferson—who believed that the early American experience showed that men are naturally equal. And there were others—like Adams, Calhoun, the Social Darwinists, and the meritocrats—who believed that the rise of social and economic inequalities established the fact of natural inequality. The Jeffersonians seemed to be saying that when men test their abilities against nature, rather than against other men in a direct competition for wealth and power, their natural equality of endowment will be demonstrated. Those who argued for natural inequality seemed to be saying that men have a natural propensity to demonstrate their worth through personal rivalry for position and preference, and that the results of their competition establish their natural inequalities.

How are we to evaluate these rival claims? On the one hand, the arguments from American history of the advocates of natural equality make considerable sense. The remarkable, if temporary, conditions of early American life did in fact reveal the possibilities of equality in freedom. The resulting "uniformity of decent competence" said something of fundamental importance about the capabilities of the average man. Still, the spokesmen for natural equality seem to have assumed the possibility of a rural, power-free, and status-free utopia—almost a nonsociety in its freedom from interpersonal competition and from all forms of hierarchy. Their argument stands, however, not as a promise of an agrarian utopia, but as a vision of the open-ended possibilities for a richer, more satisfying life available to a people who have chosen equality.

On the other hand, those who have spoken for natural inequality have less to commend their arguments. All such efforts ultimately end in a vicious circularity. When men compete with one another for scarce rewards, some emerge winners and some losers. This is, of course, a truism, which can establish absolutely nothing about the natural worth of individuals. The argument that it does is vicious because every competition is a selection of some human qualities to the exclusion of others as a test of worth. At the same time, every reward in the form of wealth or power is an advantage in the competitive struggle. Every competition rewards previous rewards, a fact that has been expressed, without its implications being fully appreciated, in the old expression that "nothing succeeds like success." The argument that natural inequality is established by social experience is circular because the competitive game is always rigged.

The Jeffersonians, at their perceptive best, understood this point. Their understanding is reflected even in their clumsy efforts to deal with the issue of slavery. Was the servitude of blacks justified by their natural inferiority? Jefferson worried over the question, and his answer was not unequivocal. But his analysis probed the heart of the question. No conclusion about natural differences, he argued, could be drawn by observing the behavior of blacks and comparing it to that of whites. For then, what we are really comparing is the results of the social inequality we are trying to test. If "the black man" is not presently equal in talents to the white, "it would be hazardous to affirm that, equally cultivated for a few generations, he would not become so."[14] Our only evidence is behavior, and behavior always reflects the social consequences of inequality. There is, therefore, only one test of whether men are naturally unequal: treat them socially as equals; give them all the same advantages by eliminating social disadvantages. Thus, in his response to the assertion that the behavior of slaves proved their "moral" inferiority, Jefferson argued "that a change in the relations in which a man is placed should change his ideas of right and wrong, is neither new, nor peculiar to the color of blacks. Homer tells us it was so two thousand and six hundred years ago." And regarding the question of intelligence, Jefferson stated, "The want of talents observed in blacks is merely the effect of their degraded condition, and not proceeding from any difference in the structure of the parts on which intellect depends." The conclusion of this analysis is that, until the question is tested by eliminating all social inequalities, any claim to natural inequality is vacuous.

John Taylor formulated the same insight more generally in his reply to John Adams's effort to ground social and economic inequalities in man's nature.[15] Adams's principle of aristocracy, he argued, cannot be established by "reasoning." Adams had therefore resorted to the age-old illusion that principles of society and government could be established by "reference to an inevitable power, calling it God or nature." This "contrivance for erecting a system, by asserting and setting out from the will of God, or from nature, is not new." The inequalities of all earlier societies and forms of government—the very ones "to which Mr. Adams refers us for instruction"—had rested on it. "'It is the will of Jupiter,' exclaimed some artful combination of men. 'The will of Jupiter is inevitable,' responded the same combination to itself; and ignorance submitted to a fate, manufactured by human fraud."

From such appeals to an "inevitable power" men have been induced to accept "the sanctity of oracles, the divinity of kings, and the holiness of priests; and now that these bubbles have become the scoff of common sense, experiment is to decide, whether there remains in America a stock of superstition, upon which can be ingrafted, 'an aristocracy from nature.'" Men would not easily be persuaded that they "ought to erect an aristocracy spontaneously"; hence the resort to the proposition that nature has already "settled the question." Once that contention has been established, the resulting system of inequality is effectively removed from examination or criticism; "the whole system, bottomed upon the concession, becomes irrefutable."

But the system becomes refutable if it is viewed in historical perspective. Taylor notes that the character of aristocracy is different in various times and social settings. Previous aristocracies have been based on conquest and on superstition, and now the mantle falls on an aristocracy of "paper and patronage." How, he inquires, can all these diverse systems of inequality be regarded as equally the fruit of an inevitable and constant nature? And he concludes: "If aristocracy is the work of nature, by deserting her accustomed constancy, and slyly changing the shape of her work, she has cunningly perplexed our defensive operations."

Taylor's point is that the diversity of criteria of inequality suffices to disclose the fraudulent character of all claims to a natural, a priori basis for any system of inequality. Men are naturally equal precisely in this sense that all criteria of inequality are socially rather than naturally determined. Nature knows only differences among men; it knows nothing of superiority and inferiority. Differences of talent, even insofar as they are natural (and even assuming that we could know how far that is), do not necessarily, of themselves, engender inequality or require that they be translated into wealth and power. They might as easily remind men of their interdependence and of the necessity for fraternity.

Equality as Moral Choice

In the development of his argument, Taylor distinguishes between the natural and the moral. The terms "natural or physical" describe events that "are the direct and immediate effect of matter, independent of abstraction." Whenever the mind's power of abstraction is involved, "moral causes" are operative. The translation of natural differences into social inequalities always rests on human abstraction from among the almost limitless diversities of natural endowment. Inequalities always follow from moral rather than natural causes. Hence, it is never possible to "deduce government from a natural fate"; it is always a matter of "moral liberty."

From their own passionate experience of equality during the struggle for independence and the formation of new governments, these men had come to understand that the very essence of a humanistic commitment to equality was the insistence that man's nature posed the problem; it did not solve it. They understood that nature is indifferent; *men* prefer equality, or they prefer inequality. Thus all inequalities should be regarded as man-made, temporary, and conditional grants of responsible power, conferred "for the common good" by men who share "an equality of moral rights and duties." Tom Paine expressed this emphasis on equality as "moral choice" in his belief that "social distinctions can only be founded upon common utility."[16] Sam Adams expressed it in his prediction that "whether America shall long preserve her Freedom or not, will depend on her virtue."[17]

Expressed in a variety of ways, the central message was that the choice of equality over inequality is most likely to promote virtue and happiness, to facilitate the most fruitful release of the creative energies of all, and to permit the continuing critical examination of all existing inequalities. It is, therefore, the only alternative consistent with man's continuing moral freedom and responsibility.

16

The Choice of Equality

Inequality, as we are so often reminded, is a characteristic of every known society. But that truth settles nothing. The decisive question is always whether a particular society has chosen equality or inequality as the standard for judging social relations. That choice determines the scope and meaning of the inequalities that will be countenanced. It determines the realms of experience to which inequality will apply; whether inequalities will have, in C. Wright Mills's phrase, "sovereign significance"; whether the inequalities will need to be constantly justified to those affected by them; whether the inequalities will maximize the creative energies of all or only of a few; whether they will inflame ambition and excite avarice, or produce mutual trust and compassionate concern; and whether they will provide grounds for the dignity of each, or will merely gratify the pride of some at the expense of others.

The crucial historical fact is that, out of their experience, the Jeffersonians came to prefer equality. The historical tragedy is that they never formulated the ideal sharply enough, or separated it clearly enough from their utopian agrarian dreams, to prevent its being transformed by later generations into a slogan of equal opportunity that concealed a choice of inequality as an individual and social ideal. But when the Jeffersonians did not permit their agrarian extravagance to warp their insight, they gave us the outlines of a theory of equality applicable beyond their own time and place.

Choose Equality

Choose equality. This is the central message of the ideas we have been examining. On what grounds may men be persuaded to choose it? Menander, in his maxim, had offered a reason—in order to "flee greed"—which was fully shared by the Jeffersonians. Their writings echo their concern for the fatal dangers of unrestrained "avarice and ambition," dangers they took to be so universally recognized as not to require much explanation. They shared implicitly the later analysis of R. H. Tawney, that the choice of inequality "sacrifices the cultivation of spiritual excellence, which is possible for all, to the acquisition of riches, which is possible, happily, only for the few."[1] The spirit of avarice, Tawney argued, "lives in an interminable series of glittering tomorrows, which it discovers to be tinsel when they become today."

Other reasons can be offered, most of which were either explicit or implicit in the American revolutionary tradition. Choose equality, the "American farmer" could say, because equality alone keeps alive the dream of a "new man"—a vision that a democracy has no business surrendering to the totalitarians of the left or right. This vision responds to a deep human need to find moral meaning in personal and social experience, a need that is denied in a competitive society that depends for its stability on cultivating, marshaling, and counterbalancing man's egoistic vices. The market society, by taking man as he is, succeeds only in making him worse.[2] The worst potentials of human nature are promoted: lying, dissimulation, manipulation, pride, arrogance, and obsequiousness. These characteristics are cultivated, as Edward Bellamy put it, through "a lifelong study to regulate every thought and act with sole reference to the pole-star of self-interest in its narrowest conception."[3] Euripides, In *Phoenissae,* captures this point in the advice he has Jocasta give to her son:

Status-seeking is quite wrong—the worst possible guide for life you could have. When that idea is current in a family or a state it always ruins those who believe in it. . . . Much better to put your money on equality, my boy: that's what makes for solidarity among friends and townships and nations. Equality is what's naturally right for men, you see: when you get the overprivileged and the underprivileged lined up against each other there's always trouble.[4]

Choose equality, because it provides the only hope for filling the moral vacuum that is the necessary condition of the countervailing power of organized group greed. "The politics of convenience," as Glenn Tinder calls it, leads to "low expectations and low demands" (and therefore produces, it might be added, still lower expectations and demands).[5] Politics is seen to be an economic, goal-oriented activity; participation, like work, involves disutility. Citizens vote and participate in other ways for the same reason they go to work—for the sake of future material rewards. The labor people expend in politics can be viewed as the cost of producing the intended benefits. Economic man triumphs, even in the domain of the political and the moral. Equality demands the recapture of the sphere of politics for the sake of the human spirit. It offers the possibility of remaking politics into a redemptive activity, calling citizens to a public office in which they are expected (though they will not always succeed) to subordinate interests to the claims of justice. In a secular world like ours, whose fate can no longer be underwritten by a benevolent nature, and whose secular God of technology has failed, equality is the only basis on which the legitimacy of a political order can be grounded. It is the only basis for the sociableness that alone can create civic decency.[6]

Choose equality, because other men, like ourselves, are choosing animals. We are all, being human, denied both the certitude of instinct on which other animals rely and the certitude of perfect knowledge of the gods. Our behavior is willed, intentional, chosen. Each of us knows this truth about ourselves immediately and introspectively. But we do not know, in the same way, that others are like us in that regard. We only observe others' actions. Since those actions may threaten our own precarious sense of importance and uniqueness, we are tempted to reduce the threat by treating others as objects and not as subjects. Only equality permits us to learn to identify with the condition of others and, in so doing, as John Wilson tells us, "we learn to see another person as he sees himself; and he sees himself as a willing, choosing creature."[7]

Choose equality, because otherwise we will continue to be blinded to the origin and causes of our current malaise. On this matter, misconceptions abound. The populist spirit of equality, its enemies tell us, is responsible for producing mediocrity and creating conformity at the lowest common denominator of tastes. By severing the connection between merit and rewards, equality undermines the basis of justice and equity in society. It destroys incentive; it destroys standards and ends the pursuit of excellence.

These misconceptions have been with us for a long time. John Adams and some of his conservative colleagues hinted at them. And in the 1830s a perceptive French observer, Alexis de Tocqueville, made them the central theme of his *Democracy in America*. Surveying the American scene, he made this dire prediction: "Thus not only does democracy make every man forget his ancestors, but it hides his descendants and separates his contemporaries from him; it throws him back forever on himself alone and threatens in the end to confine him entirely within the solitude of his own heart."[8] De Tocqueville's brilliant, prophetic insights have earned him a deserved reputation for discerning in Jacksonian America the beginnings of distinctively modern forms of alienation, of the growth of egoism and materialism, of mediocrity and conformity. At the heart of his analysis is the contention that the egalitarian dreams of the agrarian democrats—the democratization of manners, a rough equality of condition, majority rule, individual autonomy—were the sources of social ills that threatened to lead to a new tyranny of the "regular, quiet, and gentle kind."

Because de Tocqueville named equality as the cause of the potential malaise, he later became a culture hero to generations of conservatives and, now, to meritocrats. But however prescient his predictions and fears, the analysis supporting them was muddled and mistaken. The idea of equality, the triumph of which he regarded as inexorable, was in fact found only in the rhetoric of the Jacksonians, and in the opposition of a minority of radical dissenters. The social and economic reality of Jacksonian America reflected the rise of a new doctrine of inequality, thinly veiled by the romantic and sentimental slogan of equal opportunity.

De Tocqueville was taken in by the agrarian rhetoric and the historical residue of an older agrarian reality. He shared the same illusions that permitted Jacksonian liberals to imagine that the new regime of competitive inequality was an instrument for the effectuation of the old agrarian meaning of equality. He mistook the egalitarian intentions of the Jacksonians for the new inequalities of a competitive order, which reflected their own confusion, nostalgia, and, often, greed. He attributed, as they themselves did, an exaggerated importance to their political goals and victories—the principles of universal male suffrage; popular and frequent election of all government officials, including judges; and public participation in the nominating process. But these victories for political equality were not likely to shape the national character when politics itself became a casualty of the belief in the natural economic laws of free markets. The operation of an invisible hand liberated men from the duty of compassion, rewarded men's "natural" inequalities, and made political life largely superfluous.

The market process, with its emphasis on acquisition and competitive behavior, was unlikely to respond to the Jacksonian nostalgia for the "republican virtues." De Tocqueville, for all his penetrating insight into future consequences, mistook the intentions of the Jacksonians for their policies, and blamed equality for the social pathology of an inegalitarian market society. In so doing, he compounded the Jacksonians' confusion and gave it an intellectual rationale that has furnished grist for the mill of conservatives ever since. By the end of the century, his analysis was put in the service of a philosophical heritage that blinded men to the fact that the "natural selection" of an elite depended for its operation on men who had become what Hobbes and other philosophers of "possessive individualism" had imagined them "naturally" to be. This heritage has obscured the process by which a system of competitive inequality shapes individual character in ways diametrically opposed to the demands of equality; a heritage, in short, that perversely blames the spirit of equality for social pathology that flows from the competitive pursuit of inequality.[9]

Choose equality, because it is the precondition for individuality. The conformity de Tocqueville feared and predicted stems, not from equality, but from the inherent demands on the individual of competitive status seeking. It is a strange conceit, as Bellamy understood, that imagines that men would become "well-nigh indistinguishable if their bank accounts were the same."[10] It is only when men see another group of men as inferior (or superior) that they become unable to recognize their individual characteristics. Just as the assumption of inequality blinds us to individual variations, so the assumption of equality discloses them. When all men are equally human, individual humans are more, not less, likely to be appreciated for their uniquenesses.

Nor is equality the enemy of standards and the pursuit of excellence. It is, in fact, perfectly compatible with and likely to produce what Ortega, in his vastly misunderstood *The Revolt of the Masses*, described as the "true nobility."[11] The genuinely noble life, he argued, is "synonymous with a life of effort, ever set on excelling oneself, in pressing beyond what one is to what one sets up as a duty and an obligation." The key terms in Ortega's definition are "excelling *oneself*" in the pursuit of standards that "one sets up" *for oneself*. Emerson, who shared those views, provided the further insight that the one who seeks power and wealth in order to excel often does so as a substitute for his failure to reach "the mark of a good and equal life."[12]

The argument that equality is the enemy of excellence proceeds from the assumption that standards must be protected from the clamor of the populist masses for the commonplace. It implies that excellence is, therefore, safe only in the hands of the talented elites, and that inequality is the fence protecting it. Those who argue this case fail to make a necessary distinction between two meanings of the word *standards*. The enemies of standards of the first kind (institutionally sanctioned criteria for measuring the relative worth of individuals) do not necessarily oppose standards of the second kind (models of excellence for judging their own and others' achievements). Judged by any genuine standards of excellence, egalitarians are likely to argue, we are all mediocre. They warn that we are most likely to undermine the pursuit of excellence by equating it with the accomplishments of an elite, thus making it irrelevant to the pursuits of lesser mortals.

Especially in its meritocratic form, equal opportunity undetermines the pursuit of excellence by limiting it so narrowly. Brainpower, defined by IQ, is elevated into a criterion for judging relative individual worth and access to the good material life. Meritocratic justice thus destroys incentive to excellence for the losers by mocking John Wilson's insight that "nobody minds losing in one context, so long as he does not lose in all contexts and is hence counted as generally inferior."[13]

Choose equality, because it promises to maximize initiative and creative effort. Of all the criticisms of equality, none is taken so seriously and regarded to be of such moment as the charge that it would destroy incentive. Indeed, many argue, it has already gone a long way to take the temper out of the springs of human action. Here again, historical and causal relations are usually muddled. The common assumption is that the work ethic has been eroded by the egalitarianism of a creeping socialism in the form of welfare programs that destroy character and incentive by giving people something for nothing.

We need to be clear, first, about the Puritan ethic of work. Essentially, it was a statement of moral obligation. Every man, in the words of a 1647 Leveller manifesto, is "equally oblieged and accomptable to God . . . for the use of that talent betrusted unto him."[14] One of its spokesmen described the new regime of Puritan values as one in which "you will no longer value men and women according to their wealth, or outward shewes, but according to their vertue, and as the love of God appeareth in them." Men were stewards of their divinely given talents, obligated to God to develop them and put them in the service of their fellow man. Talents were not seen as competitive assets to be cultivated and spent carefully in the pursuit of individual ambition and greed.

Competitive inequality in both its capitalist and pluralist forms lived on, and lived up, the borrowed social and moral capital of a puritan, democratic, and egalitarian past. All social, political, or moral obligation was devoured by the appetites of men who were encouraged to ask, "What's in it for me?" To blame the results on equality is a cruel and vastly misleading hoax. Fortunately for the survival of both capitalism and pluralism, the work ethic was a remarkably resilient and durable idea. For generations it held its ground—in the form of such slogans as "an honest day's work for an honest day's pay"— against the corrosive spirit of: "Get as much as you can for as little as you can give." But now the capital is exhausted.[15] The middle and lower classes have learned the lesson of success, which the careers of the competitive elites have so often illustrated. "Something for nothing," after all, is the ideal dream of the economic man and the man on the make.

Competitive inequality fosters a social character that is self-centered and self-aggrandizing. It has, ironically, created a "new man," one who knows nothing of the social or moral obligation to work, on which all previous societies depended. Viewed from the perspective of the entire history of mankind, self-aggrandizement as a major incentive to work must be judged an unnatural phenomenon, alien to a creature whose needs can only be met in social interaction with his fellows.[16] But this unnatural new man exists now, and those who worry about incentive have a point. In a society in which self-interest has been legitimized and nearly universalized, the reduction of invidious rewards threatens incentive. But that is merely a statement of the cultural crisis brought on by competitive inequality in a market society. A society that believes that men will be motivated to develop their merits only when they have to prove their worth will succeed only in developing those human possibilities that diminish the humanity of the winners, deprive the losers of self-esteem, and bury the possibilities of justice.

Choose equality, because equal-opportunity liberalism failed to deliver on its dream. In both its economic and political expressions the dream was individual autonomy. The result, however, has been the centralization of power in the hands of manipulative elites and the erosion, for elites and nonelites alike, of the moral autonomy that political and economic independence was expected to produce. This result was inevitable, since the dream ignored the subtle but insidious pressure of the universal crises of getting ahead, which induces individuals to purchase wealth and prestige by spending their autonomy in small ways and small amounts until the whole inheritance is gone.

Avarice and ambition make liars and slaves of us all, as a long list of philosophers have understood. John Adams, in his honest and sophisticated conservatism, understood as well as Jefferson that universal competition for place and power gives rise to an emulation that destroys individuality and produces conformity. Human vanity produces a situation in which all men are "chained . . . to an incessant servitude to their fellow creatures." Adams's conservatism led him to the conclusion that vanity is a constant in human affairs, and that inequality is therefore man's natural state.[17] The democratic socialism of Edward Bellamy followed Adams's insight into the consequences of vanity, but reached a different conclusion: "It is always inequality which prompts the suppression of individuality by putting a premium on the servile imitation of superiors, and, on the other hand, . . . it is always among equals that one finds independence."[18]

But it was Rousseau who explored the question most fully and saw its implications most clearly. With the rise of competitive inequalities in the "rank and condition" of men, he argued, "it was necessary for men to be thought what they really were not. To be and to appear became two different things, and from that distinction sprang pomp and knavery."[19] Man, in these circumstances, comes to live not in himself, but "beside himself," in a constant comparison with others. The result is that "everything is reduced to appearances . . . honour without virtue, reason without wisdom and pleasure without happiness."

Choose equality, then, because individual authenticity requires genuine mutuality. The cultivation of one's own individuality requires variety and integrity in the personalities of others. One needs help, support, and compassionate concern in becoming oneself. No real satisfaction is possible unless one can disclose oneself to others and be appreciated for what one is—and this is possible only in interaction with other authentic selves.

Choose equality, therefore, not in spite of, but because of, the human need for praise. This need, so often viewed as the source of inequality, can in fact be satisfied only in relations among equals. Only the praise of others who are our equals really matters. All the rest is flattery, ingratiation, or condescension. Praise from our equals, of course, extends only to admiration of our specific merits—the quality of a specific performance, the nobility of a specific act of generosity, the courage of a specific demonstration of integrity.[20] We can never expect from equals a judgment of our superior worth as persons. But that is a judgment no one has a right to demand. In any event, since that judgment could never be freely and sincerely made, it would always be unsatisfying.

Choose equality, because the meritocratic world toward which we drift corrupts the democratic moral perspective. It does this by translating differences in particular natural talents into a hierarchy of human worth. Where differences in ability exist, they cannot be successfully shown to result from natural differences rather than from social disadvantages. More fundamentally, even if we assume that natural differences can be identified and measured, they do not imply a natural right to differential rewards. There is, after all, no more reason to reward individuals for their natural ability than to reward them for being born to aristocratic parents. Natural talent is, as we say, a "gift," and it is, or should be, its own compensation. On what moral reckoning should those more gifted by nature have their treasure artificially added to at the expense of the less gifted? If men had not been so thoroughly alienated from themselves, from their own possibilities and their own powers, it would not occur to them to want, and still less to believe they deserve, to be rewarded for their gifts. Indeed, it is precisely the system of competitive extrinsic social rewards that contributes so mightily to modern man's alienation.

Moreover, the talents that are judged to be worthy of economic and political reward tend, in the equal-opportunity society, to be just those acquisitive, self-aggrandizing, and technical talents that are responsible for the fact that "nice guys finish last." Hence, even the successful are led to cultivate talents that falsify their own possibilities. As Emerson said,

> The gladiators in the lists of power feel, through all their frocks of force and stimulation, the presence of worth. I think the very strife of trade and ambition is confession of this divinity; and successes in those fields are the poor amends, the fig-leaf with which the shamed soul attempts to hide its nakedness. . . . It is because we know how much is due from us that we are impatient to show some petty talent as a substitute for worth.[21]

Choose equality, because its counterfeit—equal opportunity to become unequal—promotes the arrogance of the "talented" elites it produces. Their rewards are viewed as their natural due; their status and power acquire sovereign significance. Having rewarded talent with great power and wealth, we lose, as John Taylor warned us, "the power of rewarding them at all."

Choose equality because, contrary to our ordinary understanding, the view of life as a racetrack on which the laurels go to the talented does not distinguish a democracy from other forms of social organization. In modern industrial societies of all descriptions—fascist and nominally communist as well as democratic—careers are everywhere open to talent. There are always, of course, ideological tests of eligibility to compete. In nondemocratic societies those tests are more rigid, more clearly delineated, and exact a larger toll in individual autonomy. But for most of the participants in a meritocratic system, the price, whether subtly exacted or clearly evident, is not felt as a burden or experienced as a denial of self.

Is not the question of goals as far outside the conscious choice of the aspiring American as it is of his Soviet counterpart? Opportunity for what? In both cases the answer is predetermined in the rules of the competitive race and the rewards it offers. The price of eligibility to compete is a willingness to surrender at the starting line one's own right to judge what goals are worthy of one's aspirations and what rewards are worth seeking. I doubt that the typical upwardly mobile Russian, rising on his merits through the educational and bureaucratic hierarchies, is much more conscious than the average American of the price he is paying in the loss of his "moral personality." In neither case is there likely to be much awareness that any price at all has been paid. And in both cases, the imperatives of ambition for position and promotion wed the individual to the system, and provide a powerful impetus toward mindless conformity. In democratic societies, to be sure, success is more variously defined, the system is less constraining in its ideological demands, and the penalties for dropping out are much less serious. But in every system of competitive inequality, ambition forecloses for most individuals the possibility of challenging the system by preferring, in Tawney's phrase, "other goods to those which it promises."

And Flee Greed

Equality is the only principle that offers the possibility of our regaining control over our own destinies—either individually or collectively. It is the only weapon against a meritocracy that, in the name of success, determines for us ahead of time what matters most, and spares us the task of thinking critically about where we are headed.[22] In the name of efficiency, competitive inequality has led us to a blind faith in growth and an identification of growth with progress. The triumph of the acquisitive spirit could be made tolerable only by transforming the ladder of opportunity into an escalator with running room. In order to reconcile the increasing inequalities resulting from equal opportunity with the dreams of an older equality, it became necessary, as John Taylor had foreseen, to extend "corruption to cover a fraud." As inequality of condition (and, therefore, of opportunity) increased, growth became necessary to provide enough room at the top to satisfy the universal ambition—and enough annual surplus to placate the universal avarice—that equal opportunity had unleashed.

Under modern conditions, the historical sources of growth —the frontier, an undeveloped economy with access to abundant resources, imperial and colonial adventure abroad— tend to dry up. At the same time, the pressures for growth— rooted in the unsatisfiable greed of elites, the rising expectations of the middle classes, and the new claims of the politically conscious oppressed—accelerate. Growth is the equal-opportunity society's substitute for the income redistribution that justice would require. And, as the pressures accumulate, growth becomes increasingly removed from any connection with human welfare.

To see how far this estrangement from human values has already proceeded, we need only note how insanely our "responsible" leaders see disarmament and peace as threats to a healthy economy, how mindlessly they go about multiplying nuclear power plants whose radioactive wastes cannot be safely disposed of and will threaten the lives and health of our descendants for untold generations, and how blithely they discount well-grounded fears of ecological disaster when remedial programs would interfere with the avarice of established groups and with their own political ambitions. It is no mere fantasy to imagine that we are progressing toward oblivion. And it becomes more obvious every day that the only alternative to mindless growth is a reaffirmation of the spirit of equality.

As equality opens up previously barred avenues to community with our contemporaries, so it also reminds us of our links with past and future, and with our natural habitat. The social compact, as Burke insisted, binds "the dead, the living, and the yet unborn." Only the arrogance born of competitive, acquisitive individualism has ever ignored that truth, thus freeing the living from responsibility for stewardship of a cultural and natural heritage.

Time is running out on our futile efforts to simultaneously choose equality and enjoy greed. The ecological limits on the exploitation of nature and the limits our human nature sets on living without values simultaneously foreclose that possibility, even if it were a desirable one. To save ourselves, nothing less will do than to relearn the lesson of the Revolution that began our common adventure. It is a lesson that Hannah Arendt summarized precisely and eloquently: "That all men are created equal is not self-evident nor can it be proved. We hold this opinion because freedom is possible only among equals, and we believe that the joys and gratifications of free company are to be preferred to the doubtful pleasures of holding dominion."[23]

Epilogue

The typical arguments over affirmative action, I suggested at the start, are confused; the real issues are elusive. My attempt to reduce the confusion and to define the issues more clearly has led me along paths I initially had no intention of treading. I originally set out to write a brief essay on the *Bakke* case. That done, my desk and my attention would be cleared to write a book on the larger issues of equality about which I had been worrying for a good many years. Once I embarked, however, I never came close to finding a stopping place. I found that the reasons usually offered for supporting or opposing affirmative-action programs conceal more than they reveal about the assumptions underlying them. The ways we approach the issue of racial justice, or decide to ignore it, I discovered, reflect assumptions so basic that they have been largely unconscious and unexamined. Behind every apparently simple assertion or argument was a seamless fabric of assumptions and ideas, all finely interwoven in a historical tapestry.

The result of my reflection was a series of excursions into the historical background and the philosophical implications of what has become the dominant American ideology of equal opportunity. I attempted to trace the path by which that ideology developed out of—and obscured and falsified—a different and more radical egalitarian tradition. The picture of our current predicament that emerged parallels the thumbnail collective biography of Americans sketched by Max Otto three decades ago:

> When we were young, two great ideas had power in our lives. We believed ourselves as a people to be working out on this continent a political and social commonwealth intended to guarantee the opportunity for a satisfying life to every man, woman, and child. We often fell short in practice, and our ideal was in some of its features utopian, but the thing we aimed at was vital and noble. This common faith is no longer alive in us.[1]

While the loss of our egalitarian faith, together with the failure of nerve accompanying the loss, has redefined conditions for all of us, the consequences have been especially disastrous for racial minorities. Frustrated for hundreds of years in their efforts even to secure a fair hearing regarding our professed faith in equality, they now discover that while they were waiting to be heard the meaning of equality was changed in a way that denies them redress. When whites finally listened, the great principle, which seemed to be contradicted by the plight of minorities, turned out merely to be a slogan that rationalized their condition. Minorities have been ideologically disarmed by a consensus on the meaning of equality that permits neglect of their condition to be characterized as "benign." Neglect of racial injustice is benign, of course, only for whites. But in the same way the neglect of other inequalities is benign only for the wealthy and powerful. Just as some people view colored minorities subjected to discrimination as being treated fairly, the wealthy can also view the poor as having a fair chance despite the handicap of their poverty.

In this way, not only racial inequality, but virtually all existing inequalities, are placed beyond the reach of deliberate efforts at remediation. Our helplessness is rooted in the assumption that it is dangerous, as well as useless, to admonish mankind to forsake ambition and avarice in order to pursue justice. Almost no one before our own age thought the pursuit of justice dangerous (though a few—most notably the cynics and rhetoricians of Athens in decline, and some later Machiavellians—thought it useless). But this very conclusion is inherent in the present meaning of equal opportunity. The premise that the quest for justice is socially pathological was implicit in the psychology of self-interest and the sleight of hand by which Adam Smith's marketplace translates private vices into public virtues. And it is also explicit in both the "interest-group liberalism" of pluralists and the meritocrats' denunciation and fear of populist equality.

In light of the above conclusions, I return again to reflect on the two experiences, described in the Prologue, that influenced my approach to the issue of affirmative action. How ironic it seemed, even at the time, that the teachers and administrators involved in the school incident were blinded by their own color-blind standards of justice to the racist realities that affected the black children's behavior. It is ironic that in the name of equal treatment, they refused to accord those children special treatment, thus contributing to the perpetuation and reinforcement of their unequal treatment.

If there had been an opportunity to probe with those educators the rationale underlying their color-blind posture, I do not doubt we would have found at the core of their beliefs the tandem dogmas of equal opportunity and equality before the law as I have explored them here. Only those myths could have permitted the school officials to dismiss our suggestion (which would later be called an affirmative-action approach to the children's plight) as a demand for reverse discrimination. Without such an approach, the children's wounds were unlikely to be healed, nor would the community's tensions be abated.

So it is now in our larger society where, without affirmative action, the struggle for racial justice will come to a dead end. Too many whites imagine that the problem has been solved, that justice has been achieved, that formal equality has provided a framework in which the magic of equal opportunity can do its work. At that school then, and in the larger society now, this assumption promotes a stalemate. By blinding us to the realities of racial injustice, it paralyzes our will to change those realities; by making further progress unnecessary, it makes any progress impossible.

But if whites are blinded to the personal indignities and injuries suffered by nonwhites in America, perhaps they can still be brought to see the injustice of a situation in which blacks enjoy less of the good material life *because they are black*. Perhaps whites can be convinced that there is no other decent explanation for the relative economic disadvantage of minorities. Economic parity for racial minorities, of course, is not synonymous with racial equality. But in a society like ours, in which income and occupational differentials play so large a role in measuring relative status and judging individual worth, and where economic deprivation has been so important an index of racial subjugation, economic parity is a necessary next step. Equal-opportunity programs, as opposed to affirmative-action programs, cannot be relied on to reduce group-income differentials. There is simply no way to proceed "unless we can make a political accommodation with the basic fairness of affirmative action programs."[2] It must also be a moral accommodation, made by whites as well as blacks, workers as well as intellectuals, and voters as well as bureaucrats and politicians.

Affirmative action cannot be approached as a political effort to buy the votes of racial blocs or to buy off the threat of social disorder. Nor can it be accomplished by the efforts of well-meaning white politicians and intellectuals who seek to manipulate an unenlightened white majority. It has to be done because it is the fair thing to do, or it cannot be done at all.

Affirmative action must be understood as the only fair alternative by those who will pay the cost of achieving it. It is never easy to do what is fair, where conscience and interest are at fundamental odds. And it is infinitely more difficult when the costs of fairness are not fairly distributed. Under current conditions the costs are grossly unfair, weighing most heavily on the young and the poor. Short of a radical redistribution of income that seems beyond our present vision, the only available means of achieving a fairer distribution of costs is a full-employment policy. As things now stand, affirmative action functions in an economic situation of job shortages. Because we have not devised an alternative to using unemployment as a trade-off against inflationary pressure, full employment has been virtually abandoned even as a goal of public policy. The result is to make affirmative action a zero-sum game in which the gains of racial minorities and women are matched by the losses of white males, especially at the lower end of the economic ladder. Those who are treated unfairly cannot be expected to pay willingly for fairness to others at the price of their own further disadvantage. Nor should they be expected to by those whose favored positions have insulated them from the necessary costs. Considerations like these led Lester C. Thurow to the accurate conclusion that "full employment is not a sufficient condition, but it is an absolutely necessary condition" for reducing income differentials between minorities and the majority.[3]

The sufficient condition, of course, is commitment to an ideal of equality that enables us to see that existing economic inequalities among racial groups are the result of racism, to judge those inequalities to be intolerable, and to recognize there is no way to achieve racial justice without cost to those who have been advantaged by racism. If affirmative action is conceived as a response of power brokers to group pressure, rather than as a quickening of the democratic conscience, the context in which such programs operate is raw power; the voice of justice is not raised, and conscience need not answer. But understood as an exercise of the compassionate imagination and as an effort to right a grievous wrong, affirmative action may begin to fill the hope that Nat Hentoff prematurely found in the racial turmoil of the 1960s:

> Although the odds at present are heavily against a major re-education of the electorate within this decade, the civil rights activists may startle us again. The ultimate irony in American race relations may yet be that the bitter insistence of the Negro revolt will have provided the initial impetus for basic social and economic change for all Americans. Having gone beyond

morality to power in order to achieve its aims, "the movement" may have begun to create a society in which morality
will be the normative principle in action.[4]

I return, also, to reflect on Paul Robeson's compelling challenge that excited my youthful enthusiasm: "But I'm not going
to live that long." If there is a central lesson to be drawn from
the historical and philosophical condition in which we find ourselves, it is that our task is to universalize the moral fervor
behind Robeson's statement. Although the burden of living in
an unjust society falls most heavily on the victims, in a larger
sense we are all victims. The stake each of us has in living in a
just society is independent of the color of our skin. "Why we
can't wait" was Martin Luther King's warning to whites, but it
was more than that. It was also an invitation to whites to share
the humane and egalitarian vision from which that sense of
moral urgency springs. The reason none of us can afford to wait
is that none of us, no matter our color, is going to live that long.
We will not achieve a complete victory in our lifetimes; most
likely, mankind never will. The indispensable insight is the one
contained in Albert Guerard's reformulation of the scriptural
injunction: "Ye shall *seek* the truth; and the *quest* shall make you
free."[5] The quest, of course, is open only to seekers, and only
they will reap its benefits.

In an age where winning is everything, is it surprising that
we have chosen to forfeit those difficult struggles? In a competitive social order ruled by a fear of failure, is it surprising we do
not wish to be reminded of our failures by utopian ideals? In a
world in which the claims of conscience are viewed as an intolerable impediment in the struggle to get ahead, should we
wonder that those values that make demands on conscience are
in disrepute?

At the root of our predicament is the fact that we have
redefined equality so that the ideal mirrors reality (or, at least, so
that the ideal is close enough to the reality that the gap can be
closed without testing our consciences or sacrificing our con-
veniences). We have accomplished this by substituting for the
substantive goal of equality, the procedural standards of equal

opportunity and equality before the law. These procedural standards mask our substantive failure and, by permitting us to believe we have in fact prevailed in our struggle with inequality, have removed the tension between what is and what ought to be that makes the struggle necessary.

Martin Luther King, Jr., was speaking out of understandable frustration, not out of his own prophetic vision, when he issued this ultimatum to whites: "We are not asking you to love us, only to get off our backs." Whites *have* gotten off the backs of blacks, insofar as that is possible without the love that informs compassion for the unjust suffering of equals. This is precisely the meaning of a sense of justice that is satisfied by equality before the law, and that leaves the rest to equal opportunity, without making further demands on the consciences of the dominant group. There lies the measure, and the limit, of what men who do not really believe in their equal humanity owe to one another.

The fire of equality burns at the source of democratic dreams. Ignored or neglected, it threatens to engulf us; but faithfully kindled, it offers promises of warmth to the human spirit and a friendly hearth for our common abode. It requires tending. That is why we can't wait. For, in the world we now make for our grandchildren, our reasons for not waiting will become an explanation to them of how their world became a fairer place.

Notes

Prologue

1. *DeFunis* v. *Odegaard*, pp. 336–37.

2. *Regents of the University of California* v. *Bakke*, p. 387.

Chapter 1

1. Here, and throughout the book, I have often referred to blacks to illustrate or symbolize the problems of racial oppression to which affirmative action is addressed. This emphasis is partly unavoidable in view of the legal and constitutional issues that have arisen as a result of the heritage of black slavery and "Jim Crow." In light of this history, blacks are also the "test case" for white conscience and national earnestness of purpose. But racism is, at bottom, a matter of color prejudice. I hope that my frequent references to blacks have not seemed to obscure or minimize the consequences of that fact for other colored minorities.

2. Justice Douglas's position is not, of course, grounded in the same reasons, nor does his opposition to affirmative action reach as far, as those who deny the continuing injustices of racism. In his dissent in *DeFunis* v. *Odegaard,* for example, although he reached the conclusion that "there is no constitutional right for any race to be preferred," Douglas would have allowed a "separate classification" of minority applicants in order to insure that race would not be "a subtle force in eliminating minority members because of cultural differences" (p. 335).

3. Daniel Moynihan, *The Negro Family; The Case for National Action,* Office of Policy Planning and Research, U.S. Department of Labor (Washington, D.C.: Government Printing Office, March 1965). See, especially, pp. 2–3. The equal-opportunity thesis of this monograph was smothered in a flood of controversy over its tendency to indict what the report described as "the pathology of the Negro family" structure as the root cause of relative black underachievement. Not surprisingly, this struck most blacks and many white liberals as an exercise in "blaming the victims." The resulting furor, however justified, unfortunately drowned out almost completely the report's analysis of "the new crisis in race relations." See Lee Rainwater and William Yancey, *The Moynihan Report and the Politics of Controversy* (Cambridge: M.I.T. University Press, 1967).

4. It is not self-evident of course that, in the absence of genetic racial differences, the relative deprivation of blacks can only be attributed to white racism. Alternative explanations are theoretically possible. In fact, several efforts have been made to explain away such inequalities of group results. These efforts, which are not persuasive, are critically analyzed in Chapter 5.

5. The National Urban League's report is quoted in *Poverty Law Report,* Southern Poverty Law Center, Spring 1978 (Montgomery, Ala.).

6. *Regents of the University of California* v. *Bakke,* p. 395. (Cited hereinafter simply as *Bakke.*)

7. Garry Wills identified the way in which affirmative action proposes to shorten the path to racial equality in his description of President Johnson's 1965 Howard University speech, in which Johnson boldly expressed his intent to "move blacks straight from stage one (equal rights) past stage two (equal opportunity) into stage three

(equal results)" (Garry Wills, *Nixon Agonistes* [New York: New American Library, 1969], p. 472).

8. The decisions of the Court were announced in Justice Powell's opinion, which did not have the total concurrence of a single other Justice (nor was there concurrence on many of its particular sections by any of his colleagues). A total of six opinions were filed in the case. Four of the Justices (Stevens, Burger, Stewart, and Rehnquist) joined Powell in ordering Bakke's admission; the same four Justices joined in holding the Davis special admissions program unlawful. Four other Justices (Brennan, White, Marshall, and Blackmun) dissented from the ruling that the Davis program was invalid, but joined Powell in finding that race could legitimately be used as a factor in admissions. The "Brennan four" pointed out that "no decision of this court has ever adopted the proposition that the Constitution must be colorblind" (p. 336). They found the "central meaning of today's opinions" in the verdict that "government may take race into account when it acts not to demean or insult any racial group, but to remedy disadvantages cast on minorities by past racial prejudice . . ." (p. 325). But they were promptly reminded by four of their colleagues that "only a majority can speak for the Court or determine the 'central meaning' of any judgment of the Court" (p. 408). The Court did not rule that the program was void on constitutional grounds (as a violation of the Fourteenth Amendment's equal protection clause). In fact, only Justice Powell reached that conclusion. The four Justices who joined him in finding the program invalid rested their case on the statutory ground that it violated the intent of Title VI of the Civil Rights Act of 1964.

9. Justice Powell sought to reconcile his interpretation of equal protection with the use of race as one factor by arguing that "the applicant who loses out on the last available seat to another candidate receiving a 'plus' on the basis of ethnic background will not have been foreclosed *from all consideration* for that seat simply because he was not the right color or had the wrong surname" (emphasis added). But, of course, since the "plus" was the decisive factor, the applicant who loses out will have been deprived of the seat "simply because he was not the right color." On Justice Powell's assumptions, it is difficult to follow his conclusion that the qualifications of such a rejected white applicant "would have been weighed fairly and competitively," since the decisive qualification he lacked was being colored (p. 318).

10. *Bakke*, p. 318.

11. *Bakke*, p. 378.

12. *Bakke*, p. 318.

13. *Bakke*, p. 379.

14. *Bakke*, p. 319.

15. The California Supreme Court had similarly advised the university to satisfy "the appearance of justice." Preference for disadvantaged applicants, the majority held, is constitutionally permissible. But "disadvantaged applicants of all races must be eligible for sympathetic consideration, and no applicant may be rejected because of his race, in favor of another who is less qualified, as measured by standards applied without regard to race" (*Bakke* v. *Regents of the University of California*, p. 55). At the same time, the California Court recorded its sympathy with the objective of increasing the number of minority members in the profession. Indeed, having denounced all forms of racial preference, the Court urged the university to exercise its ingenuity to increase the number of minority students by methods that do not take race into account. Where, the Court seemed to be asking the university, are your experts in dissimulation? (Actually, the university's experts had displayed abundant ingenuity in that regard in their efforts to deny that the Davis special admissions program rested on what looked rather obviously like a racial quota.)

16. Thomas Sowell, "Affirmative Action and Pious Fraud," *Inquiry*, August 21, 1978, p. 11. Sowell cites the 1977 Gallup poll.

Chapter 2

1. Mark Twain, *The Adventures of Huckleberry Finn* (New York: Lancer, 1967), pp. 374, 378–79. The account of this anecdote relies heavily on John C. Livingston and Robert G. Thompson, *The Consent of the Governed*, 3rd ed. (New York: Macmillan, 1971), pp. 441–42. Roscoe Pound first used this episode to describe an aspect of judicial decision making in "Law in Books and Law in Action," in *Readings in Jurisprudence and Legal Philosophy*, eds. F. S. Cohen and M. R. Cohen (Englewood Cliffs, N.J.: Prentice-Hall, 1951), p. 419.

2. McGeorge Bundy makes a forceful argument for affirmative action, which is extraordinarily forthright in recognizing that minority preference means white disadvantage. But even he describes Davis as having a "relatively large and rigid *goal* for minorities" ("The Issue Before the Court: Who Gets Ahead in America?" *Atlantic*, November 1977, p. 49, emphasis added). Justice Powell took up this question in his *Bakke* opinion. The university's brief, he noted, describes the special admissions program "as establishing a 'goal' of minority representation in the medical school"; Bakke's counsel, "echoing the courts below, labels it a racial quota." Powell dismissed the university's effort to distinguish between quotas and goals as a "semantic distinction" and "beside the point" (p. 389). But he then went on to reintroduce a distinction between invalid quotas (places reserved for minorities for which white applicants cannot compete) and valid goals (the use of race as one factor in admissions decisions). His new distinction suffers from the same weaknesses as the old one. Indeed, Powell's effort to demonstrate that quotas are invalid applies with equal force to goals (as he now defines them).

3. A. Lawrence Lowell, *Public Opinion and Popular Government* (New York: Longmans, Green, 1913), pp. 2–3. The absurdity of describing this situation as an instance of majority rule, Lowell concluded, reflects the fact that "the three men . . . do not form a community which is capable of a public opinion on the question involved." Jefferson formulated clearly the majoritarian test in his first inaugural declaration that: "All, too, will bear in mind this sacred principle that, though the will of the majority is in all cases to prevail, that will, to be rightful, must be reasonable. . . ." That is, the will of the majority must have resulted from and be amenable to reasoned appeals. Joseph Tussman has eloquently made the same point in his argument that a democracy is obligated to give a majority, not what they "want," but what they "think best" (Joseph Tussman, *Obligation and the Body Politic* [New York: Oxford University Press, 1960], pp. 110–12).

4. Ray Ginger's observation on what has happened to American public life since men like Peter Altgeld, Clarence Darrow, Theodore Dreiser, Thorstein Veblen, and John Dewey passed from the scene deserves to be quoted more fully. "Men like Altgeld and Darrow," he says, "had some ambitions that were far from noble, and they had more conflicts than the typical man. But in most situations they ultimately faced up to the question: What is right? The question has

gone out of style. Nowadays an effort to reach a decision is likely to begin and end with the query: Am I covered? In this shift lies the collapse of a civilization, and we still do not realize exactly what has happened or how." In line with my own analysis in later chapters, Ginger sees this moral approach to experience to be grounded in "the capacity for deep sympathy" with the suffering of others (Ray Ginger, *Altgeld's America* [New York: Funk and Wagnalls, 1958], pp. 1, 360).

Chapter 3

1. Meg Greenfield, "How to Resolve the Bakke Case," *Newsweek*, October 24, 1977, p. 128.

2. *DeFunis* v. *Odegaard*, p. 338. The boundary-line argument seems close to the heart of Douglas's position. It played a similarly crucial role in Justice Powell's opinion in *Bakke*. I discuss the substance of this issue in subsequent chapters. For present purposes, the relevant point is that the boundary line actually employed in affirmative-action programs is the "color line." To deny that such a line can be drawn is to deny that color prejudice can be qualitatively distinguished from other forms of ethnic prejudice.

3. The prize for misplaced righteous indignation about reverse discrimination goes to those who find a grave injustice in the possibility that under preferential admissions a black who has "passed" (as white) might now reclaim black ethnic status to advance his career. I discuss the racist implications of this apparent concern for "justice" in the next chapter.

4. Seymour Martin Lipset and William Schneider, "An Emerging National Consensus," *New Republic*, October 15, 1977, p. 9.

Chapter 4

1. R. H. Tawney, *Equality* (New York: Harcourt, Brace, 1931).

2. This white insensitivity to the human and moral meaning of "passing" has a paradoxical result. It is precisely the inability to share compassionately in the human plight of colored individuals that enables whites to claim the right to treat colored persons as individuals (in disregard of their color).

3. *Bakke,* p. 292.

4. *Bakke,* p. 400.

5. Powell's analysis of "post-Civil-War judicial reactionism" (p. 291) relies on and quotes from Joseph Tussman and Jacobus ten Broek, "The Equal Protection of the Laws," 37 *Calif. L. Rev.* 341 (1949).

6. *Bakke,* p. 295.

7. *Bakke,* p. 296.

8. *Bakke,* p. 292.

9. After having conjured away the white majority, Justice Powell consistently puts the phrase in quotation marks ("white 'majority'") throughout the rest of his opinion. A similar, more fully developed case for the nonexistence of a white majority was made by Nathan Glazer, *Affirmative Discrimination: Ethnic Inequality and Public Policy* (New York: Basic Books, 1975), chap. 1. The general analysis that follows from the assumption that there is no white majority parallels the arguments of pluralist theorists. The conclusion was clearly formulated by Robert A. Dahl: There is no problem of majority tyranny in America because a majority does not rule. Instead, minorities rule through the process of group bargaining and compromise. Thus, Powell argues that "the concepts of 'majority' and 'minority' necessarily reflect temporary arrangements and political judgments [and] those political judgments are the product of rough compromise struck by contending groups within the democratic process." As authority for this interpretation, Powell cites Robert A. Dahl, *A Preface to Democratic Theory* (Chicago: University of Chicago Press, 1956). This happy picture of a multigroup society in which there are no oppressed minorities has been subjected to devastating criticism by political scientists in recent years. See, for example, Peter Bachrach, *The Theory of Democratic Elitism* (Boston: Little, Brown, 1967); Henry S. Kariel, *The Promise of Politics* (Englewood Cliffs, N.J.: Prentice-Hall, 1966); Theodore J. Lowi, *The End of Liberalism* (New York: W. W. Norton, 1969); Joseph Tussman, *Obligation and the Body Politic* (New York: Oxford University Press, 1960); and Robert Paul Wolff, "Beyond Tolerance," in Robert Paul Wolff, Barrington Moore, Jr., and Herbert Marcuse, *A Critique of Pure Tolerance* (Boston: Beacon Press, 1965). The most devastating critique of pluralism as a safeguard of the rights of ethnic minorities is Daniel M. Berman's study of congressional enactment of civil-

rights legislation, *A Bill Becomes a Law,* 2nd ed. (New York: Macmillan, 1966). Justice Powell's appeal to the authority of political scientists in defense of a benevolently pluralist view of American politics is, in short, at least a decade out of date.

10. *Bakke*, p. 295; emphasis in original.

11. It is misleading to describe the white majority as being made up of white ethnic minorities. I suspect that, at least before the recent concern for discovering one's ethnic identity, most members of the white majority regarded their whiteness as much more significant than their ethnic origins. And they probably still do. One critic of affirmative action makes this point inadvertently, but dramatically: "Easy phrases like 'majority' and 'minority' obscure the important fact that there is no single American ethnic group that comes close to being a majority. Half of the American population cannot identify their ethnicity at all" (Thomas Sowell, "Affirmative Action and Pious Fraud," *Inquiry*, August 21, 1978, p. 12). If ever a proposition lent itself to easy and obvious inference, it is that nearly all of those Americans who "cannot identify their ethnicity at all" are white.

12. Powell concluded that the color line does not provide the clear standard the Constitution requires for granting "preferred status." But he confronted the same problem later in his opinion, where he sought to justify the use of race as one factor in the selection process. There, he found it useful to quote Justice Frankfurter: "A boundary line is none the worse for being narrow" (p. 318).

13. Mary Ten Thor et al., *The Bakke Symposium* (Sacramento: Uncommon Lawyers Workshop, 1977), p. 144. "How can you possibly treat [black Americans]," Ivor Kraft asked, "as 'disadvantaged immigrants' along with your Slavs, Greeks, Turks, Jews, etc.? Forced immigration, slavery, imposed illiteracy, deliberate suppression of cultural folkways, lynchings, Black Codes, Jim Crow, ghettoization with what some might consider genocide in mind, and much more—how can you possibly put this in a class with what even the most brutally exploited Greek or Jew or Swede had to put up with?" (Ibid.)

14. Eliot Marshall, "Race Certification; the Logical Next Step," *New Republic*, October 15, 1977, p. 18.

15. Tourgée's brief is reprinted in Otto H. Olsen, *The Thin Disguise: Turning Point in Negro History* (New York: Humanities Press, 1967), p. 84. In its response, the Court, through Justice Brown, simply noted that "The power to assign to a particular coach obviously implies the power to determine . . . who, under the laws of the particular state, is to be deemed a white, and who a colored person" (*Plessy* v. *Ferguson*, p. 549). Actually, there was no law in Louisiana defining who is white and who is colored, nor a need for one.

16. *Plessy* v. *Ferguson*, p. 552.

Chapter 5

1. Robert Blauner makes the crucial point: "Preferential treatment is not racism in reverse because its purpose and goal is not to turn our racial order on its head so that non-whites will be in a position of dominance" (Robert Blauner, *Racial Oppression in America* [New York: Harper & Row, 1972], p. 279).

2. *Bakke*, p. 375. After denying that the injuries sustained by rejected whites are comparable to those sustained by blacks, Justice Brennan went on to note that they are nonetheless real and "sufficiently serious to require justification." Hence, the "strict scrutiny" test is required (p. 375).

3. In the actual circumstances of the *Bakke* case, there were twenty-five minority admissions in the 1974 entering class of one hundred, sixteen having been admitted through the special admissions program and nine through the general admissions process (see Powell's opinion, footnote 6 at p. 276). Since this total number of minority admissions does not exceed the proportionate number of those minorities in the California population, it does not affect my argument here.

4. *Bakke*, pp. 355–56. The "Brennan four," later in the opinion, reemphasized the importance of fair competition when they noted that the Davis figure of 16 percent "is consistent with the goal of putting minority applicants in the position they would have been in if not for the evil of racial discrimination" (footnote 58, p. 374).

5. *Bakke*, footnote 36, p. 296.

6. John Howard Griffin's *Black Like Me* (New York: New American Library, 1960) is an account of his experiences in the South after he had undergone medical treatments to change his skin color to black and shaved his hair in order, as he said, to find out "what it is like to be a Negro in a land where we keep the Negro down." It is an important measure of the limits of white compassion that whites—judged at least from my experience with my white students—respond so much more readily to Griffin's account than to the experiences of, say, Claude Brown or Malcolm X.

7. Madison Grant is quoted by J. R. Pole, *The Pursuit of Equality in American History* (Berkeley: University of California Press, 1978), p. 233. The fact that Jews, alone among white ethnics, were treated as a racial group helps to account for their greater historical sensitivity to the distinctive badge of color prejudice in America.

8. Thomas Sowell, "Equal Opportunity or the Numbers Game," *American Educator,* Fall 1978, p. 12.

9. R. M. O'Neil, "The Case for Preferential Admissions," in *Reverse Discrimination*, ed. Barry R. Gross (Buffalo, N.Y.: Prometheus Books, 1977), p. 69.

10. An interesting perspective on the furor over preferential treatment of colored minorities is provided by a policy decision made in the California state college system in the mid-1960s. It had become evident that there were more females than males in the student bodies of the eighteen colleges. The response was to shift admission requirements from high school grade point averages (GPAs) to just that combination of GPAs and scholastic aptitude scores that would produce an equal number of males and females. (Girls statistically get better grades, while boys score relatively higher on the tests.) This was a clear-cut affirmative-action program for white males. Yet it was accomplished without fanfare or opposition; it seemed the only fair thing to do!

11. McGeorge Bundy calls attention to the significance of Blackmun's point in his essay, "Beyond Bakke" (*Atlantic*, November 1978, p. 71). It should also be noted that the constitutional footing thus provided to the use of race as a factor is limited to higher educational institutions. Moreover, as Bundy says, "The quest for diversity is not enough to give the cause of affirmative action the im-

petus it still needs. Harvard College was praising diversity long before it had a real affirmative action program—I know because I was there. In those days when we admitted an occasional well-trained middle-class Negro, we thought we were doing just fine."

12. When the Justices asked counsel for the university in oral hearings in *Bakke* whether a quota of fifty positions could be justified under the university's reasoning, they were probing compensatory quotas. In his opinion, Justice Brennan argued that, if such programs gave preferential consideration to racial minorities "in numbers significantly in excess of their proportional representation in the relevant population," they "might well be inadequately justified by the legitimate remedial objectives" (footnote 58, p. 374). But Brennan did not develop a rationale for resolving the issue.

13. The comments of Robert G. Thompson and Harold J. Spaeth were conveyed in their reviews of an earlier version of the manuscript.

14. The Nietzsche quotation is from *Thus Spake Zarathustra*, preface 4, quoted by Herbert Spiegelberg, "Defense of Human Equality," in *The Concept of Human Equality*, ed. William T. Blackstone (Minneapolis: Burgess, 1969), p. 161. Spiegelberg notes that Nietzsche here comes "dangerously close" to an "unaristocratic conclusion."

15. On the question of the time necessary to eliminate the roots of racism, J. R. Pole paraphrases a 1952 observation of Ralph Bunche: "For those who are suffering from the deprivation of inalienable rights, gradualism can never be a sufficient remedy, because inalienable rights cannot be enjoyed posthumously" (Pole, *The Pursuit of Equality*, p. 253).

16. The point that poverty, as well as racism, produces inequalities of opportunity has often been proposed as a basis for avoiding the use of race in affirmative-action programs. Why not use economic disadvantage as the criterion for preference in admissions? The answer, as the "Brennan four" pointed out in *Bakke*, is that there is simply no way to promote proportionate group results "in the foreseeable future without the use of race-conscious criteria." Relying on such neutral criteria as "disadvantage," or "poverty," or "family educational background" won't work because whites outnumber blacks at every socioeconomic level (p. 376).

Chapter 6

1. Quoted in Paul Seabury, "The Idea of Merit," *Commentary*, December 1972, p. 44. Seabury notes that Smith's predictions are "somewhat out of date."

2. Meg Greenfield, "How to Resolve the Bakke Case," *Newsweek*, October 24, 1977, p. 128. Justice Douglas made a parallel argument in his dissent in *DeFunis* v. *Odegaard:* "A segregated admissions process creates suggestions of stigma and caste no less than a segregated classroom, and in the end it may produce that result despite its contrary intentions" (p. 343). Justice Powell made the same point in *Bakke:* "preferential programs may only reinforce common stereotypes holding that certain groups are unable to achieve success without special protection based on a factor having no relationship to individual worth" (p. 298). Both Powell and Douglas neglect the importance of the fact that existing stigmas and stereotypes are decisive factors in the group's relative failure to achieve.

3. McGeorge Bundy, "The Issue Before the Court: Who Gets Ahead in America?" *Atlantic*, November 1977, p. 44.

4. J. R. Pole, *The Pursuit of Equality in American History* (Berkeley: University of California Press, 1978), p. 335.

5. On the question of how far, in social fact, the "unfair" advantages of birth replace the principle of merit, see John A. Brittain, *Inheritance and the Inequality of Material Wealth* (Washington: Brookings Institution, 1978). Brittain's evidence yields the conclusion that more than half of the net worth of wealthy men (and almost all that of wealthy women) has been derived from inheritance.

Chapter 7

1. Herbert Hoover, *The New Day; Campaign Speeches of Herbert Hoover* (Stanford: Stanford University Press, 1928), pp. 40–41. The ambiguity of the idea of equal opportunity is revealed in the fact that Clinton Rossiter could conclude that the American conservative "justifies all government activities that he has no hope or intention of dismantling by fitting them into his magic formula of equality of

opportunity" (Clinton Rossiter, *Conservatism in America* [New York: Alfred A. Knopf, 1955], p. 196.

2. The idea that equal opportunity is sufficiently guaranteed by legal equality has a long history in America. But in its earliest forms it had a different and more plausible basis. Thus, President Jackson, in his veto of the bill creating a national bank, could say: "If government would confine itself to equal protection, and, as Heaven does its rains, shower its favors alike on the high and the low, the rich and the poor, it would be an unqualified blessing." But Jackson was making the Jeffersonian assumption that, in the absence of legally established and protected privilege, no privilege would exist. This assumption denied the fact of society and overlooked the reality of slavery. But under agrarian conditions it had a certain plausibility for whites, which it would later lose.

3. R. H. Tawney, *Equality* (New York: Harcourt, Brace, 1931), p. 135.

4. John Plamenatz, "Diversity of Rights and Kinds of Equality," in *Equality*, eds. J. Ronald Pennock and John W. Chapman (New York: Atherton, 1967), p. 96.

5. J. R. Pole, *The Pursuit of Equality in American History* (Berkeley: University of California Press, 1978), p. 293.

6. The fact that equal opportunity does not function as an ideal makes it especially attractive to the antiideologists and the apologists for meritocracy. The point about postindustrial meritocratic societies is that, in them, authority has to promise only what equal opportunity can deliver. The promise of equality of educational opportunity, for example, does not need to satisfy any ideological demands of equality, but aims simply "to mobilize needed skills." See Alasdair MacIntyre, "Son of Ideology," *New York Review of Books*, May 9, 1968, p. 27.

7. Booker T. Washington, *Up From Slavery* (New York: Dell, 1970), p. 166; quoted in John K. Roth, *American Dreams* (San Francisco: Chandler and Sharp, n.d.), p. 135.

8. The results of the 1966 NORC survey and subsequent polls are described in Seymour Martin Lipset and William Schneider, "An Emerging National Consensus," *New Republic*, October 15, 1977, pp. 8–9. Lipset and Schneider offer little helpful analysis of the philosophical contradictions in the attitudes of these "average"

Americans. "Most whites," they say, "accept the reality of at least some racial discrimination, but see black problems as stemming essentially from the moral failings of individuals." This attitude, they assume, is not an expression of racism but of a widespread resentment of what whites "perceive as the unwillingness of many blacks to live by the standards of middle-class America." They see the rejection by whites of the view that "blacks are inherently inferior" as giving greater credibility to the moral argument that "not discrimination but lack of effort" is the explanation for racial inequality. I suspect that many whites are able to conclude both that blacks are "treated fairly" and that they are subjected to discrimination because the significance and consequences of social prejudice and discrimination are conjured away by the magic of individual "freedom of choice." Individualism, as romantic myth, denies the influences of society and culture. Except where the visible power of government is involved, all social institutions and cultural practices are seen merely to reflect the free choices of individuals. Even where widespread discrimination and prejudice are directed against minority groups, the result can be viewed, in Sidgewick's phrase, as only a "coincidence of the free choices" of individuals. From this perspective, paradoxically, a conspiracy to deprive others of their rights is visible only where there is overt collusion.

Chapter 8

1. *Plessy* v. *Ferguson*, p. 544.

2. *Plessy*, p. 551.

3. *Plessy*, p. 562.

4. Paul A. Freund, "Social Justice and the Law," in *Social Justice*, ed. Richard B. Brandt (Englewood Cliffs, N.J.: Prentice-Hall, 1962), p. 94.

5. The record of the Court in the cases leading up to *Brown* was uneven. As early as 1917, in *Buchanan* v. *Warley*, the Court in a unanimous decision invalidated a Louisville ordinance that had prohibited the purchase of property by a colored person in a block in which there was a majority of whites. The Court penetrated the sophistry in the formal neutrality of the ordinance, which also prohibited whites from buying in predominantly black neighborhoods.

But the decision turned less on equal protection than on property rights, and even there, on the right of a white to sell his property rather than on the right of a black to acquire it. After the decision, in any event, the purpose of maintaining racially exclusive neighborhoods was achieved by the use of "restrictive covenants" written into property deeds, which the Court unanimously upheld in 1926 *(Corrigan* v. *Buckley)* and which continued to be legally enforceable until 1948. Then, in *Shelley* v. *Kraemer,* the Court held such covenants to be legally unenforceable: "The difference between judicial enforcement and non-enforcement of the restrictive covenants is the difference to petitioners between being denied rights of property available to other members of the community and being accorded full enjoyment of those rights on an equal footing." But even here the Court was careful to maintain that the rights of individuals are protected by the Fourteenth Amendment only from "discriminatory action on the part of the States" (p. 19).

6. *Sweatt* v. *Painter,* p. 634.

7. *Brown* v. *Board of Education*, p. 494.

8. *Plessy,* p. 559.

9. Even Albion Tourgée, Plessy's lawyer, had made the color-blind argument in his brief: "Justice is pictured blind and her daughter, the law, ought at least to be color-blind." But he reached this conclusion from the "fact inseparable from human nature, that, when the law distinguishes between the civil rights or privileges of two classes, it always is and always must be, to the detriment of the weaker class or race" (Otto H. Olsen, *The Thin Disguise: Turning Point in Negro History* [New York: Humanities Press, 1967], pp. 90, 95–96). This reasoning would make race a "suspect category" only when its use is directed against what the "Brennan four" in *Bakke* described as a "discrete and insular" minority. As a unanimous Court put it in *Ferguson* v. *Skrupa:* "Statutes create many classifications which do not deny equal protection; it is only 'invidious discrimination' which offends the Constitution" (p. 732).

10. *Plessy,* p. 554.

11. *Plessy,* p. 561.

12. Reprinted in Olsen, *The Thin Disguise*, p. 102. Emphasis in original.

13. Justice Marshall made the connection between the *Plessy* doctrine and current arguments for color-blindness in his separate opinion in *Bakke*. "I fear," he concluded, "that we have come full circle." The beneficent legislation initiated by the government after the Civil War was vitiated by the Court. Almost a century of nonaction followed, with "the tacit approval of the Courts. Then we had *Brown* v. *Board of Education* and the Civil Rights Acts of Congress. *Now*, we have this Court again stepping in" to blunt "the movement to complete equality" (p. 402, emphasis in original).

14. Justice Marshall, in *Bakke*, sketched the effects of the *Plessy* decision on segregation: "In the wake of *Plessy*, many states expanded their Jim Crow laws, which had up until that time been limited primarily to passenger trains and schools." And Marshall (citing C. Vann Woodward, *The Strange Career of Jim Crow*, 3rd ed. [New York: Oxford University Press, 1974], p. 68) quotes a parody of Jim Crow laws that appeared in the *Charleston News and Courier* in 1898: "If there must be Jim Crow cars on the railroads, there should be Jim Crow cars on the street railways. Also on all passenger boats. . . . If there are to be Jim Crow cars, moreover, there should be Jim Crow waiting saloons at all stations, and Jim Crow eating houses. . . . There should be Jim Crow sections of the jury box, and a separate Jim Crow dock and witness stand in every court—and a Jim Crow Bible for colored witnesses to kiss." As Marshall says, "The irony is that before many years had passed, with the exception of the Jim Crow witness stand, 'all the improbable applications of the principle suggested by the editor in derision had been put into practice—down to and including the Jim Crow Bible' " (p. 393).

15. Hannah Arendt, *The Origins of Totalitarianism*, 2nd ed. (New York: Meridian, 1958), p. 467.

16. Harold J. Spaeth has called my attention to the racist implications in the common usage, which cites this famous case as *Dred Scott* v. *Sandford*. Why not *Scott* v. *John Sandford*? The answer is clear: Dred Scott was a slave and Mr. Sandford a slave-owner. Methods of address are, of course, crucial indicators of dignity and status. As recently as 1964, the Supreme Court reversed the conviction of a certain Mary Hamilton for contempt of court. She had refused to answer an Alabama prosecutor's questions because he addressed her as "Mary" instead of "Miss Hamilton." *(Hamilton* v. *Alabama)*

17. *Bakke*, p. 318.

18. *Civil Rights Cases*, p. 25.

19. Justice Marshall commented in *Bakke* on the Fourteenth Amendment's implicit acknowledgment of the need for preferential treatment: "The Congress that passed the Fourteenth Amendment is the same Congress that passed the 1866 Freedmen's Bureau Act, an act that provided many of its benefits only to Negroes." In response to the attacks on it as preferential legislation, "the bill's supporters defended it—not by rebutting the claim of special treatment—but by pointing to the need for such treatment." And when both the original and modified bill were vetoed by President Johnson, largely on the grounds of its special benefits for blacks, Congress passed it over his second veto (p. 397).

20. *Bakke*, p. 295.

21. *Pollock* v. *Farmers' Loan and Trust Co.*, p. 581.

22. *Pollock*, p. 532.

23. *Pollock*, p. 596.

24. *Pollock*, p. 607.

25. *Pollock* (rehearing), pp. 674–75.

26. *Pollock*, p. 518.

27. *United States* v. *Butler*, p. 61.

28. *Adair* v. *United States*, p. 175. Harlan was not completely consistent on the question of contractual freedom. See, for example, his dissent in *Lochner* v. *New York* (1905). The strong tendency of his views, however, appears to have been a commitment to the formal neutrality of government in social affairs.

29. *Adkins* v. *Children's Hospital*, p. 545.

30. Mason and Beaney note that in 1907, Joseph H. Choate, the same renowned lawyer who had argued to the Court that an income tax was "communistic," rejected an offer to prepare the defense of an Oregon ten-hour law for women. He observed that he could see no reason why "a big husky Irish woman should not work more than ten hours in a laundry if she and her employers so desired"

(Alpheus T. Mason and William M. Beaney, *American Constitutional Law* [Englewood Cliffs, N.J.: Prentice-Hall, 1964], p. 330).

31. *Adkins*, p. 562. The assumption of formal equality in the marketplace was necessary to its defense. Justice Taft's was a fundamental attack on "contractual liberty." If, as Harold Laski observed, liberalism could never bring itself to grant the obvious truth that "a contract is never genuinely free until the parties thereto have equal bargaining power," the reason was that equal bargaining power is "a function of equal material conditions" (Harold Laski, *The Rise of Liberalism* [New York: Harper, 1936], p. 18).

32. Mason and Beaney, *American Constitutional Law*, p. 335. Emphasis added.

33. Herbert Hill, "Affirmative Action and the Quest for Job Equality," *Review of Black Political Economy*, Spring 1976; reprinted in George McKenna and Stanley Finegold, *Taking Sides* (Guilford, Conn.: Dushkin, 1978), p. 199. Justice Blackmun made the same point eloquently in his opinion in *Bakke:* "In order to get beyond racism, we must first take account of race. There is no other way. And in order to treat some persons equally, we must treat them differently. We cannot—we dare not—let the Equal Protection Clause perpetuate racial supremacy" (p. 407).

34. In the *Bakke* case, the "Brennan four" stressed this distinction between an ideal future and a still-flawed present: "Against this background, claims that law must be 'color-blind' or that the datum of race is no longer relevant to public policy must be seen as aspiration rather than as description of reality. . . . We cannot—and . . . need not under our Constitution . . . let color-blindness become myopia which masks the reality that many 'created equal' have been treated within our lifetimes as inferior both by the law and by their fellow citizens" (p. 327).

35. In *The New Equality*, Nat Hentoff writes: "Until, therefore, 'special efforts' for everyone in the underclass are actually put into operation on a sizable enough basis, the particular problems of the Negro dispossessed point to the fact that it is both too late and too soon to be color-blind" (Nat Hentoff, *The New Equality* [New York: Viking Press, 1964], p. 114).

Chapter 9

1. R. H. Tawney accurately described what happened to the ideal of equality: "It is the fate of revolutionaries to supply watchwords to conservatives. It was *la carrière ouverte aux talents* which was the formula of reconciliation. . . . Guaranteed, as it was supposed, by the abolition of legal restrictions on enterprise and initiative, it supplied a satisfactory moral title to the class system which succeeded it" (R. H. Tawney, *Equality* [New York: Harcourt, Brace, 1931], p. 122).

2. I rely here on Hannah Arendt's discussion of the role of equality in constitution making. See Hannah Arendt, *On Revolution* (New York: Viking Press, 1963), especially chap. 4.

3. John Adams, *The Works of John Adams*, ed. Charles Francis Adams (Boston: Little, Brown, 1850–1856), vol. 6, p. 452.

4. Helvetius is quoted by Sanford A. Lakoff, *Equality in Political Philosophy* (Cambridge: Harvard University Press, 1964). I have relied heavily on Lakoff in this section. The quotations that follow from Hobbes, Rousseau, and Locke are found on pp. 70, 81, 99.

5. John Taylor, *An Inquiry into the Principles and Policy of the Government of the United States* (New Haven: Yale University Press, 1950; originally published in 1814), p. 224.

6. As Chief Justice Waite said, quoting the preamble of the Constitution of Massachusetts, in *Munn v. Illinois* (1877): "A body politic is a solid compact by which the whole people covenants with each citizen, and each citizen with the whole people, that all shall be governed by certain laws for the common good" (p. 124).

7. The reason a constitutional order is incompatible with ascribed group inferiority is illumined by John Rawls's discussion in *A Theory of Justice* (Cambridge: Harvard University Press, 1971). Rawls proposes that we can discover what is fair by imaginatively placing ourselves in the "original position" before the formation of society, where we are behind a "veil of ignorance" as to the positions we will occupy in society. He argues that if we asked ourselves what sensible persons would agree to, we would, then, choose equality (except for those inequalities that are to everyone's

advantage), since no one would risk a position of subjugation or worthlessness. Whatever the general merits of his formulation, it is a persuasive argument that no one would choose to risk group inequalities of the sort that define the color line in America.

8. Thomas Hobbes, *Leviathan*, ed. Michael Oakeshott (New York: Collier, 1962), pp. 119–20.

9. Henry Demarest Lloyd, *Mazzini and Other Essays* (New York: G. P. Putnam's, 1910), p. 17.

10. Douglas is quoted by Henry Alonzo Myers in *Are Men Equal?* (Ithaca, N.Y.: Cornell University Press, 1955), p. 99.

11. Tourgée's brief for Plessy is in Otto H. Olsen, *The Thin Disguise: Turning Point in Negro History* (New York: Humanities Press, 1967), p. 100. Emphasis in original.

12. In a deeply ironic way, the viciousness of American racism is attributable to the fact that slavery developed in a society committed to the Declaration's radical vision of equality. No position of "second-class citizen" was theoretically permissible; slaves had to be put completely beyond the pale of the equality that enclosed whites.

13. The men who wrote the Constitution appear to have been aware of the monumental contradiction on which it rested, as well as the crime that made it no Constitution at all for a segment of the population it governed. How else are we to explain the reluctance of the Founding Fathers even to name the relationship or write the ethnic identity of those who would be denied their inalienable right to consent to be governed? Instead (when providing that the slave trade could not be prohibited before 1808) they used the expression, "the migration or importation of such persons as any of the States now existing shall think proper to admit." When defining the basis for the apportionment of representatives, they spoke of "three-fifths of all other persons." The proverbial visitor from outer space, unfamiliar with their practices, could not have guessed that the men who wrote this document of freedom were slave-owners.

14. John P. Roche, "Equality in America," in *All Men Are Created Equal*, ed. William W. Wattenberg (Detroit: Wayne State University Press, 1966), p. 20. Emphasis added.

15. Rocco J. Tresolini, *American Constitutional Law,* 2nd ed. (New York: Macmillan, 1965), pp. 324, 234.

16. *Civil Rights Cases,* pp. 24–25.

17. Samuel Eliot Morison and Henry Steele Commager, *The Growth of the American Republic,* vol. 2 (New York: Oxford University Press, 1962), p. 87.

18. Quoted from Roche, "Equality in America," p. 30.

19. *Plessy* v. *Ferguson,* p. 560.

20. *Plessy,* p. 544.

21. *Plessy,* p. 551.

22. Most constitutional arguments against affirmative action do not adequately take into account the basic constitutional dimension of the problem. J. R. Pole, for example, grants that "the Constitution's normal gravitation pulls in the direction of equalization [of results]." But, he concludes, "the most important" limitation on that normal gravitation is that "the Constitution extends its protection equally to all—to every individual on American soil—in his or her capacity as an independent and irreducible individual. No constitutionally acceptable outcome can conflict with that obligation. It is the individual whose rights are the object of the special solicitude of the Constitution and for whose protection the Republic had originally justified its claim to existence" (J. R. Pole, *The Pursuit of Equality in American History* [Berkeley: University of California Press, 1978], p. 358). The problem with this conclusion is that the Republic which justified its claim to existence was defined by its color, and the individuals who were accorded its "special solicitude" as "independent and irreducible individuals" were white. In these circumstances, it is misleading to describe affirmative-action programs as intended, in some general way, to establish greater equality of results. At stake is an "equality of results" that applies to those groups that have been, on account of their color, outside the social contract on which a democratic Constitution rests. This equality of results can reasonably be regarded as a necessary precondition for the legitimacy of the constitutional order.

23. Milton Mayer, *On Liberty: Man vs. the State* (Santa Barbara: Center for the Study of Democratic Institutions, 1969), pp. 79–80.

Chapter 10

1. Bickel is quoted by McGeorge Bundy, "The Issue Before the Court: Who Gets Ahead in America?" *Atlantic*, November 1977, p. 44.

2. The argument is made, of course, that there is no assurance minority doctors will practice in minority neighborhoods. While this is true, the strength of the argument is vitiated by its reference to "minority neighborhoods," a phrase that implies America is still substantially a racially segregated society. The same social pressures that produce segregated neighborhoods suggest, at least, where doctors are most likely to practice.

3. Michael Kinsley, "The Conspiracy of Merit," *New Republic*, October 15, 1977, p. 24. Emphasis in original.

4. Nathaniel S. Colley, "Affirmative Action or Quotas? It Depends upon Whose Bull Is Gored" (Address to the Professional Men's Club, Los Angeles, November 15, 1972), mimeographed, p. 9.

5. This and the subsequent quote in the paragraph are from Colley, "Affirmative Action or Quotas?" p. 3.

6. Every system of social stratification, of course, implies judgments about the relative worth of persons and therefore tends to promote differential judgment about the relative value of their lives. This tendency may be partially offset in a hierarchical society characterized by a high degree of two-way vertical mobility, in which luck plays a significant role in social ascent. But the more consistently meritocratic a society becomes, the more likely its social and economic distinctions will be translated into judgments of basic human worth. Where social status continues to be a function of the invidious use of race or color, such distinctions are especially likely. Drug use became a social problem only when the children of white suburbanites became users; crime became a problem only when its victims were white. Blacks, in whose experience these understandings and memories burn brighter than they do for whites, are indeed quite likely to doubt their equal status in white-dominated examining rooms or operating rooms.

7. I am indebted to Paul Goldstene for pointing out that the children and grandchildren of present beneficiaries of affirmative action will provide the meritocratic test of the efficiency of such programs.

8. McGeorge Bundy, "Beyond Bakke," *Atlantic*, November 1978, p. 73.

9. Justice Brown is quoted in Alpheus Thomas Mason and William M. Beaney, *American Constitutional Law*, 3rd ed. (Englewood Cliffs, N.J.: Prentice-Hall, 1964), p. 326.

10. Justice Brewer is quoted in Mason and Beaney, *American Constitutional Law*, p. 327.

11. Daniel Bell, "Meritocracy and Equality," *The Public Interest*, Fall 1972, pp. 29–68.

12. Seymour Martin Lipset, *The First New Nation* (New York: Basic Books, 1963), p. 129. Lionel Gelber attributes this change to bigness: "Organized magnitude, as distinguished from feudalism or precorporate capitalism, substitutes in place of property a property of place. Incumbency is all" (Lionel Gelber, *The American Anarchy* [New York: H. Schuman, 1953], p. 107.

13. David M. Potter, *People of Plenty* (Chicago: University of Chicago Press, 1954).

14. Julian Huxley is quoted by George E. G. Catlin, "Equality and What We Mean by It," in *Equality*, eds. J. Ronald Pennock and John W. Chapman (New York: Atherton, 1967), p. 103.

15. Mark Hanan, *The Pacifiers* (Boston: Little, Brown, 1960), as quoted by John G. Cawelti, *Apostles of the Self-Made Man* (Chicago: University of Chicago Press, 1965), p. 201.

16. Calhoun went on to draw the logical conclusion that public policy must be "wealth-blind" or forfeit efficiency: "To force the front rank back to the rear, or attempt to push forward the rear into line with the front, by the interposition of the government, would . . . effectually arrest the march of progress" (John C. Calhoun, "Disquisition on Government," in *The Works of John C. Calhoun*, vol. 1, ed. Richard K. Cralle [New York: Appleton, 1954], p. 59).

17. George Harris, *Inequality and Progress* (New York: Arno Press, 1897). The Harris quotations in this section are found on pp. 7, 12, 35, 40, 45, 48, 58–59, 62, 63, 97.

18. Edward Bellamy, *Equality* (New York: Appleton-Century-Crofts, 1897), pp. 348, 351.

19. *The Best and the Brightest* is of course the sardonic title of David Halberstam's study of the political elite. (Greenwich, Conn.: Fawcett, 1969).

20. Magruder's comments and reflections are recorded by Studs Terkel in "Reflections on a Course in Ethics," *Harper's,* October 1973, p. 68. Magruder's career, like those of other members of the modern meritocracy, illustrates William H. Whyte's point that the new men of power "have concentrated on the fact of their skills rather than on the uses to which their skills are put" (William H. Whyte, *The Organization Man* [New York: Simon and Schuster, 1956], p. 308).

21. Michael Young, *The Rise of the Meritocracy* (Baltimore: Penguin, 1958). Michael Kinsley correctly describes the respective roles of natural ability and effort in a meritocratic system: "If I were about to begin the meritocratic struggle, and I were told to choose either a generous dollop of innate advantages or the opportunity to exert myself without these, I have no doubt which aspect of 'merit' I'd pick" (Kinsley, "The Conspiracy of Merit," p. 23).

22. William Graham Sumner, for example, stressed *natural* selection when he argued that: "Nature is entirely neutral. . . . If there be liberty, men get from her just in proportion to their being and doing" (William Graham Sumner, *What Social Classes Owe to Each Other* [Caldwell, Idaho: Caxton Printers, 1952], p. 70). At the same time Social Darwinists, unlike the classical economists, recognized the reality of society, and thus got themselves into theoretical difficulties. As long as Nature was held to be the judge of fitness, and as long as she is neutral in her judgments and is indifferent to all considerations except the energy and ability of those who seek her favor, those who succeed might be held to be the fittest. But Sumner was also the intellectual father of the "mores principle." A central implication of his *Folkways* (Boston: Ginn, 1907) was that the social rules of the game intercede between man and nature, and that the struggle is man against man within a given pattern of mores and folkways. *Fitness* is then culturally defined, and the argument becomes circular. A similar conflict is found in the ideas of Herbert Spencer, in the tension between his claims for natural selection and his organic conception of society.

Chapter 11

1. Sanford A. Lakoff, *Equality in Political Philosophy* (Cambridge: Harvard University Press, 1964), p. 101.

2. On the Jeffersonian attitude toward competition, see John G. Cawelti's observation that, "The older philosophy, stressing individual effort and achievement, did not place great emphasis on competition" (John G. Cawelti, *Apostles of the Self-Made Man* [Chicago: University of Chicago Press, 1965], p. 171). Hans J. Morgenthau makes a similar and persuasive case: "The conditions of the frontier push the domestic conditions of freedom and equal opportunity to their logical extreme: freedom becomes anarchy, and *equal opportunity becomes absence of competition*" (Hans J. Morgenthau, *The Purpose of American Politics* [New York: Vintage, 1960], p. 27, emphasis added). Note, also, Hannah Arendt's conclusion that "the game of status seeking is common enough in certain strata of our society, but it was entirely absent from the society of the eighteenth and nineteenth centuries, and no revolutionary ever thought it his task to introduce mankind to it or to teach the underprivileged the rules of the game" (Hannah Arendt, *On Revolution* [New York: Viking Press, 1965], pp. 66–67).

3. Rantoul is quoted by Marvin Myers, *The Jacksonian Persuasion* (Stanford: Stanford University Press, 1960), pp. 208, 209. Rantoul is not content to assert a right "to advancement in life." He makes that right dependent on a natural, divinely implanted "desire of improving our condition." This is no simple economic motivation; it is no less than "the instinct of perfectibility." See Myers, *The Jacksonian Persuasion*, pp. 218–19. The subsequent quotations from Myers in the text are found in Myers, *The Jacksonian Persuasion*, pp. 214, 135.

4. On Alger's meaning of "fame and fortune," see Cawelti, *Apostles of the Self-Made Man*, p. 110. I have relied heavily on Cawelti in this chapter and quote subsequently from pp. 105, 109, 150, 120, 207.

5. Thayer is quoted by Ralph Henry Gabriel, *The Course of American Democratic Thought* (New York: Ronald, 1940), p. 156. The quotations in the following paragraph are from Gabriel, p. 152. Despite Gabriel's generally insightful analysis of "The Gospel of Wealth in the Gilded Age," he missed one of its important elements when he

concluded that poverty was viewed as "a symbol of shame, a sort of scarlet letter proclaiming that [the poor person] was wanting in ability or character, or both." There is nothing in either the secular or ecclesiastical versions of the gospel of wealth—even as Gabriel describes them—that even hints at a natural lack of ability as a cause of failure. It was, indeed, only because poverty was attributed to a lack of effort that it could effectively serve as "a symbol of shame."

6. Tuthill is quoted and discussed by Cawelti, *Apostles of the Self-Made Man*, pp. 104–06. Cawelti describes Tuthill, mistakenly I think, as a believer in "natural aristocracy." As he notes, her heroes "spring from respectable families who have the means to educate their children" (p. 106). Her emphasis is on education, not native intelligence.

7. Cawelti properly stresses the role of luck in Alger's stories. Luck plays a similarly important role elsewhere in the gospel of wealth. Indeed, Andrew Carnegie himself, luxuriating in his pool-sized bath and gesturing toward the 30,000 acres of his Scottish estate, confided to a visiting friend: "I still can't believe all of this has happened to me, a poor weaver's son. It was nothing but blind luck. If my fortune had been dependent upon my ability, I should not have had a fraction of this" (Louis M. Hacker, *The World of Andrew Carnegie* [New York: Lippincott, 1968]).

8. Except for this egalitarian function of luck, how are we to explain American attitudes toward inheritance? It has always been a striking fact that the principle of inheritance of wealth, which patently violates every standard of individual talent, achievement, or effort, has never been seriously challenged in America. Inherited wealth and status seem, indeed, the very essence of the principle of aristocracy against which the principle of equal opportunity was arrayed. Nor, at least until recently, was inheritance justified on the basis of an assumed absolute right of property. The origin of property rights was firmly linked to individual effort, and hedged in by specific conditions. Early assertions of the personal right of private property emphasized the individual's right to acquire—but not any absolute right to dispose of—property. Certainly no right was claimed to dispose of property (as in an inheritance) that would operate to limit the equal right of all to acquire it. The right of inheritance, then, did not rest on any assumed absolute right of

disposal or on any claim to privilege by birth. In earlier years, under frontier conditions, inheritance did not seem to limit others' rights to acquisition. Later it appears more likely that it was seen as a form of luck through which the accident of birth helped to offset the inegalitarian results imputed to natural fitness.

9. On the role of effort in an egalitarian game, see John Wilson, *Equality* (New York: Harcourt, Brace & World, 1966).

10. See Irvin G. Wylie, *The Self-Made Man in America* (New York: Free Press, 1966), pp. 168–74.

11. Clark Kerr. *The Uses of the University* (Cambridge: Harvard University Press, 1963), p. 121.

12. Mill and Babeuf are quoted by Lakoff, *Equality in Political Philosophy*, pp. 126, 122. In America, the emphasis on effort kept Babeuf's question from being posed. This helps explain why Henry Ward Beecher could tell Herbert Spencer in 1866 that "the peculiar condition of American society has made your writings far more fruitful and quickening here than in Europe" (Richard Hofstadter, *Social Darwinism in American Thought* [Boston: Beacon Press, 1955], p. 18).

13. Jeremy Taylor is quoted by R. H. Tawney, *Equality* (New York: Harcourt, Brace, 1931), p. 36.

14. Mary Jo Bane and Christopher Jencks, "The Schools and Equal Opportunity," *Saturday Review of Education*, September 16, 1972, p. 37.

15. Menander's maxim is quoted by Matthew Arnold, "Equality," in *The Portable Matthew Arnold* (New York: Viking Press, 1949), p. 574.

16. Langston Hughes, "Let America Be America Again," originally published in *Esquire*, July 1936. Reprinted in Langston Hughes and Arna Bontemps, eds., *The Poetry of the Negro* (Garden City, N.Y.: Doubleday, 1949).

Chapter 12

1. William Graham Sumner, *Essays of William Graham Sumner*, eds. Albert Galloway Keller and Maurice R. Davie (New Haven: Yale

University Press, 1934). This and subsequent quotations in this section are found in vol. 1, p. 18; vol. 2, p. 254; vol. 1, p. 18; vol. 2, p. 238; vol. 2, p. 297.

2. John Hammond with Irving Townsend, *John Hammond on Record* (New York: Ridge Press, 1977), pp. 276–77.

3. Magruder's reflections are recorded in Studs Terkel, "Reflections on a Course in Ethics," *Harper's*, October 1973, p. 67.

4. Robert E. Lane, "The Fear of Equality," *American Political Science Review*, March 1959, pp. 35–51. Lane points out that all of his respondents "believed that equality of incomes would deprive men of their incentive to work, achieve, and develop their skills" (p. 45). Yet, while all the respondents agreed that status or income is central to motivation where others are concerned, they did not all believe that the same was true for themselves.

5. Michael Young, *The Rise of the Meritocracy* (Baltimore: Penguin Books, 1958), p. 85.

6. James Baldwin, *Nobody Knows My Name* (New York: Dial Press, 1969), p. 133. Emphasis in original. Quoted by Robert Blauner in *Racial Oppression in America* (New York: Harper & Row, 1972), p. 47.

7. Compton is quoted by Paul Delaney, "Growing Estrangement," *Sacramento Bee*, "Forum," March 12, 1978.

8. "The American Underclass," *Time*, August 29, 1977, p. 14.

9. *New York Times*, July 6, 1978; quoted by Allan P. Sindler, *Bakke, DeFunis, and Minority Admissions* (New York: Longman, 1978), p. 316. Professor Sindler uses this quote to illustrate his important point that "a root tension [was] caused by the mismatch between Powell's focus on educational diversity and the schools' focus on societal concerns" (p. 315).

Chapter 13

1. Eliot Marshall, "Race Certification: The Logical Next Step," *New Republic*, October 15, 1977, p. 20.

2. The analysis of pluralism in this section relies heavily on John C. Livingston and Robert G. Thompson, *The Consent of the Governed*, 3rd ed. (New York: Macmillan, 1971), chaps. 4, 5.

3. Earl Latham, *The Group Basis of Politics* (Ithaca, N.Y.: Cornell University Press, 1952), pp. 6, 51. The development of a pluralist theory of democracy owed much to the simultaneous development of voting behavior research. This research, in the 1950s, revealed that the average voter is neither informed, principled, altruistic, nor even very interested. On the assumption that the system seems nonetheless to work well, early pluralists developed a case that exactly parallels the arguments of classical economic theory. The individual vices of self-interested voters automatically produce the public virtues of stability and progress. See, for example, the final chapter of Bernard R. Berelson, Paul F. Lazarsfeld, and William N. McPhee, *Voting* (Chicago: University of Chicago Press, 1954). John Taylor, the philosopher of Jeffersonianism, clearly defined the difference between traditional and pluralist versions of democracy: "To sanction law by common consent or publick will, is one principle; by the will of a combination of interests, another" (John Taylor, *An Inquiry into the Principles and Policy of the Government of the United States* [New Haven: Yale University Press, 1950], p. 519).

4. The account here of Jim Crow in the federal service relies on, and quotes from, Nancy J. Weiss, "The Negro and the New Freedom: Fighting Wilsonian Segregation," *Political Science Quarterly*, March 1969, pp. 63, 70.

5. Roosevelt's response is recounted in Walter White, *A Man Called White* (New York: Viking, 1948), pp. 169–70; quoted by Morroe Berger, *Equality by Statute*, rev. ed. (New York: Anchor, 1968), p. 18.

6. U.S. Works Progress Administration, *Final Report on the WPA Program, 1935–1943* (Washington, D.C.: Government Printing Office, 1947), Table 25, p. 45; cited by Berger, *Equality by Statute*, p. 19.

7. Eric F. Goldman, "Liberals, Blacks and the War," *New York Times Magazine*, November 30, 1969, p. 17.

8. Daniel M. Berman, *A Bill Becomes a Law: Congress Enacts Civil Rights Legislation*, 2nd ed. (New York: Macmillan, 1966), pp. 139–40.

9. Stokely Carmichael and Charles V. Hamilton, *Black Power* (New York: Vintage Books, 1967). Quotations, including the statement of

the committee of black ministers, are found on pp. 40, 53, 49, 60. Carmichael and Hamilton incisively underscored the anomalous treatment of blacks in an otherwise pluralistic setting in their observation that "it is a commentary on the fundamentally racist nature of this society that the concept of group strength for black people must be articulated—not to mention defended."

10. Sethard Fisher is quoted by Mervyn Dymally, "Urban West Forum," *Urban West*, September–October 1967, p. 17.

11. The HUD mobile home agency is described in *Newsweek*, January 2, 1978, p. 23.

12. Alan Fox, "Is Equality a Necessity?" *Dissent*, Winter 1975, p. 50.

13. Descriptions by political scientists of the central characteristics of coalition politics offer additional reasons for the ineffectiveness of group politics in securing racial justice. One of these characteristics, for example, is the "size principle," by which "participants create coalitions just as large as they believe will ensure winning and no larger" (Eugene J. Meehan, *Contemporary Political Thought: A Critical Study* [Homewood, Ill.: Dorsey, 1967], p. 323). The principle was formulated by William H. Riker in the more technical language of game theory: "In n-person, zero-sum games, where side-payments are permitted, where players are rational, and where they have perfect information, only minimum winning coalitions occur" (William H. Riker, *A Theory of Political Coalitions* [New Haven: Yale University Press, 1962], p. 32). The circumstances in which other interests need colored minorities to form a winning coalition, and the size of the "side-payments" they will be constrained to make have no relationship to racial justice. The distinctive position of blacks and other colored minorities in the politics of pluralism is further revealed by the pluralist principle of "overlapping membership." This describes a phenomenon in which individuals typically belong to several groups. The typical individual will therefore be in a minority in some coalitions on some issues, but in a majority on other issues when the other groups to which he belongs are in the majority coalition. Thus "overlapping membership" is counted on to stabilize the system by insuring that individuals are never permanently in the minority. The proposition seems plausible (although, of course, what is described as stability may look, from a different perspective, like entrapment). But this phenomenon has little relevance to blacks,

who politically have been a permanent minority that has suffered "because of who its members *are*," not what they *do*. See
Andrew Hacker, *Political Theory* (New York: Macmillan, 1961), p.
474. Emphasis in original.

14. Paul Seabury, "The Idea of Merit," *Commentary*, December 1972, p.
44.

15. Leonard Fine, "The War Inside the Jews," *New Republic*, October
15, 1977, p. 17.

16. *Regents of the University of California* v. *Bakke*, footnote 16, p. 299.

Chapter 14

1. Eric F. Goldman, "Liberals, Blacks and the War," *New York Times
Magazine*, November 30, 1969, p. 46.

2. Hannah Arendt, *On Revolution* (New York: Viking Press, 1965), p.
84. Arendt was wrong, however, in her contention that "the only
revolution in which compassion played no role in the motivation
of the actors was the American Revolution." See John Stafford,
"Sympathy Comes to America," in *Themes and Directions in American Literature*, eds. Ray B. Brown and Donald Pizer (Lafayette,
Ind.: Purdue University Studies, 1969), pp. 24–37; and John Stafford, "The Power of Sympathy," *Midcontinent American Studies
Journal*, Spring 1968, pp. 52–57.

3. Sheldon S. Wolin, *Politics and Vision* (Boston: Little, Brown, 1960),
p. 394. The subsequent quotation from Rousseau is also found in
Wolin, p. 394.

4. Here is de Tocqueville on the relation of equality to sympathy: "It
is true that in [aristocratic] ages the notion of human fellowship is
faint and that men seldom think of sacrificing themselves for
mankind; but they often sacrifice themselves for other men. In
democratic times, on the contrary, when the duties of each individual to the race are much more clear, devoted service to any one
man becomes more rare; the bond of human affection is extended,
but it is relaxed" (Alexis de Tocqueville, *Democracy in America*, ed.
Phillips Bradley, vol. 2 [New York: Alfred A. Knopf, 1948], p. 99).

5. Aristotle, *The Politics of Aristotle*, ed. Ernest Barker (New York: Oxford University Press, 1962), pp. 79, 87.

6. John Taylor, *An Inquiry into the Principles and Policy of the Government of the United States* (New Haven: Yale University Press, 1950). This and subsequent quotations are found at pp. 67, 65, 487, 505, 448, 543, 378.

7. Rousseau examined the conditions in which people are precluded from sympathizing "with other people's woes unless we know we may suffer the same ourselves" (Jean Jacques Rousseau, *Emile*, trans. Barbara Foxley [London: Everyman, 1955], p. 185). Rousseau's views are quoted and discussed by Marshall Berman in his tremendously provocative and insightful, *The Politics of Authenticity* (New York: Atheneum, 1972), p. 100. On the moral limitations of an approach to justice rooted in the egoistic viewpoint that "it might happen to you," see also Edmond Cahn, *The Moral Decision* (Bloomington: Indiana University Press, 1955).

8. While a guaranteed white majority has in the past put colored minorities beyond the compassionate reach of the selfish altruism of "it might happen to you," recent trends in some parts of the country may undercut that guarantee. Recent demographic analyses, for example, have led to the prediction that a majority of the population of the state of California will be colored within the next couple of decades. If, under those conditions, group-interest politics were to result in a reversal of the racial hierarchy, would equality before the law and equal opportunity then appear to whites as an adequate guarantee of human rights?

9. E. E. Schattschneider, *Two Hundred Million Americans in Search of a Government* (New York: Holt, Rinehart & Winston, 1969), p. 45.

10. The analysis here of the role of the Negro in the attitudes of those who embraced the principles of the Declaration relies on, and quotes from, Arendt, *On Revolution*, p. 66.

11. This ability of whites to believe they could have both equality and white supremacy was reflected early in public reaction to the Lincoln–Douglas debates. Douglas hoped to convince the audiences of the "utter inconsistency" of Lincoln's simultaneous advocacy of natural human equality and denial of unqualified equality for blacks. Henry Alonzo Myers describes the results of his efforts: "In this hope he was disappointed. As he read passages affirming Lincoln's faith in equality, voices from the crowd shouted: 'He's right.' And when in the hope of proving contradiction he read

other passages indicating Lincoln's belief that the slaves were not ready for political and social equality, the same voices disappointed him by shouting: 'That's the doctrine' (Henry Alonzo Myers, *Are Men Equal?* [Ithaca, N.Y.: Cornell University Press, 1945], p. 90).

12. Richard Parker, *The Myth of the Middle Class* (New York: Harper & Row, 1972), pp. 199–200. Parker adds that raising the issue of equality for blacks "would have meant examining the quickly stratifying income and wealth distribution generated by industrialism, and challenging the sanctity of property which Jefferson had seen as protecting the small farmer and laborer, but which was now rapidly becoming the chief tool of the aggressive entrepreneur against the small farmer and laborer."

13. R. H. Tawney, *Equality* (New York: Harcourt, Brace, 1931), p. 122.

Chapter 15

1. The quotes from Bryce in this section appear in James Bryce, *The American Commonwealth*, ed. Louis Hacker, vol. 2 (New York: G. P. Putnam's, 1959), pp. 514–16.

2. C. Wright Mills, *The Power Elite* (New York: Oxford University Press, 1956), pp. 332, 335.

3. Jefferson is quoted on money-making by Harry V. Jaffa, *Equality and Liberty* (New York: Oxford University Press, 1965), p. 55. Warren's letter to Adams is quoted by Page Smith, *John Adams*, vol. 2 (Garden City, N.Y.: Doubleday, 1962), p. 686.

4. Thomas Paine, *The Rights of Man* (New York: E. P. Dutton, 1951), p. 151.

5. Joel Barlow, *The Political Writings of Joel Barlow* (New York: Mott and Lyon, 1796). A contrary view, that the effect of the Revolution was limited to the principles of English Whiggery, is developed in Louis Hartz, *The Liberal Tradition in America* (New York: Harcourt, Brace & World, 1955), and in Clinton Rossiter, *Conservatism in America*, 2nd ed. (New York: Vintage, 1962), especially pp. 67–96.

6. This exchange of views between Jefferson and Adams on natural aristocracy has been a favorite source for conservatives, who have

unwarrantedly concluded from it that Jefferson was not really committed to the ideal of equality. Russell Kirk even reached the absurd conclusion that Adams's argument forced Jefferson to grant the validity of Adams's defense of natural inequality. See Russell Kirk, *The Conservative Mind* (Chicago: Regnery, 1953), p. 85. Compare Hannah Arendt, *On Revolution* (New York: Viking Press, 1963), especially pp. 252–59, 279–85.

7. The quotations from John Taylor in this section are found in John Taylor, *An Inquiry into the Principles and Policy of the Government of the United States* (New Haven: Yale University Press, 1950), pp. 67, 195, 71, 196, 46, 186.

8. James Weinstein, *The Corporate Ideal in the Liberal State: 1900–1918* (Boston: Beacon Press, 1968), pp. xiii–xiv.

9. Arendt, *On Revolution*, p. 67.

10. J. Hector St. John de Crevecoeur, *Letters from an American Farmer* (New York: E. P. Dutton, 1957), pp. 35–36.

11. Benjamin Franklin, "Information to those who would remove to America," as quoted by Hans J. Morgenthau, *The Purpose of American Politics* (New York: Vintage, 1960), p. 17. William Penn is quoted in Arendt, *On Revolution*, p. 65.

12. The phrase, "the fertile and beneficent inequality of men," is Benito Mussolini's, as quoted by Henry Alonzo Myers, *Are Men Equal?* (Ithaca, N.Y.: Cornell University Press, 1945), p. 3.

13. Whitman is quoted by Morgenthau, *The Purpose of American Politics*, p. 19.

14. Thomas Jefferson, *The Writings of Thomas Jefferson*, ed. Albert Ellery Bergh, vol. 14 (Washington, D.C.: Thomas Jefferson Memorial Association, 1907), p. 463; quoted in Daniel J. Boorstin, *The Lost World of Thomas Jefferson* (Boston: Beacon Press, 1948), p. 94.

15. Taylor's analysis, described in this section, is in Taylor, *Principles and Policy*; quotations are found on pp. 42, 43, 36, 44. Taylor observed that John Adams's position "that an aristocracy is the work of nature" was "equivalent to the antiquated doctrine that 'a king is the work of God'" (p. 41). Earlier, Taylor perceptively remarked that "however lightly Mr. Adams may speak of Filmer," they are both "political fatalists" (p. 36). Taylor's analysis reaches the con-

clusion that all inequalities are matters of human judgment and choice since "moral causes, being capable of human modification, events flowing from them, possess the quality of freedom."

16. Thomas Paine, *The Rights of Man*, p. 134. Paine added: "In these principles there is nothing to throw a Nation into confusion by inflaming ambition. They are calculated to call forth wisdom and abilities, and to exercise them for the public good, and not for the emolument or aggrandisement of particular descriptions of men or families."

17. Samuel Adams's views, quoted here, are from his letters to John Winthrop and James Warren, in Samuel Adams, *The Writings of Samuel Adams*, ed. Harry Alonzo Cushing, vol. 4 (New York: Octagon, 1968), pp. 103, 213–14.

Chapter 16

1. R. H. Tawney, *Equality* (New York: Harcourt, Brace, 1931), p. 132.

2. Goethe expressed eloquently the practical consequences of our judgments about the nature of man: "When we take man as he is, we make him worse; but when we take man as if he were already what he should be, we promote him to what he can be" (Viktor E. Frankl, *From Death Camp to Existentialism* [Boston: Beacon Press, 1959], p. 110). Edmund Burke made the same point: "If you treat men as robbers, why, robbers sooner or later they will become" (Lee Cameron McDonald, *Modern Political Theory* [New York: Harcourt, Brace & World, 1968], p. 424).

3. Edward Bellamy, *Equality* (New York: Appleton-Century-Crofts, 1897), p. 356.

4. Euripides is quoted in John Wilson, *Equality* (New York: Harcourt, Brace & World, 1966), p. 32.

5. Glenn Tinder, *Political Thinking* (Boston: Little, Brown, 1974) p. 159.

6. The Reverend John Wise, a Puritan democrat, rested his case for equality on the political necessity of sociableness, "since no man can live a sociable life with another that does not . . . respect him as a man" (John Wise, *A Vindication of the Government of New*

England Churches [1717]; reprinted in P. Miller and T. H. Johnson, *The Puritans* [New York: American Book Co., 1952], p. 262). Equality, Wise went on to argue, "is to be cherished and preserved to the highest degree as will consist with all just distinctions amongst men of honor, and shall be agreeable with the public good." If men correctly understand the stakes, they will "yield the precedency to nothing but to superior virtue and wisdom." The status they confer on persons who possess those qualities will be granted only conditionally, in ways that protect the equal rights of all to participate in making the moral choices on which temporary inequalities rest.

7. Wilson, *Equality*, p. 160.

8. Alexis de Tocqueville, *Democracy in America*, ed. Phillips Bradley, vol. 2 (New York: Alfred A. Knopf, 1948), p. 99.

9. The perceptively accurate phrase "possessive individualism" appears in C. B. Macpherson, *The Political Theory of Possessive Individualism: Hobbes to Locke* (Oxford, England: Clarendon, 1962).

10. Bellamy, *Equality*, p. 347.

11. José Ortega y Gasset, *The Revolt of the Masses* (New York: W. W. Norton, 1932), p. 65. This book has often been interpreted as an elitist attack on "the masses." This misses a central point of Ortega's analysis, which is that the meritocratic elites of modern mass societies are themselves mass men.

12. Ralph Waldo Emerson, "Politics," reprinted in Alpheus Thomas Mason, *Free Government in the Making* (New York: Oxford University Press, 1949), p. 468. Emerson added, "Like one class of forest animals, they have nothing but a prehensile tail; climb they must, or crawl."

13. Wilson, *Equality*, p. 180.

14. Quoted from Sanford A. Lakoff, *Equality in Political Philosophy* (Cambridge: Harvard University Press, 1964), p. 65.

15. On the cultural contradiction between capitalism and Puritanism, see Daniel Bell, *The Cultural Contradictions of Capitalism* (New York: Basic Books, 1978), pp. 54–76. Bell's analysis is provocative and persuasive, but in its emphasis on the late stages of capitalist

consumerism it understates, I believe, the inherent conflict between capitalism and both Puritanism and political democracy.

16. On the unnaturalness of personal gain as an economic incentive, see Karl Polanyi's still timely and brilliant *The Great Transformation* (1944; reprinted, Boston: Beacon Press, 1957), especially chaps. 4, 7, 10.

17. Adams's observation on human vanity is quoted from Joseph Dorfman, "The Regal Republic of John Adams," in *Origins of American Political Thought*, ed. John P. Roche (New York: Harper & Row, 1967), p. 132.

18. Bellamy, *Equality*, pp. 347–48.

19. Jean Jacques Rousseau, *The Social Contract and Discourse on the Origin of Inequality*, ed. Lester G. Crocker (New York: Washington Square Press, 1967), p. 245.

20. On the important distinction between equality of esteem and a respect for excellence in particular performances, see J. R. Pole, *The Pursuit of Equality in American History* (Berkeley: University of California Press, 1978), p. 350; and John C. Livingston, "Tenure Everyone?" in Bardwell L. Smith and Associates, *The Tenure Debate* (San Francisco: Jossey-Bass, 1973), pp. 66–67.

21. Emerson, "Politics," reprinted in Mason, *Free Government in the Making*, p. 468.

22. Meritocracy, by narrowing the meaning of success in an equal-opportunity society, supports Santayana's complaint that "in a country where all men are free, every man finds that what most matters has been settled for him beforehand" (Alan Valentine, *The Age of Conformity* [Chicago: Regnery, 1954], p. 62).

23. Hannah Arendt, "Reflections: Truth in Politics," *New Yorker*, February 25, 1967, p. 62.

Epilogue

1. Max Otto, *Science and the Moral Life* (New York: New American Library, 1949), pp. 44–45.

2. Les Thurow, "Toward a U.S. Incomes Policy: Strategy and Tactics," *ADA World,* June–July 1978, p. 11.

3. Thurow, "Toward a U.S. Incomes Policy," p. 9.

4. Nat Hentoff, *The New Equality* (New York: Viking Press, 1965), p. 241.

5. Albert Guerard, *Testament of a Liberal* (Cambridge: Harvard University Press, 1956), p. 10. Emphasis added. Quoted by Marc R. Tool, *The Discretionary Economy* (Santa Monica, Calif.: Goodyear, 1979), p. 19.

Table of Cases

Index